FAST-FORWARD FAMILY

Fast-Forward Family

Home, Work, and Relationships
in Middle-Class America

**Edited by ELINOR OCHS
and TAMAR KREMER-SADLIK**

UNIVERSITY OF CALIFORNIA PRESS

Berkeley   Los Angeles   London

University of California Press, one of the most distinguished
university presses in the United States, enriches lives around the
world by advancing scholarship in the humanities, social sciences,
and natural sciences. Its activities are supported by the UC Press
Foundation and by philanthropic contributions from individuals and
institutions. For more information, visit www.ucpress.edu.

University of California Press
Berkeley and Los Angeles, California

University of California Press, Ltd.
London, England

Illustrations and photos appear by permission of CELF.

Library of Congress Cataloging-in-Publication Data

Fast-forward family : home, work, and relationships in middle-class
America / edited by Elinor Ochs and Tamar Kremer-Sadlik.
    p.   cm.
  Includes bibliographical references and index.
  ISBN 978–0–520–27397–9 (cloth : alk. paper)
  ISBN 978–0–520–27398–6 (pbk. : alk. paper)
  1. Middle-class families—United States.   2. Work and family—
United States.   I. Ochs, Elinor. II. Kremer-Sadlik, Tamar.
  HQ536.F388   2013
  306.850973—dc23   2012027301

Manufactured in the United States of America

22 21 20 19 18 17 16 15 14 13
10 9 8 7 6 5 4 3 2 1

In keeping with a commitment to support environmentally responsible and sustainable printing practices, UC Press has printed this
book on Rolland Enviro100, a 100% post-consumer fiber paper that is
FSC certified, deinked, processed chlorine-free, and manufactured
with renewable biogas energy. It is acid-free and EcoLogo certified.

To the thirty-two families that inspired this study

Contents

Illustrations

FIGURES

MAP

TABLES

Acknowledgments

This volume distills highlights of a decade-long endeavor undertaken by the UCLA Sloan Center on Everyday Lives of Families (CELF). Beyond the editors and chapter authors the CELF project benefited vastly from our entire corps of researchers and technicians who worked closely together in collecting, archiving, and analyzing family life from dawn to dusk and beyond.[1] All the researchers are indebted to Paul Connor, CELF Digital Laboratory director, who created a cutting edge technical infrastructure that was key to the success of CELF at every step of the way. His efforts culminated in the multimedia CELF Archive, an exceptionally rich documentation of middle-class America at the turn of the twenty-first century.

At the top of our list of acknowledgments are the thirty-two CELF families that graciously allowed us the extraordinary privilege of entering their homes and private lives. Over the years that the CELF team examined video recordings, photographs, timed observations, and other information gathered for each family, we developed a great affection and admiration for these parents and their children. It was simply breathtaking to log the nonstop activities that undergird households and the intricate coordination required for family members to accomplish them. Hats off to the CELF families!

We credit Kathleen Christensen, founder and director of the Workplace, Workforce, and Working Families Program at the Alfred P. Sloan Foundation, with the inspiration for the CELF project. The intellectual bedrock of our study is Kathleen's vision of dual-earner parents as faced with managing three jobs—two of which are paid employment plus the work of raising a family—and her mission to systematically document how parents actually live this challenge from one moment to the next. Throughout the CELF study Kathleen and the Sloan Foundation provided extraordinary support and shepherded our research so that it would be both scholarly and publicly relevant and accessible.

CELF also benefited from the community of scholars created by the Alfred P. Sloan Foundation as part of the Sloan Workplace, Workforce, and Working Families Program. In particular, through Sloan support two sister centers were established in Italy, iCELF, whose principal investigator (PI) is Clotilde Pontecorvo; and Sweden, sCELF, Karin Aronsson, PI. Our studies of middle-class American families were enhanced greatly by lively dialogue and collaboration with scholars across our three research sites. CELF has also had the luxury of working closely with Barbara Schneider, who codirected the Alfred P. Sloan Center on Parents, Children, and Work at the University of Chicago. Collaboration between our two centers on a documentary film and publications has demonstrated the power of integrating databases and methodologies to generate new ways of understanding the uneven interface of family and workplace.

Throughout the course of this project the CELF team relied on the exceptional talents of our administrative coordinators. Mary Hsieh was indispensable in the early years of the project. Thereafter, Johanna Romero and Adrian Meza independently and together were organizational geniuses who saw that family-researcher contacts, stipends, purchases, travel, budgets, reports, working papers, weekly meetings, colloquia, conferences, and other critical arrangements too numerous to specify were carried out with efficiency, grace, and taste. In the past two years, as CELF gathered its research findings to produce this edited volume and a photoessay book, *Life at Home in the 21st Century: 32 Families Open Their Doors*, we had the great fortune to have Aleksandra Van Loggerenberg as our chief editorial assistant. Aleks worked her magic on individual chapters to create a sense of coherence across the volume.

The specific CELF studies presented here greatly benefited from the valuable and sustained assistance of researchers Tatyana Plaksina and Julie Bernard. Maggie McKinley brought her anthropological sensibilities and media skills to create an impressive video documentary on working families. Satomi Kuroshima ran like clockwork the CELF Digital Laboratory, where 145 undergraduate students transcribed and coded all the data that compose the CELF Archive. We are also grateful to Anna Corwin and Keziah Conrad, whose watchful eyes and deep knowledge of the subject matter has guided the final editing of this volume. We also wish to express gratitude to UCLA for providing the ideal habitat for CELF activities, granting each Sloan-supported graduate student a Dissertation Year Fellowship, and maintaining the CELF Archive beyond our funding period for years to come.

Finally, we wish to thank our own partners and children for holding down our respective households while we spent long days recruiting, visiting, recording, tracking, and interviewing the families in the study. CELF researchers have learned a great deal about the efforts required to create resilient, loving families, which we hope will nourish our own homes and those of our readers.

NOTES

1. CELF was administered by Elinor Ochs, Center Director; Tamar Kremer-Sadlik, Director of Research; Paul Connor, Digital Laboratory Director; and our administrators, Adrian C. Meza, Johanna Romero, Mary Hsieh, and Aleksandra Van Loggerenberg. CELF Core Faculty were Jeanne Arnold, Thomas Bradbury, Linda Garro, Charles Goodwin, Marjorie H. Goodwin, Kris Gutiérrez, and Rena Repetti. CELF Postdoctoral Fellows included Margaret Beck, Belinda Campos, Jeffrey Good, Anthony P. Graesch, Carolina Izquierdo, Wendy Klein, Chi-Young Koh, April Leininger, Alesia Montgomery, and Amy Paugh. CELF Graduate Student Fellows were Mara Buchbinder, Leah Dickinson, Rachel George, Jeffrey Good, Anthony P. Graesch, Wendy Klein, Tali Klima, Heather Loyd, Angie Mittman, Angela Orlando, Diane Pash, Darby Saxbe, Merav Shohet, Karen Sirota, Jaqueline Sperling, Eve Tulbert, Shu-wen Wang, Heather Willihnganz Huffman, and Leah Wingard.

Note to the Reader

In this book a number of symbols are used in the excerpts of dialogue captured in interviews and during filming of families' everyday lives. These are transcription conventions designed to capture how speech was delivered.

OVERLAPPING TALK AND PAUSES

[	A single left bracket in two successive lines indicates the commencement of overlapping talk.
=	An equals sign indicates that there is no break or pause between words.
–	An en-dash after a word or part of a word indicates interrupted speech.
((pause))	Pauses are noted by the word *pause* in italics, within double parentheses.
((long pause))	Notably long pauses are indicated by the words *long pause* in italics, within double parentheses.
(.)	A period within parentheses indicates a micro pause, usually less than 0.2 second.
(0.4)	Numbers in parentheses indicate the length of a pause in tenths of a second.

INTONATION AND SPEECH DELIVERY

:::	Colons indicate the elongation or stretching of the sound that immediately precedes them.

?	A question mark indicates rising intonation.
.	A period indicates falling intonation.
(hi)	Words in single parentheses in a transcript indicate that the utterance is not clearly audible and that this is the transcriber's best guess.
hhhh	The letter *h* marks audible in-breaths or out-breaths. These may be associated with breathiness, laughter, or crying.
(xxx)	*x*'s within single parentheses indicates words that are unclear to the transcriptionist.
WORD	Uppercase letters in part of a word or a whole word indicates a very loud voice.

OTHER CONVENTIONS

(( ))	Double parentheses around an italicized word or phrase indicates descriptions of gesture or conduct.
. . .	Ellipsis indicates that some lines of transcript were omitted.
[ ]	Brackets indicate additions made by the author(s) to clarify the text.
Word	Italics indicate emphasis or importance.

Introduction

ELINOR OCHS AND TAMAR KREMER-SADLIK

In spring 2000 Kathleen Christensen, program director at the Alfred P. Sloan Foundation, traveled to Los Angeles on business. On a Friday afternoon, before returning to the airport, she called Elinor's home number to see if she could stop by. Elinor was at UCLA, and her husband, Sandro, took the call. On arriving at home Elinor was surprised to see a town car parked in front of the house and then to find Kathleen in the living room chatting with Sandro about Sloan endeavors. Kathleen's impromptu visit was occasioned by an exciting research project on American dual-earner middle-class families. The Sloan Foundation had launched a program to investigate the exigencies of raising a family while managing a paid job so that workplaces could better meet the needs of working families. Would Elinor be interested in joining this effort by designing and directing a research project dedicated to this end? Kathleen asked. Thus the UCLA Sloan Center on Everyday Lives of Families (CELF) began.

For months on end a team of UCLA scholars from diverse disciplines gathered to design a study of family life unlike any conducted previously. Anthropologists, who had traveled to faraway field sites, retooled their ethnographic methods for the "natives" of urban Los Angeles. Archaeologists, used to uncovering the material remains of past societies, turned their excavation skills to unearthing the avalanche of possessions filling contemporary American middle-class homes and to deciphering how homes are inhabited as lived spaces. Clinical psychologists, used to analyzing how people behave inside laboratories in short periods of time, developed ways to analyze stress, emotions, and family relationships over days in the midst of chaotic life at home, in the car, and in all sorts of community settings. And education specialists, who had a good sense of teaching and learning in all sorts of classrooms, sought to capture how middle-class parents strove to promote their children's learning—with varying degrees of success—in education-relevant family routines.

Families evince the historical times in which they live. The family is both the crucible of culture—where children first learn what matters in life—and the bellwether of how societal aspirations and concomitant pressures affect the vitality of persons and relationships. This volume offers entry into the private worlds of middle-class families. CELF researchers video recorded weekday mornings when parents woke their sleepy-eyed children and propelled them through routine preparations to get out the door to school and themselves off to work. Their evening video recordings laid bare how parents returning home immediately shed their workday mind-sets to attend to a sea of tasks. And they recorded weekend moments when children crawled into their parents' bed to snuggle and whisper sweet exchanges or when families lazily made pancakes for breakfast before heading to a soccer game.

The intimate access to daily life granted to CELF researchers exposed the bumps and lumps of raising a family. Inevitably, the rolling cameras caught tensions that flared between couples when collaboration broke down and intransigencies between parents and children when they did not see eye to eye about what needed to be done. While some households ran more smoothly than others, the intent of this volume is not to prescribe a right or a wrong way of being a family but rather to bring to light the intricate work exacted and the bravery demonstrated as parents crafted families, along with the inevitable misfires and dramas that ensued.

THE HISTORICAL MOMENT OF THE CELF STUDY

CELF began its study in the emotional and political aftermath of the searing tragedy of September 11, 2001, when many Americans suffered a sense of heightened vulnerability and craved the trust and intimacy that family can provide. In addition, in October 2002 working parents returned home to televised news flashes of a sniper still at large in the Washington, D.C., area, as the prelude to reuniting with their children in the next room. In 2004, as the Iraq war was in full force, an eight-year-old boy in one of the CELF families told his mother that he feared Saddam Hussein might enter their house and hurt them: "What if he's over here? What if he's in California right now?" "Would you die if he shot you right here, Dad?" In this climate CELF parents were mindful of keeping a watchful eye on children, accompanying them to their after-school organized activities and monitoring their playtime at home. Some wistfully recalled their own, more carefree childhoods, when it was possible to roam the neighborhood unsupervised on bikes or on foot.

At the same time, the years in which CELF researchers documented family life (2002–5) were a period of rapidly rising home prices, heightened consumerism, widening disparities between the super rich and the middle class, and parents burning the candle at both ends—working long and hard toward the American Dream of home ownership and a satisfying family life. CELF parents had jobs, owned their homes, purchased numerous possessions, and paid for educational and recreational opportunities for their children.

As CELF researchers wrote up their findings a few more years into the twenty-first century, parents in the United States were facing a bleaker way of looking at their wallets and their children's economic prospects. In the wake of the 2008 financial meltdown, the confidence in upward mobility and material rewards that dominated the late twentieth century and that CELF researchers documented at the turn of the twenty-first has been repackaged as the Age of Hubris, Excess, and Greed. Wall Street has been the primary target of these attributes, but households all along the great American middle-class continuum also, either out of economic necessity or moral consciousness or both, have recently looked inward, critically, at their lifestyle and consumption habits. Of Wall Street the middle class furiously inquires, "How could you do this?" But the question that some middle-class parents pose to *themselves* is, "What were we thinking?"

At the time of data collection, CELF researchers did not consider the possibility that they might be documenting a passing social, economic, and cultural era of American middle-class households, but, retrospectively, that may be exactly what CELF findings represent.[1] Yet, while some ways of life may ultimately prove emblematic of an era that no longer exists, many of the socioeconomic realities and cultural expectations that CELF captured will continue to influence everyday family practices and challenges in the near future. Parents who work will *still*—in the midst of a sagging economy—be contending with extraordinarily full days and will *still* be grappling with norms and expectations generated by their social class. Indeed, as we write this introduction, the press reports that despite the depressed economy, consumer spending is on the rise. In short, family life—especially intimate family life that transpires behind closed doors in the privacy of one's home—will continue to be the keystone that supports, on one side, the arc of previous assumptions about the way things are supposed to be and, on the other, the arc of present-day pressures, contingencies, and hopes.

PRIVATE LIFE

Private life in the United States is idealized as something that takes place out of the public eye, concealed, protected, and relatively sacred. We have laws and rules of decorum that draw boundaries between public and private worlds. Public life means conducting oneself as expected for an audience, whereas in private life people feel that they can be less conventional and freer to be themselves.[2] The eminent sociologist Erving Goffman portrays the middle-class home as a "backstage" region, where family members feel that they do not have to perform for others.[3] Certain areas of the house, such as the bedroom and the bathroom, are more backstage than others.

Researchers have been reticent to cross over the public-private threshold to observe the intimate moments of family life in middle-class households. Entering middle-class homes, where privacy is conceived of as a cultural entitlement of the highest sort, was indeed a fearsome challenge for the CELF team. In 2001, when we began our study, parents expressed trepidation that their private lives could become someone else's reality show or might be circulated on the Internet. In response to these concerns, CELF researchers treaded carefully and gratefully. Although we hoped to be a fly on the wall observing the countless engagements that consume families' waking hours, our physical presence and equipment made that impossible. Sometimes we were able to fade into the woodwork, sometimes we lent a helping hand, and sometimes we were sounding boards to someone wanting to be heard.

In the course of this delicate dance CELF amassed an extraordinarily rich archive of the backstage realms of twenty-first-century middle-class households usually out of bounds to scholars. Thousands of photographs taken by CELF researchers display homes as they are inhabited, filled with casually placed objects. Timed observations tell us how and how often family members used different rooms in their homes at ten-minute intervals. More than 1,500 hours of video recordings capture casual encounters between family members and moments of solitude. In addition, CELF measurements of each family member's stress levels indicate how experiences throughout the day affect their well-being. Finally, in-depth interviews lasting hours bring to light family members' dreams, convictions, and concerns about health, education, work, and relationships.

CELF FAMILIES

The thirty-two families in our study lived across the vast metropolis of Los Angeles, stretching from the San Fernando Valley to the South Bay and from Santa Monica to Pasadena. Some parents were first-generation immigrants from Latin America, Europe, or Asia; some had moved from the Midwest or the East Coast; some had lived all their lives in Southern California. Most families were headed by a mother and a father; two were headed by gay fathers. The families included biological and adopted children and children from previous marriages. All parents worked, some in professions like law and medicine; others held technical, administrative, or teaching positions. Some had to watch their wallets; others enjoyed more financial flexibility. All were inspired by the middle-class American Dream of buying their own home and filling it with nice things to make it beautiful and comfortable.

Above all else, what united CELF parents was that they were experiencing one of the most demanding times in their lives. They were primarily in their mid-thirties and forties, when their career opportunities were at a pivotal point of growth, determining future earning power. They had two to three children, most of whom were in elementary school. In line with middle-class expectations surrounding childrearing, CELF parents felt that they needed to provide considerable hands-on assistance to their children—not only basic care (feeding, dressing, hygiene) but also homework and chauffeuring to extracurricular activities and play dates. They worried that their parental actions—big and small—were crucial to their children's futures. They devoted a lot of time to thinking about the best path to developing self-esteem, academic success, special talents, and the like. The combination of these home- and child-related aspirations, along with the realities of Los Angeles living—high home prices and dependency on two cars per family—led to continuous commitments of time and money. Yet these involvements defined and enriched working parents' sense of themselves and gave meaning to their lives.

Let us look briefly at a day in the lives of four of the households in the study.

The Reis Household. Pam and Jerry Reis's household ran like clockwork. Pam used to produce films but changed jobs to have time to "produce" her family with Jerry, a lawyer. Both were highly involved in their children's school, sports, and getting them through their activity-packed days. On the kitchen wall hung a special calendar to keep track of their complicated family schedule. As Pam explained, "This is our magnetic calendar that we designed to try to keep this family in order. . . . Like today is the twenty-third. Mike has PE, and later on tonight Allison goes fencing. See, tomorrow, Ally has PE, Mike has tennis, his five-pitch baseball practice, and we have dinner at Bubby's [Grandma's]. Friday, two spelling tests, hockey, Ally goes to school, and Ally has basketball practice. You get the idea."

With such a busy schedule, there was a lot for Pam and Jerry to coordinate on weekday mornings. For example, one morning we filmed Pam making breakfast while Jerry prepared lunchboxes for school. Intermittently, they checked on the children's progress getting dressed and completing unfinished homework. While Pam ironed clothes for work, Jerry packed duffel bags with sports equipment for afternoon activities and loaded them into Pam's SUV. The SUV itself was an icon of organization—brimming with snacks, drinks, sports paraphernalia in plastic bins, school supplies in zippered bags, and lap boards for the children to do homework in the car. After Pam downed a glass of juice, she confirmed with Jerry practice pickup time, got the kids into the car and on the way to school, quizzed her daughter for her spelling test—all before driving herself to work.

The Sato Household. Debra and Kent Sato's household operated on a different cycle. Debra worked long hours as a municipal executive, which her young daughter, Kate, sometimes found difficult. One afternoon she phoned her mother to ask, "When are you coming home?," adding, "I miss you," before hanging up. Debra's work schedule was partly compensated for, however, by Kent's ability to leave his computer programmer job early, pick up the children, and telecommute in the afternoons. While working at home Kent answered homework questions and supervised music practice. At 5:00 P.M. one afternoon he shut off the computer and announced, "I'm off work now." On some days he took the children to basketball practice; on other days the three played basketball in the yard. On a day when Debra worked late, Kent and the children ate at a fast-food restaurant; on another day when Debra arrived earlier, Kent cooked a simple family dinner. During the meal there was a sense that nothing else competed for the family's attention and time: the food was shared and appreciated; conversation was relaxed.

The Puri Household. In another neighborhood Shanta and Vashkar Puri worked especially long hours and devoted almost all their free time to promoting the educational success of their two boys. Vashkar owned and ran two small businesses, Shanta was an elementary school teacher, and together they managed family rental property. They lived modestly on the ground floor of one of their properties but chose to send nine-year-old Harun to an excellent private school more than an hour away. When Harun and his younger brother returned home from school, Shanta gave them extra homework exercises. In between attending to the demands of several businesses, Vashkar stopped off at home in the late afternoon to see the family and eat a quick meal before leaving again. On Saturdays Shanta drove Harun to an early morning piano lesson, then to one of Vashkar's business establishments, where the Spanish-speaking manager gave Harun a private Spanish lesson. Vashkar explained that knowing Spanish was imperative to being a successful entrepreneur in California.

The Moss Household. In the San Fernando Valley, Jeri and Jeff Moss had the benefit of a nanny to help with their three children—eight-year-old Anna, five-year-old Isaiah, and nineteen-month-old Joshua. Nonetheless, there was plenty to do. Jeri arrived home first from her social welfare job, two hours before Jeff, a middle manager in a small firm. On one afternoon Jeri no sooner walked through the door than she began preparing dinner and helping tired and hungry Anna with her homework while the nanny took Isaiah and Joshua for a walk. Jeri served Anna and Isaiah dinner at the same time that the nanny fed Joshua. Around 6:00 P.M. the nanny left, leaving Jeri to monitor Isaiah taking a bath, Joshua watching TV in the living room, and Anna needing constant help with her homework. Jeri needed to be in three places at once, leading to perpetual movement from room to room. By the time Jeff arrived home Anna's homework was done, the kitchen was clean, and the children were bathed and in pajamas. As he walked through the door, Jeri and the children were cuddled in front of the TV set. Exclaiming "Look who's here!," Jeri prompted the baby to toddle toward his father. Then she wearily rose from the couch to warmly welcome Jeff home.

The demands depicted across these four family scenes are just the tip of the iceberg. A lot more transpired in CELF households in the aftermath of spending hours in the workplace and school, including the effort of maintaining couple as well as parent-child relationships. Couples had to contend with the practical urgencies at hand and still try to attune to one another's and their own emotional states. Couples—some more smoothly than others—divided the manifold tasks of raising a family. How they did so affected the quality of their relationship. Connecting with one another

Figure I.1. CELF mother after work.

in the evenings at home was not easy on days when their jobs were particularly stressful.

CELF cameras routinely documented parents multitasking at home n the evenings, usually a working mother (Figure I.1), running in circles from room to room, checking on a child with a homework problem, monitoring a pot on the stove, tidying up, and redirecting another child who should be doing homework but was instead watching TV or playing video games.[4] In the midst of all this, parents also had to take conference calls, check email messages, or prepare files for work. The workplace crept into the home and competed for mental space in the already full schedule of childcare and housecleaning responsibilities.

Looking at scenes from the Reis, Sato, Puri, and Moss households, we are not surprised that a good deal of family life transpired at home. In the CELF study, however, the home was not just the backdrop of family relationships and events; it was a central protagonist in defining middle-class families. Its centrality rested in no small way on its status as one of the jewels of the American Dream, one that required high monthly mortgage payments.[5] Beyond the financial outlay, however, the house, including the objects that filled it, shaped family identities and well-being on a daily basis. The CELF study shows what houses look like when they are used and loved—not the idealized, carefully arranged homes featured in architectural magazines but homes packed with sentimental photos, mementos, and all sorts of purchases deemed desirable or necessary. The possessions that filled CELF houses tell us a lot about the kinds of objects that middle-class American families prize (what counts as "taste") and how they want to present themselves to their friends, neighbors, and one another.

What the CELF study also makes clear are the non–American Dream consequences of living in the most materially saturated dwellings in human history.[6] Household possessions were so numerous that they overwhelmed houses and flowed into garages, pushing cars onto driveways or streets. Food bought in bulk at mega-discount stores was stockpiled in second refrigerators, cupboards, and garage floors. And children's bedrooms burst with clothes, costumes, trophies, sports gear, books, art supplies, and toys. When Mike Reis described his room, he proudly declared why it is his favorite part of the house: "Here is why: All these toys and toys and toys and toys and toys and toys and toys and toys and toys and toys and toys and toys and toys and toys and toys and toys and toys and toys. My bed is eventually somewhere. Look at all these toys, though." What many parents coming home from work realized was that the sheer number of possessions surrounding them demanded attention. Managing clutter and cleaning was a ceaseless activity and, in some families, a source of stress.

Families are profoundly influenced by social understandings of what it means to be a parent, a child, and a spouse and the significance of home. It is all too easy to think of our own ways of being a family as natural and obvious. The contribution of anthropology has been to disabuse us of this occluded vision and offer a view of family as a product of society's cultural values at a particular historical moment. How members of a family act, think, and feel shifts with the winds of prevailing values and practices across generations and communities. The earliest moments of a child's life are organized by cultural ideas about raising children to become competent members of society. These ideas, in turn, inform how parents relate to children and to one another.

In the 1970s one of this volume's coeditors, Elinor Ochs, documented young children growing up in a Samoan village.[7] Samoan caregivers encouraged toddlers to pay keen attention to people around them and show respect by doing things for them. By the time they were six or seven, along with attending school, children helped with housework, yard work, infant care, procuring food from gardens, serving meals, fetching needed objects, and transmitting oral messages across family compounds. In the households of middle-class Los Angeles, another cultural expectation prevailed: parents believed it was essential that they accommodate the needs and desires of children well beyond the preschool years.[8] CELF parents helped their children in all kinds of tasks—practical, academic, and recreational. Recall, for example, the extensive efforts of the Reis parents in just one morning.

The Reis parents took enormous pleasure in organizing their children's activities. Pam Reis remarked, "That's our time—that's my time with them . . . I'm there for them . . . when they do the things that they do, when they take their lessons, when they learn something new or they—whatever. I'm there for them. That's our time together." Yet other parents found it quite challenging, on top of housework and job-related commitments, to be so heavily involved in children's homework and extracurricular activities. One CELF mother longingly contrasted her middle-class mothering to the domestic load of her own working mother: "She would come home and cook dinner and that was—that was all she did. See, I come home and cook dinner and help my son. . . . I would come home while she was working, [sit] at my desk until six o'clock at night, and do my own homework and finish it. Very rarely she would have to help me." While the first CELF mother embraced her involvement as an intrinsic part of good parenting, the second, full of nostalgia, reflected on her childhood to question all-embracing, child-centric parenting as a moral imperative.

BACK TO THE FUTURE WITH MARGARET MEAD

It is tempting to think that raising a family at the start of the twenty-first century presents unique challenges, and to some extent that temptation is validated by the staggering sociocultural and economic transformations that brought about the steep rise in dual-earner parents who must manage their work and family in tandem. Yet these transformations have characterized life in the United States for quite a while, and the middle-class family in particular has been positioned as the pivotal institution responsible for fostering an adventurous future generation. In a lecture delivered at Harvard University in 1950 Margaret Mead argued that middle-class Americans raise their children to reject the old and "outstrip their parents" and to be "alert and ready to face a relatively new and uncharted world."[9] Key to Mead's argument was the idea that parents are distinct from grandparents and siblings as caregivers. Parents are old enough to have wisdom, yet still open to change themselves. Mead urged middle-class parents to grow along with their constantly changing children as a new age ushered in television, automation, Sputnik, the arms race, youth culture, and rising affluence.

The difference between middle-class family life in the 1950s and that in the early years of the twenty-first century may be one of scale in regard to gender roles and expectations. While many women joined the workforce during and after World War II, even the intrepid Margaret Mead saw herself as an outlier and depicted mothers simply as beneficiaries of economic prosperity and smaller families, while "the father is making his way, actively, in a world of change and commerce, a world of entrepreneurship and profit."[10] In this perspective, women were assumed to be mothers and teachers, and their singular challenge was to be a creative mentor: "She must give up any over faithful clinging to the particulars of her own past."[11] Since that era radical cultural and economic transformations in U.S. women's roles, rights, and agency in and outside the workforce have reorganized middle-class expectations and realities with regard to what it means to be a life partner as well as a parent.

Mead's insights were child-focused, concentrating on the middle-class imperative to nurture children to invent themselves in a constantly evolving modern world. As this volume reveals, however, the *entire household*—the couple, father-child, mother-child, and sibling relationships—invents itself each and every day. The chapters that follow take us to the epicenter of the middle-class American household to see how family members dance to the beat of the ever-changing expectations of peers, schools, workplaces, and the media and of one another, and, ultimately, themselves.

NOTES

1. It will, of course, take some time for scholars to systematically discern which domains of middle-class family life have been affected by foreclosures, unemployment, furloughs, and other ramifications of the current economic meltdown and which ideologies and practices perdure.

2. Goffman 1959; Sennett 1974.

3. Goffman 1959.

4. Good 2009.

5. The rise of dual-earner middle-class families in recent decades has been attributed to several factors, among which is the abiding desire for home ownership and the soaring cost of home prices and mortgage payments (Chris-

tensen and Schneider 2010; Warren and Tyagi 2003). Regardless of whether parents want to pursue careers, many feel constrained to do so in order to live in a home in a safe neighborhood with decent schools for their children.

6. Arnold et al. 2012.
7. Ochs 1988.
8. See also Ochs and Schieffelin 1984; Ochs and Izquierdo 2009.
9. Mead [1950] 2001, 56.
10. Ibid., 56.
11. Ibid., 59.

1 Coming Home

ELINOR OCHS AND BELINDA CAMPOS

This chapter is the first of several in this volume to document parents and children coming home from work and school and their challenges and triumphs in forging connections as a family. The concept "coming home" is filled with sentimentality in American society, and adages that capture these feelings abound: home is where the heart is; home is where one belongs; homeward bound. Yet these adages are misleading in assuming that familiarity and belonging are rewards that naturally await home-bound working adults and children. Rather, such rewards are the result of an interactional endeavor that begins the instant that family members arrive home. Seemingly trivial behaviors like greeting or noticing a returning family member turn out to be consequential for opening lines of communication and nourishing parent-child and couple relationships.

In his classic article on human interaction the sociologist Emanuel Schegloff argued that ostensibly mundane routines such as an exchange of greetings actually require a great deal of coordination and are best understood as complex interactional achievements.[1] You might imagine that people who do not know each other well or who see each other rarely may have to pay attention to how they initiate and respond to each other's social overtures when they meet. But what happens when parents and children and couples meet one another on a daily basis after returning home from work and school? Is it also an effort for them to greet and reengage one another after going their separate ways during the day? The message of this chapter is, yes, initiating face-to-face social interaction between family members at the end of the work- and school day demands a degree of cooperation that is not always forthcoming in different families or in the same family from one day to the next or on the same day between one family member and another. Working parents may be warmly welcomed home by some members of their family but treated as if they were invisible by others. When CELF working parents arrived home, they often encountered family members who were content to see them but distracted by their own concerns. Garnering attention and reconnecting as a family was not a matter of course; rather, at times it was quite an undertaking.

To get a sense of the vicissitudes of family reunions at the end of the day, we invite you to look at what transpired among members of the Gruvich family on two separate days after work and school. On one of these days Ray Gruvich had already arrived home from work and was sorting through the mail when his ten-year-old son, Tim, burst through the door calling out, "Hi Dad!" Ray asked, "How are you::: kiddo?," and Tim replied, "Fine!" Ray was buoyant: "Excellent. Good." They embraced. Next through the door was six-year-old Becky, followed by her mother, Beth. Ray approached them, greeting Becky with a long "Hello:::!," a kiss, and the observation, "You found your jacket, huh?" While Becky clamored for more attention, Ray and Beth greeted and kissed each other. The family had successfully reunited at the end of the day.

Lest we think that this twenty-first-century family comes straight out of a 1950s TV series, let's observe how the Gruvich family welcomed each other on another day that week. On this day Ray's parents had picked up the children from school and brought them to their house. When Ray arrived at his parents' home after work, Tim and Becky were glued to the TV set watching a cartoon. While the reunion between Ray and his children began well, with Tim embracing his father and reporting on homework progress, Becky remained transfixed by the television and did not acknowledge her father. Even when Ray opened his arms for a hug and called, "Becky," she merely flashed him a nanosecond's glance. Ray then exclaimed, "Ah!," wryly noting his daughter's minimal acknowledgment of his presence. This lament prodded Becky to say, "Hi," but she did so while watching the cartoon. At this point Ray dropped his arms in exasperation, sighing, "Well, hi to you *too*," to deaf ears. And then an argument ensued. Ray asked Becky about her homework; she mumbled something, continuing to be entranced by the television; Ray pulled away the bottle of soda she had in her hand; reaching for the bottle, Becky protested, "No::! that's mi::ne!" Holding on to the bottle, Ray insisted, "Talk to me," until Becky resentfully responded to a stream of questions reminiscent of an interrogation: "Did you finish your homework?" "Who checked your homework?" "Is that your trash?" "When are you going to throw it away?" "I'll be back to check, okay?" Shortly after this rebuff,

Ray's wife, Beth, arrived and greeted the children but overlooked him. As she passed him to help her mother-in-law in the kitchen, Ray twice called out "Hey!" to catch her attention, then entreated, "Say hi first, then you can go help." Beth retraced her tracks to affectionately greet her husband.

The Gruvich family illustrates the challenges that working parents in the CELF households in Los Angeles encountered when reconnecting with the rest of the family after a day apart. Parents and children knew little about what happened in each other's lives during the day, including plans that affected the rest of the family. The first moments after returning home were imbued with parental anticipation of affection and information that was not always forthcoming.

This daily pattern of being apart for at least six hours a day during the work- and school week contrasts with family life in a number of other societies, where school-aged children are isolated from family members for shorter periods. For example, many rural Samoan children attend school on the edge of the village close to their homes.[2] While some parents work in the capital, other adult family members remain in the village. The path to some of the family plantations runs past the schoolhouse, allowing family members on their way to or from cultivation to overhear children's recitations or relay information if necessary. Children return home at midday and immediately become immersed in a thicket of family tasks. In such communities family members encounter each other intermittently throughout the day and are integrated through cooperative activities. If a child or spouse is out of sight, his or her whereabouts are easily gleaned from others who monitor the comings and goings of extended family members and neighbors.

For better or for worse, working parents and children in the United States do not typically reside in family compounds or small communities. In Los Angeles, CELF parents and children generally commuted to work and school. While grandparents play a vital role in American family life, middle-class parents typically live apart from their own parents in nuclear households.[3] Most of these parents are unable to benefit from the kind of childcare commonplace in Samoan communities (see Introduction). In only a few CELF households, like that of the Gruvich family, did grandparents routinely take care of their grandchildren at certain times during the week. Children's schools are often not close to workplaces, and school policies may discourage parents from entering the classroom or otherwise contacting children at school except in emergencies. Beyond notice of illness or other calamities, parents in the United States usually receive little or no information about their children until late in the day. These long hours of separation make the vital process of reuniting more difficult; family members who spend the majority of their time in separate worlds may habituate to this arrangement and find it challenging to share their life-worlds spent apart in the relatively few hours that they are together in the home. The challenges imposed by the separate worlds of work and family mean that end-of-the-day reunions provide one of the few, and thus significant, opportunities of the day to show regard and affirm family bonds.

As important as it is for family members to reconnect at the end of the day, the transition to being a family after a day apart is not always easy. As working parents know in their bones, children and adults can be exhausted as a result of the day's exertions, and their moment of reunion may be strained. During the week parents returning from work may be preoccupied with household- or workplace-related tasks; children usually have homework to complete; everyone may be hungry and grouchy. As in the Gruvich family, American children may sometimes give parents the silent treatment when seeing them in the late afternoon or evening. Television and other media may also contribute to such comportment. The homecoming transition is potentially tense when weary parents and emotionally needy young children reengage one another.[4]

Given its importance, we wondered how the CELF families in our study managed to reconnect at the end of the day. To what extent did they generally enjoy positive reunions? To what extent was the delicate process of reuniting as a family hampered by a family member being distracted?

To address these questions and others, a team of psychologists and anthropologists analyzed the video recordings of families getting together after work and school.[5] In our study, we focused on the thirty families headed by a mother and father—twenty-one with two children and nine with three children—to understand how the parents experienced reuniting with their children and partners. We focused on what happens in the first two minutes after mothers and fathers walk through the door from work. We asked the following questions: What kind of reception do working parents receive from their children and spouses? When working fathers arrive home, do they receive the same kind of welcome from their families as working mothers receive when they arrive home, or are fathers and mothers treated differently? Across the thirty dual-earner CELF families there was the potential for 120 reunions at home. But family members often reunited outside the home, at school or elsewhere. As recording conditions made it difficult for these reunions to be captured consistently on video, they were not included in this study. In addition, some parents did not reunite with the rest of their families at the end of the day because their jobs (e.g., as pilot, firefighter, sheriff) required them to work during that time. Our analysis includes a total of 44 reunions that took place at home. These reunions capture the first encounters with family members immediately after nineteen working fathers and ten working mothers returned home.

WHY WE GREET

Before getting to the results of our study, we want to consider how people all over the world encounter one another after having been apart for a period of time. The sociologist Erving Goffman noted that every person has a "face"—a valued image of the self that he or she wants to project and maintain in particular social situations.[6] Relating this idea to working families, we can say that when family members come into contact at the end of the day, each has a face (i.e., an image of herself or himself as mother or father, daughter or son, sister or brother, or partner in a couple) that they want other family members to uphold.

Birds do it; even bees do it. Not falling in love but *greeting*. Among the many interaction rituals of face appreciation, greetings have an important place. When we enter into one another's social sphere after a certain stretch of time apart, we support the face of the other by greeting him or her. The presence of a greeting distinguishes persons as valued. As Alessandro Duranti has written, "In many societies children and servants are not greeted. The absence of greetings then marks these individuals not only as nonproper conversationalists or strangers but also as not worth the attention implied by the use of greetings."[7]

If one person greets there is a strong expectation that the person greeted will return the greeting. If a person does not return a greeting, its absence is noticeable.[8] When we reciprocate greetings (I greet you, You greet me) we signal to each other that we find the other worthy of recognition. Each person demonstrates positive sentiments (e.g., respect, affection) toward the other and sets the emotional tone of downstream interaction. In the first set of greetings in the Gruvich family, for example, Ray appeared absolutely delighted when his son, Tim, called out, "Hi Dad!," as he burst through the front entrance. Ray nearly cooed his greetings to both his children and his wife, and they responded in kind, displaying their affection for one another. Alternatively, when one person issues a greeting and it is not reciprocated, an asymmetry in deference and face support results. The person greeted becomes a focus of attention and appreciation but the person who greets does not. On the evening when his daughter ignored him after he arrived from work and called out to her with his arms held wide open for a hug, Ray appeared upset. An important message is that no matter how intimate we are with another person, most of us (including members of our own families) in most circumstances have the desire to be acknowledged with a greeting.

Even the simplest greeting has the potential to elicit a reciprocal greeting if not more conviviality. As such, greeting rituals help human beings to come together as a social unit. Social engagement may terminate with the greeting response: "Hi Dad"; "Hi Susie." Alternatively, the greeting may open the door to more sustained communication ("Hi Dad." "How are you::: kiddo?" "Fine!" "Excellent. Good"). This property renders the greeting a powerful medium for coming together as a family after a long day apart. Taking only a few seconds to produce, a greeting is an efficient ritual gateway to connecting to family members.

ARRIVING HOME

It struck us that the parent who returns home earlier (or first) might be having a different homecoming experience from that of the parent who returns home later (or second). The *first* parent to return home, for example, does not have the opportunity to be welcomed home by his or her partner (because he or she has not yet returned), while the second parent can enjoy this possibility. At the same time, the first parent to return home is also often the parent who has picked up the children after their school and extracurricular activities. The first parent home, therefore, may be more likely to encounter children who are more eager to greet positively and share news about their day.

The *second* parent returning home has to reckon with family members absorbed in a stream of ongoing activities. The children have homework, which usually involves supervision by the first parent. The first parent also has usually been preparing dinner and monitoring other household tasks. In some families the children may be absorbed by TV watching or other media activities. These conditions affect how the second parent is welcomed by his or her children and partner.

It probably will come as no surprise to those documenting the lives of working women that the thirty working mothers in the CELF study had first contact with the children on 76 percent of the weekdays observed, whereas their spouses had first contact with the children on 20 percent of them and a babysitter or grandparent had first contact on 4 percent of them.[9] Typically, the second parent arrived home to the partner and children roughly two hours later. Of the two weekdays that we video recorded during the workweek, mothers arrived home earlier 60 percent of the time, twice as often as did their spouses.

That CELF mothers more often had first contact with their children and arrived home earlier than did their spouses makes sense when looking at the working hours of these mothers and fathers. CELF fathers worked about two hours a day longer than the mothers in the study. These parental differences in picking up children and returning home are compatible with other findings that contemporary working mothers assume the lion's share of childcare responsibilities.[10] But overlooked in other studies is the possible *effect* that these arrangements may have on the integration of fathers into family life when they arrive home after mothers and children have been together. Let us now turn to how CELF mothers and fathers were integrated into the family when they returned home after work.

WAYS OF WELCOMING WORKING PARENTS

How did family members welcome home working mothers and fathers? To answer this question, we created five categories of welcoming behaviors exhibited by children and partners: positive behaviors, reports of information, logistic behaviors, negative behaviors, and distraction. Sometimes a reunion was characterized by just one kind of welcoming behavior, while in other reunions, a family member displayed two or more kinds of welcoming responses to the returning parent.

Positive behaviors included instances in which family members greeted ("Hi Dad!") and acted affectionately. Greetings and acts of affection not only included words; bodily expressions counted as well (e.g., waves, high five signs, hugs). The first Gruvich family reunion illustrates such positive behaviors. Positive behaviors support the face wants of a returning parent by demonstrating that the parent's arrival home was noticed and/ or appreciated. Positive behaviors toward a returning parent also opened the door to the possibility of continued social engagement between family members.

Reports of information included exchanges in which a family member welcomed a returning parent with information about what happened during his or her day. Often these reports accompanied positive behaviors like greeting or noticing a returning parent. In just such an exchange, eleven-year-old Sandra Anderson ran toward her arriving father, then showed him a school paper that had received a good grade. Her father, reading the teacher's comments, responded "That's *cool*. Oh that's coo::l. That's great."

Logistic behaviors included requesting help or information from the returning family member or talking about housework, school, or workplace obligations. For example, when working father Thomas Banks pulled into the driveway, his wife, Roberta, and daughter, Kayley, were cleaning the inside of Roberta's car. Kayley yelled, "Hey Daddy? Uh—can—can—uh—Can you get the vacuum cleaner out?" After being prompted by her mother, Kayley added, "Please," and a justification: "so that we can vacuum in the car." Thomas then teasingly turned on the ignition and started backing out the driveway, as Kayley chased him, flung open the door, repeated over and over, "You have to get it out," and tugged on him until he acquiesced.

Negative behaviors by family members included overt displays of anger, criticism, and whining. When working mother Julia Dorbin emerged from her car and walked toward the front door, for example, her eight-year-old son, Josh, complained, "Mom, you said that you'd be here earlier." Julia corrected him: "This is earlier. Yesterday I didn't get home until five thirty." After asking, "What time is it?," and finding out that it was "a little after four," Josh cocked his head and raised his arms in exasperation, muttering sarcastically, "Big difference." As Julia entered the house she concluded the matter with the words, "Well, it *is* a big difference." In another CELF household, Anita Goodson arrived home before her husband, Chad, to discover that he did not refrigerate the chicken that the family was to eat for dinner. She called Chad on his cell, and when he arrived home she greeted him with, "So does that mean that's all spoiled? What did you do *that* for?" After Chad cautiously responded, "Well, I'll have to look at it and see," Anita walked away, insisting, "But you need to answer my *question*." To no avail it turns out, as Chad did not respond.

Distraction occurred when a family member did not display recognition of a returning parent, either by being completely oblivious or by treating the parent as a secondary concern while primarily involved in another ongoing activity. For the returning parent distraction was not a desirable response. But unlike in the case of "negative behaviors" the distracted family member was not overtly angry or upset with the returning family member. Especially in the case of children, distraction was more often an outcome of absorption in an ongoing activity such as playing a video game. The second homecoming of the Gruvich family is a good example of distraction. Becky remained glued to the television as her father tried to greet her. In many households, screen media were powerful rivals for children's attention.

To find out how CELF working parents were welcomed home, we turn first to how couples welcomed each other and then to how children welcomed fathers and mothers.

HOW COUPLES WELCOME EACH OTHER

Husbands and wives generally welcomed their partners home positively but were also distracted, with wives being more distracted than husbands. Now let's look at the numbers.

Positive Behaviors. Recall that there were many fewer occasions in which CELF working mothers returned to family members already in the home relative to CELF working fathers. Yet five of the nine times (56 percent) that mothers returned and their husbands were already at home, the husbands behaved "positively"; that is, they greeted or showed affection. Mothers were positive to their returning husbands even more frequently, in nineteen of twenty-nine reunions (66 percent).

Information Reports. Husbands reported information about the day's events to returning wives on four occasions (44 percent). Wives delivered information to their returning husbands more frequently, on seventeen occasions (59 percent).

Logistic Behaviors. Husbands *never* asked their returning spouses for help or inquired about housework that needed to be done or their spouses' work obligations. Wives instead asked their husbands about such things in almost a third of the reunions (28 percent). This difference may appear to confirm the gender stereotype of men being more reluctant than women to elicit assistance. An alternative possibility, however, is that men may volunteer less to do housework and childcare, which may create a situation in which women feel compelled to take the lead and ask.

Negative Behaviors. Couples rarely expressed negative feelings when reuniting after work. We documented only one occasion (11 percent) of a husband acting negatively toward his returning wife and one occasion (3 percent) of a wife acting negatively to a husband.

Distraction. Husbands were distracted in 33 percent of the occasions when their wives returned home from work later than they did. Wives, however, were distracted even more often—45 percent of the occasions that their husbands returned home. Wives were not oblivious to their husbands' arrival. Rather, they were usually caught up in a swirl of tasks—monitoring children's homework, TV watching, and playtime, along with meals, laundry, and other household chores—that precluded giving their husbands their full attention. These activities were in full swing by the time working fathers walked in the door—well after the arrival home of the mothers. Preoccupation with housework and child-care and the later hour of fathers' arrival home cannot fully account for these observed levels of distraction, however. It takes only a few seconds to turn one's attention away from what one is doing to greet a returning partner, and fathers frequently were not granted even the briefest whiff of recognition.

HOW CHILDREN WELCOME PARENTS

A *Doonesbury* cartoon strip a few years ago portrayed a father opening the door to his teenage son's room and asking if it is okay to come in.[11] His son assures him, "Adults your age are invisible to us. You walk into a room of kids, no one will stand or acknowledge you in any way." After his father sighs, "Yeah, I hate that," his son continues, "I mean, unless you are holding a gun or a pizza or something." Is this how the CELF children responded to their returning parents? To address this question, we asked, "To what extent did each child display positive behavior, report information, engage in logistic talk, display negative behavior, or distraction toward their returning fathers and mothers?" Then we asked a different question: "To what extent did returning fathers and mothers receive positive behavior, report information, engage in logistic talk, display negative behavior, or distraction from *at least one of their children?*" This second question gives us a glimpse of the psychological experience of a parent returning home. For example, a positive reception from at least one member of the family may buffer a returning parent from feeling completely ignored.

The picture we found for reunions between working parents and their children, especially for working fathers, differs from what we saw for couples reuniting at the end of day. Here are the details.

Positive and Negative Behaviors. Children welcomed returning fathers differently from mothers on their arriving home from work. The children welcomed their fathers with positive behaviors—greeting, hugging, or otherwise demonstrating affection—in only 44 percent of the homecomings, compared to 59 percent of the homecomings of their mothers. When we looked at the possibility of fathers and mothers being welcomed positively by *at least one child,* however, it was comforting to find that both fathers and mothers were greeted positively by at least one of their children every time (100 percent) they returned home from work. Thus, while fathers did not experience positive attention from children more than half of the time they reentered the household, they could count on one of their children to greet them positively. Moreover, on the optimistic side, children very rarely acted in a *negative* manner to either returning fathers (4 percent) or returning mothers (2 percent).

Information Reports. Differences in how children welcomed home fathers and mothers showed up in other behaviors as well. Children gave reports of their day less often (39 percent) to returning fathers than to returning mothers, who received such reports on nearly half of the occasions (48 percent) they arrived home. This difference is even more striking when we look at the possibility that *at least one child* recounted events about their day to a returning parent. While working fathers heard reports about events from at least one child on 66 percent of occasions they arrived back home, mothers heard at least one child's report 93 percent of the time. These differences suggest that the children were more willing or perhaps more used to sharing their experiences with their mothers than with their fathers.

Logistic Behaviors. Although children infrequently brought up a logistical matter in the first moments of their parents' arrival home, it is striking that they engaged returning mothers in the logistics of homework assignments, lost belongings, items to purchase, and the like twice as often as they engaged father in such concerns (22 vs. 11 percent). Again this difference may indicate that the children had different expectations of their mothers and fathers or even of their relative pragmatic usefulness. Alternatively, it could be that fathers' later arrival home meant that certain practical problems were handled earlier by the first parent in contact with the children (i.e., the working mother).

Distraction. The great American humorist Ogden Nash quipped, "Children aren't happy without something to ignore, and that's what parents were created for."[12] Nash's witticism predates Gary Trudeau's *Doonesbury* caricature[13] and attests to a long-standing cultural resignation about American children disregarding their parents. Given this American disposition, we were curious about the extent to which the CELF children were partly or completely distracted when their mothers and fathers returned home from work. Notably, our observations are concordant with Nash's and Trudeau's insights, *but* children's levels of distraction differed for mothers arriving home compared to fathers arriving home. When mothers arrived home from work children were distracted on 22 percent of the occasions. When fathers returned home, however, the children were distracted far more often, on 38 percent of the occasions.

Looking at the possibility that *at least one child* was distracted when a parent returned home, we found an even more striking difference for working mothers and fathers. Mothers were met by at least one distracted child on 44 percent of their homecomings, but fathers were met by at least one distracted child on 86 percent of their homecomings. In other words, while mothers were frequently ignored, fathers were *characteristically* ignored by at least one of their children. Based on these findings, Nash's witticism might be rewritten as, "Children aren't happy without something to ignore, and that's what *fathers* were created for." As argued for other differences we observed, the high degree of distraction toward working fathers may be partly an effect of the later time they return home, when children were preoccupied with other activities.

GOOD NEWS, BAD NEWS

This study conveys both good news and bad news regarding the fate of men and women who seek to reconnect with their partners and children when they return home from work. The good news is that the reunions between working parents and the rest of their family are more positive than popular media suggest. Over half of the reunions between CELF couples were positive. Moreover, returning parents *always* found that at least one of their children greeted, approached, or displayed affection to them. Despite the challenges inherent in the urban life worlds of our CELF families—long hours of work-school separation and nuclear rather than extended family arrangements—they tried to capitalize on the brief opportunities embedded in the routine of the day to reconnect with one another and affirm family bonds.

On the flip side, we have to ask ourselves as researchers (and as parents) why partners and children did not display positive behaviors more often to welcome parents home. Given that across societies most people greet and convey positive sentiments when they reunite,[14] it is striking that the middle-class American children in this study did not demonstrate such behaviors in 56 percent of the reunions with their fathers and 40 percent of the reunions with mothers returning home from work.

One explanation could be that working parents were unconcerned about whether or not their child or spouse said hello or gave them a sign of affection. Our video recordings indicate, however, that it mattered a great deal. CELF parents relished positive contact with their children when they arrived home and were disappointed when such attention was not forthcoming. Indeed, these small moments set the tone of subsequent interactions throughout the evening. Positive greetings gave way to smooth, rewarding social exchanges, while distraction disappointed the returning parent, which may have contributed to fathers spending less time with other family members on weekday evenings.[15]

A major culprit hindering reconnecting as a family at the end of the day was distraction. In many homes, a returning parent had to compete for attention with ongoing involvements, and sometimes this was a losing battle.[16] Fathers returning home were more invisible than were returning mothers. It is likely that fathers' relatively late arrival in the evening (working on average two hours longer than mothers) contributed to their less than compelling reentry into the family scene. Distraction, however, is not an entirely satisfactory explanation. After all, it takes less than a minute for a child or partner to produce a greeting. It may well be that sometimes middle-class American working parents were simply too exhausted or preoccupied with their own unfinished business to compete with distractions absorbing family members' attention. Some parents may have reconciled themselves to the disappointment of being ignored or being a secondary concern of their children or spouses when they walked through the door at the end of the day. Over time, these habits of disconnection can adversely affect the quality of family relationships.

Of course, a greeting proffered by a parent to a child or by one partner to another is only one of many moments in which to communicate with one's family. The whole evening lies before parents and children and couples. In the chapters that follow we will see just how these moments are seized by family members, including the extent to which the family comes together as a vital social institution.

NOTES

1. Schegloff 1987.
2. Ochs 1988.
3. Clavan 1978.
4. Kendall 2006.
5. Ochs et al. 2006; Campos et al. 2009.
6. Goffman 1963, 1967.
7. Duranti 1997, 71.
8. Sacks, Schegloff, and Jefferson 1974; Schegloff 1968.
9. Good 2009.

10. Bianchi, Robinson, and Milkie 2006; Hochschild and Machung [1989] 2003; Schneider and Waite 2005.

11. Trudeau 2004.

12. Nash 1933.

13. Trudeau 2004.

14. Duranti 1997; Goffman 1963, 1967.

15. Campos et al. 2009.

16. Pigeron 2009.

2 **At Home**

ANTHONY P. GRAESCH

Family counselors, newspaper columnists, academic researchers—even bloggers—all agree on a core problem of contemporary American families: there is too much to do and too little time to get it done. One of the most salient findings documented by the broader CELF study is that young, dual-earner families are extraordinarily busy. A typical week for parents and their children includes at least five consecutive days of work and school, each so jam-packed with appointments, meetings, classes, after-school activities, and commutes that many families spend more waking hours apart than together. Although broader survey-level studies of time use suggest that families have more time together now than in the past,[1] other studies reveal that parents are increasingly concerned with the degree to which career choices and work-related obligations limit their ability to participate in daily life as it unfolds at home.[2]

Parents' perceptions of time shortages are partly a result of trying to cram more activities into limited windows of nonwork time.[3] Children are at the center of this scheduling whirlwind, and parents' increasing levels of involvement in children's lives have amplified subjective experiences of busyness.[4] A now standard—if not *expected*—middle-class practice of enrolling children in several after-school activities has cascaded into additional time commitments, including coordinating transportation, communicating with program leaders, maintaining parental social networks, monitoring child performance, and attending children's events. As Darrah argues, busier parents are not necessarily working harder or longer hours but instead are having to reconfigure their lives around a growing number of bids for their attention before and after employed work.[5]

Indeed, there is much evidence to suggest that parents perceive

heightened levels of busyness as affecting how and *how often* they interact with their spouses and children.[6] However, what is not apparent in
most previous sociological, psychological, and other formal studies of
contemporary American life is how heightened levels of family busyness
are affecting the lived experience of parents and children in their homes.
Specifically, there is a dearth of ethnographic data that speak to daily
life as it unfolds moment by moment in the home. To this end, the CELF
study fills a gap in our much broader understanding of the "time crunch"
in and among American families.

This chapter brings to light a unique data set that addresses how parents and children use unscheduled opportunities to spend time together
when at home. These data were gathered with an ethnographic observation technique called scan sampling. Originally developed by etholo-
gists, the method entailed an ethnographer walking through premapped
home spaces at carefully timed intervals and systematically recording the
specific location and activities of each parent and child.[7] Person-centered
observations were recorded every ten minutes and are unique from our
corpus of video data in that they reflect the simultaneous activities of
all family members who were in the home, regardless of whether these
people were captured on film (Figure 2.1).[8] The resulting data set provides
important insights into the everyday lived experience of dual-income
households: how often parents and children spend time with each other,
where time is spent, and the mediating roles of home spaces and family
possessions in the co-construction of life at home. Some of these data may
be alarming in that they show a trend toward family member isolation
despite ample opportunity for direct, face-to-face interaction. This has·
implications not only for parent-child affectional relationships but also
for spousal intimacy. Other data, however, implicate new strategies for
maintaining social and emotional bonds between parents and children in
the midst of navigating within and between the spheres of work, school,
and family life. And some of the CELF ethnographic data complicate our
normative understanding of gendered contributions to childcare.

Opportunities for parents and children to co-construct daily routines
and achieve family-level cohesion are perhaps greatest when family
members are within a thirty-second walk of each other in the home. But
how often are these opportunities used, and how often do these opportunities arise? Few readers will be surprised to learn that most parents and
school-aged children in dual-income households spend more weekday
waking hours outside the home than in. Moreover, among the families
participating in the CELF project, it was rare to find parents and children

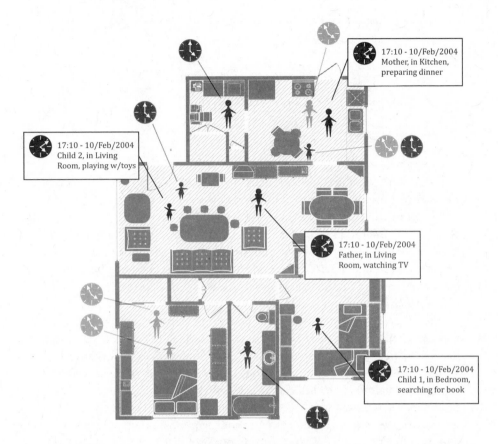

17:10 - 10/Feb/2004
Mother, in Kitchen,
preparing dinner

17:10 - 10/Feb/2004
Child 2, in Living
Room, playing w/toys

17:10 - 10/Feb/2004
Father, in Living
Room, watching TV

17:10 - 10/Feb/2004
Child 1, in Bedroom,
searching for book

Recency of Observation

Mother

Father

Child

Highly Mobile Families

After all family members returned home, parents and children gathered
in numerous person-space combinations. When I embarked on our very
first visit to a family's home, I was surprised to learn just how mobile
parents and children could be over the course of an evening.

Although many activities were localized in kitchens, I observed family
members moving between spaces so frequently that I abandoned our
initial plan to record observations every 20 minutes in favor of a
10-minute sampling interval. Even this scan sampling strategy could not
fully capture the frequency at which parents and children moved between
spaces and engaged in different activities.

Figure 2.1. Weekday time at home.

Table 2.1. Parents' Average Daily Work and Commuting Time

	Work (hrs.)	Commuting (min.)
Fathers	10.1	60.2
Mothers	8.6	45.4

simultaneously at home on weekdays. In fact, only 687 (37 percent) of 1,840 scan sampling observation rounds on weekdays found all family members in their homes at the same time.[9] Not surprisingly, we consistently recorded two spans of time during which all members tended to be under the same roof: (1) in the early mornings, after parents woke up their children and before everyone left for work and school; (2) in the late afternoons and evenings, after family members returned home and before children were put to bed.

As might be expected, weekday mornings were somewhat hurried and almost always a little chaotic. Breakfasts needed to be eaten, lunches needed to be made, transportation logistics needed to be organized, and permission slips required signing. On average, it took seventy-four minutes for parents and children to accomplish these and other morning tasks before rushing out of the house. For some families, the morning routine was fluid and without complications. For most others, the experience was hectic: there was always competition for use of the bathroom, and there was little time for interactions that did not center on getting ready for school and ushering people over the threshold.

Opportunities for parents and children to be together on weekday afternoons and evenings were largely determined by fathers' and, to a lesser extent, mothers' schedules. The return to home after work and school was often staggered over several hours. Mothers and fathers typically commuted to and from work in separate vehicles, sometimes transporting children to and from school along the way. In some families, children arrived home before either parent, having taken the bus, walked, or been met and transported by a nanny. In most families, mothers and children arrived home before fathers.

Fathers' later arrivals at the home were attributable in part to significantly longer work hours than those reported by mothers (Table 2.1).[10] But commutes also factored into parents' late arrivals. Across the United States the number of workers traveling more than two hours per day has increased significantly over the past decade, so much that the U.S. Census Bureau recently coined the term *extreme commuter* to characterize people who spend more than two hours on a *one-way* commute.[11] Among CELF families, the average duration of round-trip commutes reported by all parents was 105 minutes, or 1.8 hours. Some daily drives were as short as twenty minutes, but others were as long as four to six hours, qualifying as extreme commutes. Overall, longer workdays coupled with longer commutes may explain why fathers were usually the last to return home in the evening. Due to these late arrivals, and because most children were put to bed between 8:00 and 9:00 P.M., it was not uncommon for both parents and one or more children to have fewer than four hours' opportunity for face-to-face interaction on returning home.

WHEN UNDER THE SAME ROOF

The cumulative time demands imposed by work, school, extracurricular activities, and commuting are now sufficiently immense as to prevent most or all family members from physically reuniting until well after the sun has set. Given the short span of time separating parents' homecomings and the point at which children are put to bed, and given parents' growing concerns with spending time together as a family, one might expect parents and children to maximize the time they spend together as a group when under the same roof. Of course, the simple act of being at home does not guarantee that family members will spend time in the same room. Furthermore, even if parents and children are in the same room, they may or may not interact. There are many responsibilities and activities—not the least of which are homework and work-related tasks— that affect decisions about where family members locate themselves in the home. Indeed, such decisions can result in parents and children being at opposite ends of a floor plan.

Even so, members of most families in the study rarely *if ever* came together as a group in the home. When all members of each of the thirty families were at home (and awake) they congregated in the same home space, on average, for only 14.5 percent of scan sampling observations. Although there was some important variability among families, most tended to spend less rather than more time together as a group. In half the families studied (n = 15), parents and all children were together in the same room in fewer than one in four observations. In as many as eight of the other fifteen families, parents and children *never* shared space as a group at any point in time. Only in two families did both parents and all

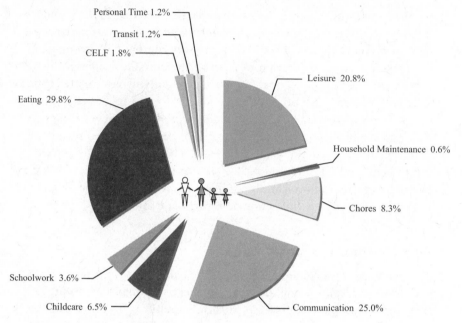

Figure 2.2. Parents' activities with children at home.

of their children come together in greater than 40 percent of all weekday observations.

These low instances of families coming together may in part be attributable to family-specific circumstances that make it difficult or merely improbable for parents and all of their children to be in the same space for very long on weekday afternoons and evenings. We observed, for example, some parents putting infants to bed several hours earlier than older children. This staggering of children's bedtimes afforded fewer opportunities for the family to come together as a group. Nevertheless, even when the definition of "together" is expanded to include instances in which both parents and one or more (but not necessarily *all*) children were in the same room, the average rate at which families shared a home space was only slightly higher (25.9 percent vs. 14.5 percent).

Of course, sharing space with others does not always translate into social interactions. Indeed, some of our observations of parents and children reflect transient uses of home spaces rather than sustained group activities. That is, at the point of recorded observation, sometimes parents and children were simply walking through the living room (often in different directions) rather than participating together in a conversation

Table 2.2. Classifying Activities

Activity Category	Examples
1 Leisure	watching TV, playing, reading, playing video games
2 Household Maintenance	opening mail, paying bills, planning renovations, remodeling
3 Chores	cleaning, taking out trash, preparing meals, mowing lawn
4 Communication	talking or listening to family members, talking on phone, emailing friends/family
5 Childcare	feeding, bathing, dressing, or grooming child; reading to child
6 Schoolwork at Home	doing homework, checking homework for accuracy, assisting with homework
7 Work at Home	emailing work-related contacts, any activity pursuant to goals of employers
8 Eating/Snacking/ Drinking	eating breakfast, lunch, or dinner; snacking or drinking between meals
9 CELF Activity	filling out questionnaires, saliva sampling, talking to researchers
10 Spousal Relations	hugging, kissing, or massaging spouse
11 Transit	walking or running through home spaces
12 Personal Time	sitting and doing nothing, staring out window, napping
13 Personal Care	brushing teeth, combing hair, grooming, showering

or activity. In fact, while the rate at which both parents and at least one child came together in a room was typically low, the rate at which they also co-participated in an activity while sharing space was even *lower* (18.7 percent of observations, on average, when all family members were at home).

This additional layer of data—the activities in which parents and children co-participate when together—provides some insight into the socially centripetal and centrifugal effects of particular activities at home. After categorizing all focal activities recorded with scan sampling observations (Figure 2.2 and Table 2.2), we found that the most common shared activities were eating, communication, and leisure. In fact, CELF data indicate that these three activities accounted for over 75 percent

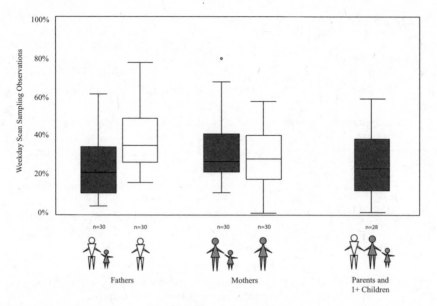

Figure 2.3. Mothers' and fathers' time with children, alone, or with spouse and children on weekday afternoons or evenings.

of the observations when both parents and their children were simultaneously sharing space and focusing attention on the same activity. In contrast, activities classified as chores, childcare, and schoolwork ranked fairly low when both parents and one or more children were in the same room. These latter three activities occupied a more significant portion of families' schedules when mothers or fathers spent *one-on-one* time with their children.

The number of observation rounds in which we documented one parent and one or more children sharing space greatly outnumbered the number of rounds where all family members were together. Often we observed parents simultaneously spending one-on-one time with children. That is, mothers were documented spending time with a child in one area of the house (e.g., the kitchen) while the father was with another child in a different space (e.g., the living room). However, hands down, mothers spent significantly more time with children. Our scan sampling data reveal that mothers shared space with one or more children for an average of 34.2 percent of observations on weekdays, whereas fathers shared space with children in only 25.1 percent of observations (Figure 2.3).[12]

Differences in mothers' and fathers' contributions to raising children and performing routine housework is a hot topic among researchers addressing family life in the United States. This is attributable in part to the persistence of gendered roles in routine domestic work in spite of the fact that more women are working full-time jobs outside the home. After working a full day at the office, women appear to still be saddled with a greater proportion of that which Hochschild labels "second-shift" work,[13] including house chores and a range of activities that revolve around the care of children, including monitoring schoolwork.

Nevertheless, characterizing inequities in mothers' and fathers' daily contributions to dual-income households is increasingly a complex task. Some researchers argue that a focus on domestic work in studies of gendered household roles should be replaced with an adaptive partnership model, or an approach that considers the *totality* of contributions.[14] Bianchi and colleagues, for example, use time-diary data to demonstrate that men's and women's total contributions to the household—including the sum of childcare and paid work outside the home—are roughly equivalent among contemporary dual-income families.[15] In general, these findings resonate with patterns observed in CELF questionnaire and scan sampling data. That is, most fathers worked more hours than mothers outside the home (see Table 2.1), but most mothers took on a greater proportion of household chores.[16]

However, it is important to note that parents in CELF families spent time with children in qualitatively different ways. The data in Figure 2.4 show that when fathers engaged with one or more children, the most popular activities were "leisure" (27.9 percent of all activities shared with children), "communication" (25.7 percent), and "childcare" (19.9 percent). In contrast, mothers were more likely to have participated with their children in "childcare" (30.3 percent), "communication" (21.7 percent), and "leisure" (13.7) activities. In fact, the average sum of *nonleisure* activities with children (or "household maintenance," "chores," "communication," "childcare," and "schoolwork") for mothers (76.6 percent) is notably higher than that for fathers (62.5 percent).

The age of a child can certainly affect the frequency and type of parental investment, with infants and toddlers typically requiring the greatest energy and time expenditures. When child age was factored into the analysis, we found that fathers with children age five or younger did not spend significantly more or less time sharing space with their kids or more or less time alone than fathers with older children. In short, having younger or older children seemingly did not affect how often fathers spent time with their kids. In contrast, mothers with young children (≤ 5

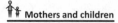 **Mothers and children**

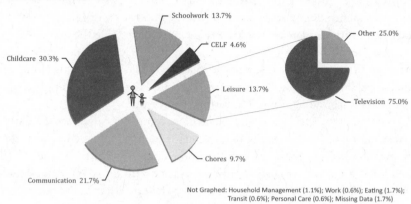

Schoolwork 13.7%
Other 25.0%
CELF 4.6%
Childcare 30.3%
Leisure 13.7%
Television 75.0%
Chores 9.7%
Communication 21.7%

Not Graphed: Household Management (1.1%); Work (0.6%); Eating (1.7%); Transit (0.6%); Personal Care (0.6%); Missing Data (1.7%)

Fathers and children

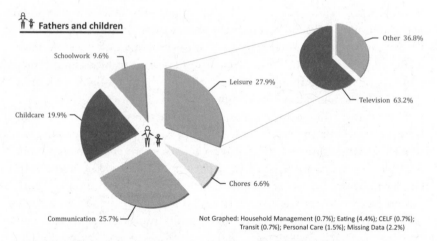

Other 36.8%
Schoolwork 9.6%
Leisure 27.9%
Television 63.2%
Childcare 19.9%
Chores 6.6%
Communication 25.7%

Not Graphed: Household Management (0.7%); Eating (4.4%); CELF (0.7%); Transit (0.7%); Personal Care (1.5%); Missing Data (2.2%)

Figure 2.4. Mothers' and fathers' activities with children at home.

years old) spent significantly less time alone than did mothers with older children (>5 years old).[17] Seemingly, the greater demands made on CELF parents by younger children fell mostly on the shoulders of mothers.

Overall, when compared to mothers, CELF fathers spent less time with children and a proportionally greater amount of time interacting with their kids in leisure activities. These findings are neither new nor surprising; other researchers have revealed similar patterns concerning fathers' behavior at home.[18] Clearly, if we apply the adaptive partnership model and take into account the differences in parents' employed work hours, then fathers in the CELF families appear less like shirkers and gender inequities in household contributions are less striking.

A key assumption of this model, however, is that the family is a self-balancing system in which mothers and fathers adjust their labor contributions in concert with one another.[19] That is, if mothers increase their paid work hours outside the home, then fathers will increase their time spent with children.[20] Yet CELF survey and observational data do not support this idea. In fact, among the thirty families headed by a mother and father, there was a moderately strong negative correlation between the number of hours mothers reported spending at work each week and the proportion of observations in which fathers were present with children on weekdays.[21] In other words, the more mothers worked outside the home, the less fathers shared space with children inside the home. Incidentally, there was no correlation between the number of hours fathers worked outside the home and the time they spent with children.

But in families whose mothers worked more hours than their husbands, were the roles reversed? That is, did fathers who worked *less* than their spouses take on a greater share of the childcare at home? Among the thirty families studied, only seven fathers reported working fewer hours than their spouses, and, on average, they did not spend comparatively more time at home or with their children. When compared to fathers who reported working *more* than their spouses (n = 22), the seven fathers were home earlier and more often on weekday afternoons but did not spend a significantly greater proportion of time at home with their children. These patterns were the same across all weekday afternoon and evening observations and not just those when all family members were in the home.

Much of the CELF scan sampling data do not support an adaptive partnership model, at least not in ways that help us to better understand differences in how and how often mothers and fathers spend time with their children. Even when their wives earned more money, most fathers still did not spend more time with children. Using surveys of much larger American and Australian populations, Craig has shown that even when mothers and fathers spend equivalent amounts of time with their children, mothers still shoulder more of the work at home by virtue of being better at multitasking.[22] It would seem that in spite of a growing awareness of gendered differences in contributions to childcare, including time spent with children, as well as the emergence of the ideal of father as co-parent,[23] fathers still are not contributing as much to childcare as mothers when at home.

These generalizations, however, are based on sample *averages*, and a more nuanced analysis of our scan sampling data suggest that fathering practices are slowly changing. For example, despite differences in average time spent with children by mothers and fathers, there is much variability in the extent to which fathers shared space with one or more children. In nine families, fathers spent *more* time with children than mothers, and in three families fathers and mothers shared space with children in an equivalent number of scan sampling observations. In another three families, the difference between mothers' and fathers' time with children was less than 10 percent. All in all, fathers in nearly half our sample spent almost as much, the same amount, or more time with children as mothers. This finding would not have surfaced had we focused only on sample averages.

In a similar vein, we found that although mothers spent overall more time with children, they spent proportionally less time *engaged* with their children when compared to fathers (77.1 percent and 85.5 percent, respectively). That is, when fathers shared space with children, they were more likely than mothers to engage their kids in various activities. Importantly, leisure did not always dominate father-child time together. Again, although the *average* amount of leisure time fathers enjoyed with children is greater than that for mothers, the extent to which individual families vary around this mean is of interest. In fact, fathers in as many as twenty of the thirty families spent proportionally more of their interactive time with children engaged in nonleisure activities. These data complicate otherwise normative depictions of mothers' and fathers' unequal contributions to raising children.

PARENTS ALONE AND ALONE TOGETHER

Parents' desires to spend more time with their children may be strong, but parents also seek the occasional "me" moment, or a portion of time to carve out for themselves and maybe some one-on-one interaction with their spouse. This sentiment is compellingly captured in the 2004 film *Before Sunset* when Ethan Hawke's character reflects on married life with children: "I feel like I'm running a small nursery with someone I used to date." Children can significantly affect opportunities and motivation for spousal intimacy.

Before children were put to bed at night, working parents rarely spent time together without one or more children being present. On average, parents were in the same room without a co-present child in fewer than

10 percent of observation rounds when all family members were in the home, and they shared an activity in only 7.6 percent of these observations. On those few occasions when they were alone together, parents' shared activities included communication (33.3 percent of parents' shared activities), chores (28.1 percent), and leisure (26.3 percent).

These findings resonate with the results of other studies of how U.S. parents spend their time at home. Survey data, for example, suggest that the time working parents spend together without children has declined from twelve hours per week in 1975 to only nine hours in 2000.[24] The underlying reasons for this trend are not clear, although we might speculate that longer work hours are intruding on quality spousal time. Yet among the thirty families in our study, there was no correlation between the time mothers and fathers individually spent at work and the amount of time they spent with their spouses on weekdays (without children present).

The extraordinarily small amount of time parents spent together without children likely speaks volumes to the substantial time demands made on parents by children and household chores. With so many bids for their attention when children were at home and awake, parents saw little opportunity to spend quality time with their spouses. That said, and when children were not around, we were surprised to observe mothers and fathers alone far more often than together. In fact, we recorded both parents *simultaneously* alone (e.g., the mother was in the living room while the father was in the garage) in home spaces in an average of 15.2 percent of weekday scan sampling observations. Simply put, spouses often spent more time alone than together before kids went to bed, even when both parents were at home.

Of course, parents may have spent more time together after kids went to bed and after we left their home. Nevertheless, these "simultaneously alone" times were missed opportunities for spouses to reconnect, and these data may indeed implicate social withdrawal—perhaps resulting from a combination of job-related stress and the stress of working so hard at home—as an explanation for diminished time together.[25] Furthermore, stress and the reaction to it may be differentially experienced. When all family members were at home and awake, fathers were found in home spaces without co-present spouses and children significantly more often than mothers (38.9 percent vs. 29.9 percent, respectively).[26] In fact, we observed fathers alone in home spaces more often than any other person-space combination (see Figure 2.3). That is, fathers were more often alone than with one or more children, whereas the opposite was true of mothers. When fathers were alone, they tended to prioritize "leisure" activities (19.5 percent of fathers' activities when alone), followed by "chores" (18.8 percent) and "communication" (17.7 percent). In contrast, when mothers were alone, their three most common activities were "chores" (35.4 percent), "communication" (12 percent), and "CELF tasks" (11 percent).

THE CENTRALITY OF KITCHENS

When family members came together, regardless of who was involved, they usually came together in the kitchen. Interactions involving both parents and one or more children, in particular, were often located in kitchen spaces. Similarly, mothers' and children's time at home often coalesced in the kitchen. Kitchens, in general, were one of the most frequently trafficked and intensively used rooms in families' homes, despite the fact that these spaces tended to be small and highly compartmentalized.[27]

The popularity of kitchens as frequented loci of parent-child interactions is also reflected in a study of American families by researchers at the University of Chicago Center on Parents, Children, and Work. Using time-diary survey methods, Chicago researchers found that the majority (42.3 percent) of instances in which both parents and one or more children shared space were documented in the kitchen.[28] Of note, these data came from a much larger sample of American households than that addressed by the CELF study. Although the University of Chicago study generated only a fraction of the observations that the CELF study recorded for any particular family, the time-diary data on kitchen use reflect trends across 465 families in as many as eight U.S. cities.

Sample size aside, there is a great deal of evidence to suggest that kitchens play a centripetal role in families' everyday lives at home. Some of this evidence emerges from our ethnographic observations of in situ family interactions and activities. For example, the bulk of children's homework and parents' off-hours from employed work transpired in kitchen spaces. Children in many of the families had access to desk spaces in their bedrooms but regularly rejected these spaces in favor of kitchen tables for doing homework.[29] Furthermore, the location of the table rather than any intrinsic features of the table itself was crucial to children's decisions about *where* to do homework. In eleven of the twelve houses that featured two multiperson tables—a large table in a formal dining room and a modest-size table in the kitchen—the smaller table in the kitchen was always the more frequently used. In fact, in twenty-five of thirty single-family homes, one of the two most intensively used home spaces—often the kitchen—contained a modest-sized table.

Kitchen tables were typically nexuses of activity on weekday afternoons. These were also anticipatory spaces, or places to stage any number of objects that anticipated activities outside and beyond the home. Photographs of these surfaces on weekday mornings reveal backpacks, lunchboxes, homework, papers, and other objects staged for transport to school and work. On weekday afternoons and evenings, inventories of these surfaces reflect a new assortment of laptops, keys, mobile phones, mail, and new homework. The cycle of artifact depletion and renewal would begin the next day as parents and children returned to this hub of family life.

Other data sets, in particular those that address family material culture, also compellingly show that kitchens and the objects they contain play a central role in parents' choreography of family time. Refrigerators are among the most important of these objects. Aside from functioning as cold repositories for food, refrigerators are multisurface bulletin boards to which all things pertaining to the scheduling of working family calendars are attached. Over half the families in our study used between 45 and 90 percent of the total visible surface area of refrigerators for posting calendars, school lunch memos, to-do lists, and the like. Some families displayed as few as five items on refrigerator surfaces; others posted up to 166, with an average of 52 objects attached to each appliance.[30] As many as 104 calendars were documented in the kitchens of twenty-nine families, and the majority of these were attached either to refrigerator surfaces or refrigerator-adjacent cork boards.

Clocks are also important. Despite the ubiquity of digital clocks on various appliances (e.g., coffee makers, microwaves, ranges), many parents hung large, analog clocks on walls that could be most easily viewed from nearly every vantage point in the kitchen, especially the kitchen table.[31] This intentional saturation of kitchen spaces with clocks, calendars, and other scheduling-related items implicates a family-level concern with monitoring the use of time in relation to a host of individual and collective obligations. The frequent co-occurrence of these objects also implicates a concerted effort on the part of parents to organize children's attention to the management of time and to build participatory frameworks for achieving numerous tasks related to work and school.[32] Materially, kitchen assemblages index a culture of busyness that has come to define middle-class families in the twenty-first century.

MEASURING FAMILY TOGETHERNESS

There is a growing body of research suggesting that active participation in the daily routines of life at home is critical to forging affectional
bonds between family members, nurturing positive social values in children, and discouraging maladaptive behavior in adolescents.[33] There is
also evidence that American parents (and not just social scientists) are
drawing connections between notions of family happiness, well-being,
cohesiveness, and time spent together. In fact, many dual-income parents
are now gauging their *quality of life*—a social and economic measure of
household well-being and life satisfaction—in terms of family cohesion
and warmth.[34] Indeed, being together is an important quality of family cohesion when cohesion is viewed as a characteristic of an ongoing,
enacted process between family members.[35]

That members of most dual-earner families spend more weekday time
outside the home and apart than inside and together is chief among a
constellation of factors impeding unscheduled opportunities for parents
and children to co-construct daily routines. Among the thirty families
headed by a mother and father, we found there were typically fewer than
four waking hours during which both parents and one or more children
simultaneously were at home on weekday afternoons and evenings.
Parents' work schedules, children's school schedules, and myriad extracurricular and sports-related activities committed parents and children
to a life more apart than together for five days of the week. Opportunities
for togetherness were limited in particular by parents'—especially
fathers'—late arrival at the home on weekday afternoons.

Our analysis of scan sampling data did not reveal a correlation between
the amount of time parents spent with children and the number of hours
parents worked each week, despite long workdays and long commutes.
Nor was there a correlation between parents' commute time and time
spent with children. The simple fact of the matter is that longer workdays
and longer commutes cannot be definitively linked to parents spending
more or less time with children among the families that participated in
the CELF study.

Nevertheless, given the short span of time in which parents and children were under the same roof, we might expect family members to have
spent a good deal more time together when they finally did return to
the home. Instead, we found that the extent to which they shared home
spaces and activities was highly varied and sometimes infrequent. Of
course, an underlying assumption made throughout this chapter is that

emotional connections are forged and maintained when two or more people are in close proximity, such as when they share a home space (e.g., a living room).

It is important to note that over the past two decades Americans have witnessed a proliferation of electronic and digital devices marketed as helping families keep in touch during the course of an average weekday. Mobile phones, text messaging, and instant messaging via computers, for example, are increasingly incorporated into busy parents' strategies for staying in touch with their families. At the time of our study, major cellular phone networks were running television ads that depicted American moms extolling the virtues of text messaging and "family-share" cellular service plans for staying connected with their spouses and children. As recently as 2007, married couples with school-aged children had higher rates of cell phone usage and subscription to broadband computer services when compared with other household types.[36] However, at the time of our visits to CELF project family homes (2001–4), many of the devices available today, such as the iPhone and the BlackBerry Smartphone, were not available, and texting was less common. Importantly, very few of the children who participated in the CELF study had their own mobile phones.

Technology aside, it is unlikely that many of today's parents would concede that phone calls or text messaging are emotionally gratifying substitutes for face-to-face interaction with loved ones, especially those with whom they live. Yet amidst the hustle and bustle of daily life, the problem for many parents is finding time for these face-to-face interactions. For most dual-income families with school-aged children, opportunity for parents to reconnect with each other and their children is often limited to brief windows of time that bracket daily work and school schedules. This was definitely true for CELF project families, most of whom also had to contend with the reality that there was so little weekday time when all family members were at home and awake.

Yet by linking notions of family cohesiveness to measures of spatial proximity we also may underestimate the importance of other practices, such as parents maintaining availability and temporal flexibility.[37] Certainly, among the families that participated in the CELF study, parents and children infrequently came together as a group in the home, but children often shared space with individual parents. Given the high mobility of family members in the home, these findings suggest that frequent but intermittent interaction between parents and kids is one strategy for reconnecting while simultaneously attending to ever-present schoolwork, dinner preparation, laundry tasks, pet care, and numerous other household obligations on weekday afternoons and evenings.

It is worth noting that low rates of family congregation in home spaces may not be solely attributable to decisions on the part of parents. That is, although analyses in this chapter assign primacy to parents' decisions about where to locate themselves when at home with their spouse and children, the low rates of group congregation may also be attributable to children's decisions. For example, some of the times when mothers or fathers were observed alone may have been the result of children leaving spaces in which parents had otherwise actively positioned themselves to interact with them. A more nuanced analysis of the scan sampling data (with an emphasis on tracking sequential movement of family members) is necessary before we can address intentionality in people-space combinations.

Importantly, scan sampling data cannot be used to gauge the emotional tenor and quality of time spent together. Other CELF researchers compellingly show how video recordings are better suited to questions addressing the emotional tone of verbal and nonverbal interactions in everyday family life.[38] Our analytic emphasis on close proximity as a measure of togetherness also may not be an accurate reflection of family members' *perceptions* of togetherness. Merely being under the same roof as their children, for example, may be just as emotionally gratifying for parents as being in the same room. In the same vein, parents sharing car space with children may have used commutes as opportunities to "check in" and reconnect on some emotional level.[39] Back in the home, the act of being in *conjoined* home spaces (e.g., contiguous family room and kitchen spaces) also may have resulted in perceptions of togetherness similar to those achieved by sharing a single space (e.g., just the family room). Many of the single-family residences in our study were small (less than 1,500 square feet) midcentury homes that were subdivided internally into numerous small spaces, thus making it difficult for families to comfortably come together as a group while attending to a wide range of afternoon and evening activities.[40] Yet although the layout of walls and other architectural features in these small homes play a role in families' decisions concerning interactions and activities, there is no clear relationship to discern. On the one hand, if the analysis of scan sampling data were broadened to include instances in which family members were situated in contiguous spaces, our yardstick of togetherness—spatial proximity— would reflect a higher measure of interaction among the thirty families. On the other hand, because the houses of most CELF project families were highly compartmentalized, being in contiguous but separate spaces often meant that family members could not clearly see or hear each other.

Nevertheless, many of the patterns in families' use of time on weekday afternoons and evenings evident in the scan sampling data are not apparent in data sets generated with broader time-use surveys, questionnaires, and/or time-diary methods. Notably, CELF scan sampling data show that simply being at home does not mean that members of dual-earner families are spending that time together or that parents are spending a majority of time at home with children. Indeed, our ethnoarchaeological data suggest that patterns of family interaction are far more complex than those suggested by other time-use studies addressing American families.

Scan sampling data also reveal that kitchens in single-family homes are the nexus of family communication, child socialization, and logistical organization. These were also spaces in which children repeatedly located homework activities on weekday afternoons and evenings, despite having ample desk space in personal bedrooms. This patterned behavior suggests that children seek to maximize contact with either or both parents as other activities, especially food preparation, unfolded in kitchen spaces. Although the time that both parents and all children spent together as a collective was limited, the number of interactions between individual parents and individual children were numerous. Assessments of family togetherness or cohesion may require that we rethink the significance of brief albeit frequent interactions between children and parents over the course of their limited time together at home.

Our data also show that mothers spent considerably more time with children than fathers. However, the differences in how and how often mothers and fathers spent time with their children suggest that we cannot view parents' contributions to the household in terms of a simple ledger sheet on which employed work hours are balanced against time spent on childcare. Simply put, the ledger sheet does not balance, and neither employed work hours nor income help to explain the disparities in mother's and father's contributions to childcare. Of course, fathers' behavior in some families more or less exemplified some long-standing and normative depictions of fathers as semipresent parents who contribute only modestly to daily childcare. However, the time that fathers spent with children was highly variable among the heterosexual CELF families, and fathers in approximately half the families spent as much (if not more) time with their kids than mothers. In light of recent generational shifts in how fathers *talk* about parenting,[41] with more parents voicing awareness of gendered disparities in childcare and household work, these ethnographic findings may indicate important changes in "on-the-ground" fathering practices in the twenty-first century.

Finally, although other time-use studies suggest that married couples are spending more time at leisure than ever before,[42] dual-earner parents in the CELF study rarely spent time together without their kids before kids went to bed. In the few instances in which we did observe mothers and fathers alone together, they were more likely to engage in interactions centered on household logistics and chores rather than leisure. In the span of time between families' return to the home and the point at which kids are put to bed, kids place substantial time demands on parents. Then again, parents may intentionally try to maximize the amount of waking time spent with children, and spouses may spend more one-on-one time together after children go to bed. Given that family members tend to spend more time apart than together on the average weekday, CELF parents strived to maintain and reinforce affective relationships with their school-aged children. After all, sharing space with children, even if only for a moment, is a strategy for improving on perceptions of otherwise diminished time together.

NOTES

1. E.g., Bianchi, Robinson, and Milkie 2006; Robinson and Godbey [1997] 1999.

2. Jacobs and Gerson 2004.

3. Gillis 2006.

4. Gergen 1991; Gutiérrez, Izquierdo, and Kremer-Sadlik 2010; Kremer-Sadlik and Gutiérrez, this volume; Zeitlin et al. 1995.

5. Darrah 2006, 383.

6. Brannen 2005; Hochschild 1997; Kremer-Sadlik, Fatigante, and Fasulo 2008; Kremer-Sadlik and Paugh 2007; Southerton 2003.

7. Details on variation in person-centered observations and scan sampling methods can be found in Broege et al. 2007; Campos et al. 2009; Graesch 2009; Klein et al. 2009; and Ochs et al. 2006.

8. Over the course of two weekday visits with the thirty participating families that featured both a mother and a father, CELF ethnographers completed 1,840 short walks (or observation rounds) through family homes and recorded 8,248 observations of parents and children in their home spaces.

9. For the thirty-family data set, there were 2,942 person-centered observations recorded when all family members were simultaneously in the home.

10. Independent samples t-test; $t(52) = 3.80$, $p = .000$, when outliers (Families 13, 20, 31) were removed from the analysis.

11. Pisarksi 2006.

12. Paired samples t-test; $t(29)$ = -2.597, p = .015. These observations do not include instances in which mothers *and* fathers shared space with one or more children.

13. Hochschild 1997.

14. Craig 2007b; Meissner et al. 1975.

15. Bianchi, Robinson, and Milkie 2006.

16. Klein, Izquierdo, and Bradbury 2007; Klein, Izquierdo, and Bradbury, this volume.

17. Independent samples t-test; $t(28)$ = 2.12, p = .043.

18. See, e.g., Beck and Arnold 2009; Broege et al. 2007; Coltrane, Parke, and Adams 2004; Craig 2007a.

19. Craig 2007b.

20. E.g., Bianchi 2000; Bianchi, Robinson, and Milkie 2006; Crouter and McHale 2005; Peterson and Gerson 1992.

21. Pearson product-moment correlation; r = -.39, p = .03.

22. Craig 2007b.

23. E.g., Pleck and Pleck 1997.

24. Bianchi, Robinson, and Milkie 2006, 104.

25. Repetti, Saxbe, and Wang, this volume.

26. Paired samples t-test; $t(29)$ = -2.61, p = .01.

27. Graesch 2009.

28. Broege et al. 2007, 142.

29. Graesch 2006, 2009.

30. Graesch 2009.

31. We documented 76 digital clocks in the kitchens of 32 homes.

32. See, e.g., Goffman 1981; Goodwin 1994; Murphy 2005.

33. E.g., Crouter et al. 1990; Fiese et al. 2002.

34. E.g., Coontz 2005; Mintz 2004; Stevens et al. 2007.

35. Ochs et al. 2006.

36. Kennedy et al. 2008.

37. Budig and Folbre 2004.

38. Campos et al. 2009; M.H. Goodwin 2007; Goodwin and Goodwin, this volume; Ochs and Campos, this volume.

39. E.g., C. Goodwin 2006.

40. Graesch 2004, 2006.

41. E.g., Pleck and Pleck 1997.

42. Voorpostel, van der Lippe, and Gershuny 2009.

3 Dinner

ELINOR OCHS AND MARGARET BECK

On the eve of Thanksgiving 2010, *USA Today* gave celebratory prominence to a recent Pew Research Center survey finding that 89 percent of Americans reported that they will gather to have Thanksgiving dinner with their families, as if, after all, at this quintessential family moment, eating together continues to matter to American society. It reported, for example, that "Barry Antonelli, 37, of Baileyton, Tenn., says he, his wife, and four young kids will drive to Baltimore this Thanksgiving because being with his father for the holiday has always been 'real important' to him."[1]

Meanwhile, the French publication *Philosophie Magazine* dedicated its entire December 2010 issue to the provocative cover theme "La Famille est-elle insupportable?" (The Family, Is It Unbearable?), with articles on the pervasiveness of irksome extended family dinners, undeniable Oedipal tensions, and a philosophical disdain for familial suppression of individual creativity. A representative comment expressed the idea that "la famille était une réalité biologique formalisée par le politique" (the family was a biological reality formalized by politics).[2]

Did *USA Today* and *Philosophie Magazine* capture two different cultural ideologies of family mealtimes? Yes and no. Like the French report, U.S. surveys, news outlets, and blogs find cracks in the image of the contemporary American family as a cohesive, engaged social unit. Most notably, the media lament the decline of family dinnertime and implicate the overscheduled lives of working parents as somewhat responsible for this moral slippage. Twenty-first-century American parents, for one reason or another, appear to be unable to prioritize the ritual of family dinner. The *USA Today* survey disclosed, for example, that only 50 percent of families said that they eat together every day, 34 percent a few times a week, and 14 percent rarely or never.

To discern possible cultural differences it is useful to look more closely at the *reasons* that American and French family members give for why it is so difficult to gather as a family and share a meal. *Philosophie Magazine* reported that the French public harbor an acute sardonic awareness that family gatherings, especially meals, seethe with tensions arising from the twin desires for attachment to and freedom from a family that one can never completely renounce. In this accounting, family gatherings inherently evoke feelings of ambivalence. Alternatively, Americans cling to the ideal of family commensality as an elixir for personal and societal ills (e.g., children's vulnerability to drugs, smoking, and obesity) and as de rigueur for kindling children's school success.[3] Many parents regret that for pragmatic reasons they cannot routinely prepare and enjoy a meal together as a family. They cite busyness—workplace obligations, children's extracurricular and school activities, and scheduling conflicts—as occluding this opportunity.[4] Some strive to create alternative sites of family involvement, as suggested in Lisa Belkin's insightful *New York Times* article, "The Pangs of Family Mealtime Guilt."[5]

Yet the CELF study reveals that the busy lives of family members outside the home are not the only culprit in the saga of the American family dinner. Even when all members of a family were at home, eating dinner together was a challenge in many households. Why?

Two less acknowledged reasons for why family dinners were a challenge for the CELF families stand out: (1) convenience foods filling refrigerators and cupboards supplied individualized snacks and meals for family members; and (2) family dinnertime often gave way to intergenerational conflicts surrounding children's food choices. The consumption of preprepared convenience foods, many of which are packaged as individual meals, stand alongside busy schedules as a root factor in undermining dinner as a family event. The "story" of the decline of family dinners that emerges from the CELF study begins in the supermarket with large-scale purchases of packaged convenience foods. The story continues with these convenience foods flooding the home space. We systematically documented where convenience foods were located, how they were consumed as snacks, and how they were prepared and eaten as dinner dishes. We noted who in the family ate dinner, with whom, for how long, and where. Researchers also examined parental scrutiny of children's food preferences.[6] We indicate the ways in which families buy, prepare, eat, and talk about food have cumulative effects on the social vitality of dinnertime.

Tensions between individual and family desires that the French press reports wreak havoc on family gatherings find expression as well in the

Los Angeles CELF households. Children resisted parental biddings to eat dinner with them, and children's individual food wants conflicted with parentally imposed food selections.[7] In some households, the ubiquity of microwaveable, individual-sized, packaged snacks in the home undermined children's interest in even coming to the dinner table, much less their willingness to eat what had been prepared for them. In these households, parents' insistence that children eat the foods that were on the table was undermined when children asked for one of the individual meals stored in the refrigerator or freezer that they knew could be easily popped into the microwave and in minutes be ready to eat anywhere in the house. To gain further insight into the story of family dinnertime in Los Angeles we invite you to look over the shoulders of the CELF ethnographers who photographed and video recorded the moral life of food at home.

FOOD STOCKPILING

To gain some perspective on the abundance of food in the CELF households of Los Angeles, we briefly turn to another food-loving society, namely, Italy. Italian families tend to have smaller refrigerators (with smaller freezer sections) than are found in most U.S. kitchens. Italian middle-class families typically do not have second refrigerators or freezers. It is hard to tell if refrigerator size organizes grocery shopping habits or the inverse, but Italian families characteristically purchase food more frequently (often daily) and in smaller quantities than was typical of the CELF families in Los Angeles. While neighborhood grocery stores abound and super-sized markets are becoming increasingly popular, they are usually located on the outskirts of Italian towns and are not (yet) ubiquitous. It is common for Italian families to purchase many of their everyday food items at bakeries, fruit and vegetable vendors, butcher shops, fish markets, and open markets.

In contrast, Los Angeles families manifested a different set of food shopping habits. The omnipresence of hypermarkets in Los Angeles prepared CELF researchers to document food purchased in large quantities and packed inside large refrigerators. Despite these expectations, however, we were awed by the sheer abundance of food stockpiled in homes.[8] Parents purchased food in massive quantities. Enormous boxes and plastic-sealed packages of items of the same kind filled kitchens and spilled over into utility rooms and garages. Enormous cases of soda, fruit drinks, and alcoholic beverages occupied floors, shelves, and the tops of

Figure 3.1. Kitchen refrigerator with freezer.

refrigerators. Food items came in multiples and giant sizes—from pancake mix and cereal to popcorn.

Los Angeles family refrigerators were brimming with food. The freezer compartment in American refrigerators is capacious and often has a separate door, as seen in figure 3.1. Some families owned a second refrigerator or a freestanding freezer, usually located in the garage. Kitchen refrigerators were dominated by large bottles of juice drinks, soda cans, and multiple gallon containers of milk. Individual-sized containers of flavored yogurts and other packaged fruit treats were often stacked inside as well. Refrigerator doors were lined with bottles of ketchup, mustard, barbecue sauces, salad dressings, syrups, and other condiments, along with tubs of margarine, butter, and cream cheese. Refrigerator bins often contained "sandwich fixings"—slices of prepared meats and cheeses—for the children's lunches. In some refrigerators, small quantities of fresh fruit and greens could be found. The second refrigerator was mainly used to hold surplus sodas, juice drinks, and beer that could not fit inside the kitchen refrigerator.

The freezer compartment in kitchen refrigerators and stand-alone freezers in garages allowed busy parents to preserve a large quantity of food items over extended periods. When the authors of this chapter were growing up, freezers were used primarily for three items: raw meats, vegetables, and ice cream. The freezers in the homes of the twenty-first-century families in the CELF study contained raw meats, vegetables, and ice cream but were often buried under an avalanche of frozen convenience snacks and meals, especially individual-sized, preprepared items that can be microwaved. Because they were packed in large boxes and purchased in great quantities, these food items were bulky and occupied a lot of freezer space. For example, the freezer shown in Figure 3.1 is filled with boxes of frozen pizzas, tacos, fish sticks, chicken strips, frozen yogurt bars, and sugar-free popsicles.

The hyper-consumerism of these convenience foods, especially their bulky packaging, explains in part why American families "require" large freezers, sometimes more than one, in their homes. Beyond the size and number of freezers and refrigerators, however, the cornucopia of convenience foods stored in family homes played an important role in the viability of CELF family dinners.

RIPE FOR THE PLUCKING

In some CELF households, parents made sure that their children were supplied with raw fruit, vegetables, and nuts to eat as snacks after school and on weekends. In other CELF households, packaged foods piled in refrigerators, freezers, cupboards, and elsewhere were "ripe for the plucking," that is, ready and waiting for children and other family members to eat. In these homes, snacking involved simply opening a package and consuming its contents. Some children asked permission before snacking (Son: "Can I have a Fruit Roll-Up, and can I give Justin one too?" Mother: "Yeah, sure"). Other children were encouraged to open the freezer or refrigerator, choose the snack they wanted, and, in some cases, microwave frozen food for themselves.[9] In one household, a mother who worked late afternoon and evening shifts filled a large thermal container with ready-made snacks for the kids to grab when they returned home after school.

What was culturally striking across the households was the abundance of individual-sized packaged foods for children. Figure 3.2, for example,

Figure 3.2. Individual-sized packaged cookies.

shows a shopping bag full of small packages of cookies, designed for a child's school lunch bag or afternoon snack. The individual packaging itself facilitates a child's consumption of the food item, as there is no need to take, pour, or cut a portion from a larger quantity. In addition, each package holds the child's own portion, obviating the need for napkin or plate. Some child-oriented yogurts and fruit purees, for example, can be squeezed directly into the child's mouth.

The commonplace practice of providing individually packaged snacks for children was noted during our health interviews with parents. During the interview we asked them to open the kitchen refrigerator and talk about its contents. On one occasion, Rhoda Anderson, a working mother, peered inside the freezer compartment and pointed out snacks that her children like to "grab": "And there's some frozen yogurt that they grab in here. There's also some more candy. And sometimes they grab that.

That's what's in the freezer." Individualized snacks were purchased for each child. Rhoda explained, "Laura loves ((*pause*)) these applesauce things that you just kind of squirt it in your mouth. . . . And Laura likes— Molly—they like, um, Go-Gurts. So it's like a yogurt thing that you just squeeze. . . . It's kind of fun." Rhoda supplied each child with a "fun" snack that was thought to be relatively nutritious—fruit in "applesauce things" and milk in Go-Gurts.

Snacks were part and parcel of refueling children after a long, hard day at school and beyond. Everyone knows, however, that eating snacks has consequences later on in the evening when dinner is ready. Consider, for example, what transpired between Susan Marsden and her eight-year-old daughter, Courtney, at dinnertime. Susan had brought home take-out food from a local restaurant for the whole family to eat, but Courtney, watching television and eating a snack, was not interested in joining them:

SUSAN: Hey lounge lizard.

COURTNEY: (Hello).

SUSAN: You want, um,—want something to eat?

COURTNEY: No. I don't like [name of restaurant].

SUSAN: I didn't get [name of restaurant], and what are you eating now? Goldfish again?

COURTNEY: ((*Nods*))

SUSAN: So what do you want? Salad and a quesadilla?

COURTNEY: ((*Shakes her head*))

. . .

SUSAN: Come on. ((*pause*)) What do you want to eat, I'll make you something to eat and then we're turning off the TV, Courtney.

SUSAN: What do you want to eat?

COURTNEY: I don't want anything.

SUSAN: You don't want, um ((*pause*)) a salad or an apple or ((*pause*)) what.

COURTNEY: ((*Shakes her head*))

In this exchange, Susan started out in a lighthearted manner but soon became alarmed that her daughter was eating "Goldfish again," suggesting this snack was habitual. After volunteering to prepare for Courtney what she would like as an alternative to take-out, Courtney responded categorically, "I don't want anything," affirming this once again when her mother proposed some food options. This exchange is emblematic of the state of dinnertime for many families in the United States: children prefer to munch on a snack of their own choosing while engaged in a separate activity of their own choosing, such as watching a television program, rather than join the family around the dinner table.

A similar scenario transpired in the Roland-Santos household. Five-year-old Pablo voiced reluctance to eat chicken nuggets or a fish stick that his mother offered him for dinner. Even after his mother, Ann, quietly directed him, "Eat your dinner," he still hesitated. His mother then put forward an explanation: "I know you're probably not very hungry because you ate lots of pizza." In response Pablo minimized the amount of pizza he had eaten but finally admitted to also eating an entire package of Cheetos, a cheese-flavored cornmeal snack, earlier in the day.

> PABLO: I—I only ate one piece of pizza and—and like one—and one piece of Cheetos.
>
> ANN: Only one piece of Cheetos?
>
> PABLO: I mean, only one Cheeto.
>
> ANN: Only one Cheeto?
>
> PABLO: I only ate—all of the Cheetos in the pack.

After a few more unsuccessful attempts ("Mommy, I don't really feel like all of this"), his parents changed gears and came to the realization that Pablo was simply not up to this endeavor ("Are you done? Oh, you're so tired").

HOME-COOKED MEALS

Convenience foods occupied an important place as ingredients in the dinner meal itself.[10] The arrival home from work, school, and extracurricular activities was a particularly challenging time of the day for family members. As reported widely for working families across the United States,[11] CELF mothers assumed an especially heavy domestic set of responsibilities after returning home from work. They tended to arrive home about two hours before their spouses[12] and, like mothers elsewhere,[13] managed the multiple tasks of helping with homework, dinner preparation, and readying children for bed, among other household tasks.[14] Under these circumstances, many of the parents sought to streamline dinner preparation.

Margaret Beck documented exactly what families ate for dinner.[15] At first she was surprised that an impressive 73 percent of the weeknight dinners were "home-cooked"! That is, they were prepared by a family member at home. These home-cooked dinners did *not* include take-out or delivered restaurant food. Mothers (sometimes with assistance of other family members) prepared over 90 percent of the home-cooked meals.[16]

When Beck looked more closely at the ingredients that constituted "home-cooked" dinners served during the workweek, however, another picture emerged.[17] Most of these meals contained preprepared convenience food items. In fact, only 22 percent of the so-called home-cooked weeknight dinners were prepared with little or no convenience foods. That is, only a fraction were made primarily from fresh or raw ingredients. This percentage is lower than reports based on surveys,[18] perhaps because CELF researchers relied on direct observation rather than self-reports.

What did these dinners look like? Main dishes included, for example, chicken nuggets (frozen, cooked in oven), chicken and dumplings (made with Chicken Helper commercial mix), Trader Joe's orange chicken (frozen, cooked in oven), and ribs in barbecue sauce (commercial, microwaved). Accompaniments were french fries (commercial, frozen, cooked in oven), mashed potatoes (commercial, microwaved), cornbread (Marie Callender's mix, cooked in oven), biscuits (commercial roll of dough, cooked in oven). In one household, the home-cooked dinner consisted of individualized meals: (1) hamburger meat (defrosted in the microwave, then cooked in a skillet) mixed in ramen noodle soup (commercial, cooked on stovetop) for the parents; (2) chicken and Rice-A-Roni (leftover, heated in microwave) for the daughter; and (3) chicken noodle soup (canned, cooked on stove) for the son.

The home-cooked meals took an average of 34 minutes of hands-on time and a total of 52 minutes to prepare (Figure 3.3). As the term suggests, preprepared "convenience" foods should take less time to prepare than cooking from scratch with fresh or raw ingredients. Heavy reliance on commercial food did reduce hands-on time significantly, but the difference was only 10 to 12 minutes.

Moreover, there was *no* significant difference in the *total cooking time* for dinners made primarily from convenience foods and those made primarily from fresh ingredients or a combination of fresh and some or limited convenience foods. This finding suggests that relying mainly on commercially prepared foods for dinner does not actually save a great deal of time for busy parents. As Davies and Madran note,[19] the

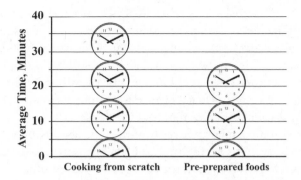

Figure 3.3. Preparation time: Cooking from scratch and preprepared foods.

preference among some adults for preparing convenience foods may be motivated by *perceived* time pressures, while the preference among other adults for cooking fresh or raw ingredients may be based on a moral orientation to meals as both enjoyable and important events.

CELF dinners included a range of one to seven dishes. Interestingly, dinners made primarily from fresh ingredients typically contained three or fewer dishes, for example, a protein, a starch, and a green vegetable. Only 18 percent of dinners made from scratch consisted of more than three dishes. In contrast, 52 percent of dinners relying on heating up packaged commercial foods consisted of more than three dishes. As we will see below, dinners from scratch with fewer dishes were communal meals, with family members eating the same dishes. Alternatively, dinners with numerous dishes correlated with individual family members eating different dishes. The higher number of commercial dishes corresponded less to a "breaking bread together" type of dinner and more to an atomistic version of this meal. The stockpiling of individual-sized convenience foods in freezers allowed parents to prepare a separate meal for a family member. At the start of dinnertime, some children requested that a parent get up and heat a commercial food not on the table that was more to his or her liking.

EATING TOGETHER AND APART

So what did dinnertimes look like in the CELF households? Did family members eat together or apart? To address these questions, we analyzed the two weekday dinners and one weekend dinner that CELF researchers video recorded.[20] Across thirty households we documented the extent to which family members ate at the same time and/or in the same place. Sometimes all family members ate together at the same time and place. Sometimes a family member was not at home, but the rest of the family ate together. At other times family members ate in staggered fashion at different times (beginning to eat at least ten minutes after others started to eat) or scattered in different rooms of the house.

On the communal side, 77 percent of the families ate dinner *together* on at least one evening during the study. When everyone was at home during the week, 59 percent of the fifty-eight dinners recorded were eaten together as a family. When one or more members of the family were not at home during the week, 67 percent of the dinners were eaten together by the family members who were at home.

Alternatively, only 17 percent of the families ate dinner all together across the three days of recording, and 23 percent of the families *never* ate all together. In 50 percent of the households, a family member, usually the father, was not at home at least one evening. In 63 percent of the households, family members ate at different times (i.e., began eating more than ten minutes after others were already eating) or ate apart from one another in different rooms. Of the fifty-eight weekday dinners recorded, 41 percent were fragmented in this way.

How does one weigh the social and moral import of these observations? For those who have written off family dinnertime as a relic of the past, the CELF findings that families still eat together at home during the week is a pleasant surprise. For survey researchers who paint a rosy picture of young children eating a home-cooked meal together with their family based on children's self-reports,[21] it is sobering to find that eating at home may frequently be temporally or spatially disjointed, as exposed by the ethnographic lens of the video camera. When a child reports in a survey study that he or she had dinner at home, it cannot be assumed that he or she is sharing a meal face-to-face at the same time with the rest of the family. Indeed, fragmented dinners at home may be salient in many twenty-first-century U.S. families.

Could there be a link between the kind of meal eaten for dinner and the extent to which CELF family members ate apart or together? The short answer is yes. To address this question, we matched the contents of dinner meals with each family member's time and location at dinnertime. In 68 percent of the weekday dinners that were eaten *at different times or in different rooms,* family members ate meals made entirely or mostly of *convenience foods* or dishes brought home from a restaurant or take-out.

In contrast, in 76 percent of weekday dinners eaten *all together,* family members ate meals prepared mainly with fresh ingredients.

Although heavy reliance on convenience foods does not predict a scattering of family members at dinnertime, their individual packaging and low-skill (but not significantly less time-consuming) preparation may encourage family members to eat at different times and places, even when the whole family is at home. The expectation that individual-sized convenience foods can be heated up and eaten apart by a family member whenever or wherever was apparent late on a Sunday afternoon in the Marsden household. Thirteen-year-old Darrin asked his mom to heat up his convenience meal right away for him to eat. When his mother, Susan, countered that she wanted him to eat his "special dinner" together with the family, Darrin was bewildered.

> DARRIN: Where's my dinner?
>
> SUSAN: ((*Gives Darrin "the look"*)) hhhh ((*Taps a pan*)) In that special pan right there.
>
> DARRIN: Special?
>
> SUSAN: Your special dinner.
>
> . . .
>
> DARRIN: Could I have my dinner now?
>
> SUSAN: No, you're eating with us.
>
> DARRIN: I know that's why I said could I have my dinner now.
>
> SUSAN: We're all sitting down together. We don't get to sit down and eat very much . . .

Like other children in the CELF study, Darrin assumed that "you're eating with us" meant eating his individualized meal at home regardless of where in the house the eating took place. That assumption was evidenced when his mother had to make explicit, "We're all sitting down together," and lamented, "We don't get to sit down and eat very much."

EMOTIONS AT DINNERTIME

Children may prefer to eat on their own for any number of reasons, including in order to avoid conflicts over their eating habits.[22] Parents and children in the CELF study frequently entered into food negotiations, complete with bargaining, enticements, and threats. Some parents insisted that children eat certain foods considered healthy. Dinnertime, for these families, became a match of wills.[23] Many parents dwelled on the nutritious value of food items and expressed appreciation for the meal. In contrast, children, especially at the start of dinner, often expressed their distaste for the food prepared for them.[24] When some children were called for dinner and saw what they were to eat, they complained.

In these dinnertime tussles with children, parental confusion over nutrition was evident.[25] At the start of one family dinner, eleven-year-old Sandra asked to have some of the pink lemonade that her parents had placed on the table for themselves. Her parents pressed her to drink a glass of milk first. Sandra refused. Her mother offered an alternative: "If you are not going to have milk, you can have string cheese. " But Sandra had a counterproposal: "I'll have a Go-Gurt." Her parents agreed to this compromise. They likely did not realize, however, that alongside the healthful ingredient of milk, each Go-Gurt contains more sugar per ounce (4.89 grams) than does that brand of lemonade (3.6 grams) or even Coca-Cola (3.25 grams).[26]

Similarly, during the Dorbin family dinner, eight-year-old Josh did not want to eat a "meatless meatball." His mother, a vegetarian, used a confused logic of nutritional value to change his mind, ending with a full admission of ignorance.

MOTHER: Eat at least one of these.

. . .

because it has your vegetable
and protein in it.
I mean your protein.
Or your vegetables.
Or something.

FATHER: Or all of those things.

MOTHER: I don't know.

Parents the world over want their children to eat healthy meals, yet many middle-class parents in the United States focus children's attention on the nutritional properties of a food item to the extent that they forget about developing their appreciation of its taste. In contrast, middle-class parents in Italy frequently direct children's attention to the pleasurable qualities of food. Looking in on family dinners in Rome, Elinor Ochs and her Italian colleagues found that parents described different foods using emotion-filled language forms.[27] Instead of talking about a piece of meat with the plain word *pezzo* (piece), they used the word *pezzettino* (an appealing morsel). This language infused kinds of cheeses, pasta sauces, and other dishes with sentiments. We do not wish to imply that food standoffs between parents and children are confined to the United States.[28] We do wonder, however, if parents' vocal preoccupation with savory foods as what children *must* eat for health reasons, instead of talking about these foods as delicious and what children *want* to eat for pleasure, may amplify the potential for power plays between generations.

It may be surprising to learn that children's reluctance to eat dinner is tied to parents' choice of *convenience foods* as meals. Children in middle-class households in the United States are sometimes fussy eaters. Here we point out that preprepared meals in CELF households were not exempt from children's standoffish relation to food. Children commonly voiced their dislike for some ingredient inside a preprepared convenience meal for dinner, as illustrated in the following dinnertime excerpts.

On not liking sauce in preprepared spaghetti dinner:

JAKE: I told you I don't want spaghetti sauce.

· · ·

I don't like these noodles.

· · ·

MOTHER: Okay then don't eat them but that's what's for dinner.

On not liking vegetables in packaged soup:

MOTHER: *Oh,* you took the celery out too?

ADRIAN: Mm hm.

MOTHER: Oh.

FATHER: I thought you liked [celery.

MOTHER: [Adrian.

ADRIAN: *I don't like it in it.*

· · ·

ADRIAN: *I DON'T want carrots.*

MOTHER: Go wash your hands.

ADRIAN: I'm taking out all the stuff I don't like it.

On not liking mixture of cereals in bowl for dinner:

BILL: What is—Dude!

That's not the right kind!

MOTHER: Hhh ((*pause*)) Sure it is!

BILL:	((*laughing*)) That's not the right KIND!
MOTHER:	I don't know what you're talking about.
BILL:	MOM! What happened?
MOTHER:	Nothing happened. It's perfectly fine. ((*laughs*))
MICHELLE:	What is it?
BILL:	No!
MOTHER:	It's nothing.
BILL:	*She didn't get me Cinnamon* [*Toast Crunch.*
MOTHER:	[No, I did!

It's in there.

It's just I had to fill it up with a little bit of Cinnamon Crunchers. ((*pause*)) It's a special mom mix tonight.

On not liking sauce on pizza:

ANNA:	Mom, ((*pause*)) So can I eat it up to there?

I don't like all of the sauce like right here

((*pause*))

so can I eat it up to there?

. . .

MOTHER:	That's fine I—
ANNA:	No for real Mom can I eat it up to here?

MOM!

MOTHER:	You don't have to eat the crust.
ANNA:	*No* ((*pause*)) see that's what I'm talking about . . .

I—I mean I don't like the crust and I don't like this part.

. . .

But Mom see that red sauce and that red sauce that's the part ((*pause*))

[I don't like all the red sauce.

MOTHER:	[Eat around it Annie

((*pause*))

you've eaten it before.

ANNA:	No–
MOTHER:	I'm going to give you one chance to do it

I'm not going to negotiate with you and ((*pause*)) fight over this.

On not liking premixed salad dressing:

FATHER: Oh *I* love this salad ((*pause*)) okay

((*pause*)) this is good

LAURA: I hate the dressing

FATHER: Yeah yeah ((*pause*))—this is sort of like ((*pause*)) daddy style [so:

LAURA: [It's gross!

MOLLY: It's *gross!* ((*pause*)) Yuck.

In these circumstances, convenience foods reveal their decidedly inconvenient affordances. As prepackaged items, convenience foods make it difficult to modify a dinner dish to accommodate the taste of a family member. For example, it is difficult to withhold an ingredient, as one might do in a meal prepared from scratch. Even when bottles of condiments are used as salad dressings or sauces, they contain premixed spices in preset proportions that cannot be easily modified for the palates of particular family members. These properties of packaged foods play a role in configuring dinnertime as a site in which children's individual tastes and wills reckon with the morally infused expectations of their progenitors.

DINNER AND FAMILY LIFE

Anthropologists have long noted that sharing a meal is a universal opportunity for strengthening the ties that bind a family.[29] CELF researchers were heartened to find that most of the families in our study ate dinner all together at least once across the week of our observations and that when a family member was not at home most dinners were eaten together by those who were at home. These figures indicate that the desire to "break bread" together continues to be valued in many households.

Yet a sizable portion of the dinners (41 percent) were eaten in fragmented fashion—with family members eating whenever and wherever even when they were all at home in the evenings. Whether or not family members ate together could not be explained away by work schedules, as the number of hours CELF parents were at their jobs did not influence their presence at dinnertime.[30] Some fathers who worked long hours managed to come home to eat with the rest of the family while some fathers who worked fewer hours did not. Getting family members within earshot of one another to sit down at a single location and time was too much of a challenge in some households. What is going on?

Family members in other societies sometimes eat at different times.[31] In some communities high status persons eat first and then others follow. In other communities family members eat opportunistically when they have finished their labor. Yet in these circumstances eating is still commonly a social activity. Other family members usually are there to converse with whomever is eating. What was striking about the fragmented dinners in the CELF families was that family members eating these meals were often only briefly in social contact. Most (67 percent) of the shortest dinners (less than fifteen minutes) were eaten by family members at different times or places at home. Most (92 percent) of the longest dinners (more than forty-five minutes) were eaten all together around the table as a family.

CELF family members, of course, did find other moments to communicate with one another. Yet the whole family was rarely home at the same time on weekdays. Generally, children returned home first, followed by mothers and then fathers. Even when at home family members were hardly ever all together in the same room; in some CELF households, family members were *never* all together in the same space at the same time.[32] Family life at home mostly transpired in dyads (e.g., a parent and a child) or individually in separated spaces. One of the very few moments when CELF family members were observed to gather, however briefly, was dinnertime, making it even more important as a locus of solidarity and communication about events, problems, and moral perspectives.[33]

Pulling together the threads of our observations, it appears that two practices may undermine the valorized family dinner. First, the prevalence of convenience foods became the silent partner in constituting the ephemeral condition of family dinnertime. Convenience foods flooded the home environment in the form of individual-sized, easy-to-prepare snacks and meals packaged in portable containers. These foods encouraged children to eat at will and apart. Surprisingly, they did not significantly reduce the burden of hands-on food preparation time, saving only ten minutes for the multitasking working mother.

The heavy reliance on convenience foods in some families may instead indicate either a lifestyle preference or lack of skill in purchasing and cooking basic foods. Convenience foods have been the bane of those concerned about childhood obesity. Yet both relatively healthy and high calorie convenience foods may have an impact on the social quality of family mealtimes. Dinners dominated by convenience foods may disassemble the family body. Heavy reliance on convenience foods in some households clustered with fragmented, rushed dinners, whereas meals prepared mainly with fresh, raw foods clustered with longer dinners eaten all together as a family. Convenience foods did not even escape the fussy tastes of children, who sometimes recoiled at the fixed combination of ingredients in a preprepared pasta or taco.

Second, dinnertime as a site of family connectedness was sometimes squandered when food became a locus of control at the dinner table—by parents issuing confusing health imperatives and children trying to withdraw to eat something else and somewhere else. And here we return to the opening theme of this chapter: in contemporary postindustrial societies like the United States and France, family meals are the Petri dish where personal and shared tastes and identities are cultivated together, and their cultivation can be relatively seamless (rare) or fraught (common). Taste is, ultimately, a sensual, private experience that is shaped by public, moral scrutiny, creating a lifelong tension between children's desire for freedom and their desire to affiliate with their parents, including how they value food and the ritual of dinnertime.

NOTES

1. Klinck 2010.
2. Lacroix and Legros 2010, 56.
3. See Baselon 2008; Neumark-Sztainer et al. 1990; Patrick and Nicklas 2005; National Center on Addiction Abuse at Columbia University 2010; Weinstein 2005.
4. National Center on Addiction Abuse at Columbia University 2010.
5. June 14, 2007.
6. Paugh and Izquierdo 2009.
7. Such familial battles of wills are not restricted to American families; Aronsson and Gottzén (2011), for example, analyze a Swedish family dinner conflict around a child's food decisions.
8. Arnold et al. 2012.
9. Garro 2011.
10. Beck 2007.
11. Bianchi, Robinson, and Milkie 2006; Christensen and Schneider 2010; Hochschild 1997; Hochschild and Machung [1989] 2003.
12. Campos et al. 2009.
13. Offer and Schneider 2010.
14. Good 2009; Ochs et al. 2010.
15. Beck 2007.
16. Ochs et al. 2010.
17. Beck 2007.
18. Sloan 2006.

19. Davies and Madran 1997.

20. Ochs et al. 2010.

21. Several surveys report high frequency of young school-aged children eating dinner frequently with their parents, then declining to do so toward adolescence (Child Trends Data Bank 2003; RMC Research Corporation 2005; Bradley et al. 2001).

22. Intergenerational conflicts surrounding food desires are common sources of tension during family dinnertime in the United States and other postindustrial societies (Aronsson and Gottzén 2011; Ochs, Pontecorvo, and Fasulo 1996; Paugh and Izquierdo 2009).

23. Paugh and Izquierdo 2009.

24. Campos et al. n.d.

25. Garro 2011; Paugh and Izquierdo 2009.

26. Hubpages website: http://hubpages.com/hub/Go-Gurt-Ingredients -List-Sugar-Sugar-Sugar.

27. Ochs, Pontecorvo, and Fasulo 1996.

28. Anderson-Fye 2004; Kleinman 1988; Shohet 2004.

29. Lévi-Strauss 1969.

30. Ochs et al. 2010.

31. Ochs and Shohet 2006.

32. Campos et al. 2009.

33. Ochs and Shohet 2006.

Mountains of Things

JEANNE E. ARNOLD

American families have more material goods per household than any society in history. Even middle-class families with modest incomes have for decades enjoyed the ability to acquire a dizzying variety of inexpensive goods from every corner of the world. During the early 2000s, U.S. incomes were generally robust, unemployment was low, credit was easy to obtain, and persuasive marketing stimulated Americans to accumulate objects at startling rates. These trends characterized much of the later twentieth century as well.

The levels of material affluence that families attain, whatever the culture or status, are most clearly expressed *within* in the home. This is where people display and use the particular sets of goods they have selected from all those available to them through the primary sources of shopping, gifting, and inheritance. Since the home is the main locus for self-expression through things, it is ironic that while any of us can see the clothes and cars owned by neighbors, coworkers, and strangers when they venture into public spaces, our opportunities to scrutinize and admire the great majority of their possessions are nonexistent unless we happen to be engaged in carpet installation or door-to-door sales.

Tucked behind closed doors in neighborhoods across the country, rooms full of possessions serve as a source of satisfaction to hardworking parents, constantly reaffirming through their very presence in the house the sense that the family has done well. Yet U.S. cultural norms exert incessant pressure to acquire more. Home-design programs on TV and commercial advertisements in glossy magazines show how the respectable home ought to look, with a new spa-like master bathroom or stainless steel kitchen appliances. Through conversations and the rumor mill, parents constantly gauge whether they are keeping up with peers in ongoing materialistic competitions among family and neighbors, typically centering on upscale renovations and the latest vehicles and electronics. The imperative emerging from these material contests is more often than not that the time is ripe to purchase another round of new cars, toys, and television sets.

Significant tension besets middle-class parents who are trying to respond to financial demands coming at them from many directions. On the one hand, they need to meet the basic economic challenges of raising a family, including clothing, educating, and entertaining their growing children; buying a house (or paying the rent); and provisioning themselves with the goods and knowledge to perform competently as parents. All the while, they must keep pace with cultural trends and the frenzied, shop-until-you-drop environment that has prevailed in the United States for decades. By the closing years of the twentieth century, things had ratcheted up to such a fever pitch that being a successful middle-class family entailed substantial purchasing of discretionary and luxury consumer goods and the accompanying dangers of serious indebtedness.

It is fair to say that this material affluence, truly a defining feature of the time, comes at a steep cost, affecting not only the pocketbooks but also the states of mind of American parents. Families routinely succumb to overwhelming pressure to try new fashions and shoes and foods and just-released electronic gadgets, not to mention the latest marketing icons from blockbuster films. Resistance is nearly futile. Witness the frenzy that surrounds the release of a new-concept laptop or gaming console; people actually camp outside stores for hours to be among the first buyers. Advertisers set enormously effective consumer traps for families with young children, pressuring parents primarily through marketing directed at kids to buy a whole new suite of products to replace last year's toys, clothes, and sweets with new styles, new colors, and new brands.[1] Ever the dutiful consumers, families respond just as they have been socialized to do, by purchasing enough to trump the neighbors. Heaps of older toys and passé jeans and furnishings are shuttled to closets and basements. It should come as no surprise that after a few short years families amass more than the house can hold.

Economists and consumer historians closely track global production and sales in hundreds of categories of goods, and the data on annual manufacturing volume and the purchasing habits of the U.S. population are widely available. Staggering quarterly profits garnered by retailers make clear to even the most casual observer that millions of U.S. families are buying mountains of things. We can count and measure in various ways the billions of dollars' worth of goods that go out retailers' doors. But we have a limited grasp of how America's consumer frenzy plays out in measurable ways family by family and within people's homes. Since the home is the repository for nearly everything families own—that is, if they do not rent an off-site storage facility to absorb excesses—it stands to reason that we must delve into home spaces to document how many possessions households have, the kinds of objects they own (including older goods), where they place them, and how they use them. We also need to be in the home and hear directly from home owners to assess how they are coping emotionally with such material abundance. As simple as it sounds, this kind of systematic documentation of assemblages of goods in ordinary homes has never been recorded for any global industrial or postindustrial society. The material world of Americans at home—perpetually occluded from view—is seriously underexamined.

I led a team of archaeologists setting out to close this gap in our record of middle-class American life by introducing a group of methods focused on documenting material culture within and around the thirty-two homes in the CELF study.[2] We systematically assembled data on possessions and their uses within the Los Angeles houses using digital photography, scan sampling, and filming. We collected detailed family commentaries on rooms and objects that shed light on the meanings of possessions for contemporary families through family-narrated video home tours.

The homes of most (but not all) families in our study are strikingly crowded with things. In some, toys and clothes overflow bedroom closets; in others, food is stockpiled in garages and pantries; electronic gadgets are everywhere; and indoor objects spill into backyards. In about half the L.A. households, a clutter crisis results from an imbalance between house size and sheer numbers of artifacts owned. High levels of accumulation swamp bedroom closets and other storage areas, leaving stuff with no (hidden) place to go. Add to this the propensity for youngsters to leave their things strewn around, and we have the perfect recipe for daily cluttering of the house.

Clutter—particularly if it is someone else's—fascinates us. We see impossibly crowded closets or garages of some hapless couple on TV and feel better about our own. Those who try to provide assistance to resolve the problem of clutter or who discuss it as a contemporary phenomenon, however, rarely if ever explicitly define what it is. In the current study, in order to compare households and spaces and people's behavior, we need to portray materiality and clutter in quantitatively meaningful ways such as in terms of the *density* of possessions in a given space. The numbers of accumulated objects *per square foot* tell us whether a family is absorbing material goods in numbers consonant with house capacity. In a small house, of course, high densities of objects are reached quickly, and a cluttered look is difficult to avoid. The White House, on the other hand, at 55,000 square feet, or Elvis Presley's Graceland, at 17,552 square feet, would take gargantuan shopping sprees to fill and transform into cluttered spaces.

Density plays a major role in what constitutes clutter, but it is not the whole story. We must recognize two other components, both difficult to quantify and thus largely subjective. These are whether objects are tidily or messily arranged and whether they are visible somewhere other than where they belong. People will always have different thresholds in defining and tolerating clutter in their own homes, but generally speaking we all know clutter when we see it. One thousand neatly arranged DVDs are a model of organization; the same items scattered about on the floor and on tabletops are a visual blight. Some individuals with extreme minimalist taste might even consider one thousand DVDs on a shelf an example of clutter, but everyone will agree on the case of the strewn disks because they are clearly *unkempt* and *out of place.* Among the L.A. families, it appears that most households are losing the clutter battle. Fully 75 percent of the families in our study, and across much of Los Angeles, have acquired so much stuff that they have shifted masses of household objects into garages and expelled one or all of their cars onto adjoining driveways and streets.

The consumer one-upsmanship that produces these high densities of goods in homes eats up as much time as it does money. On the work side of the equation, there is an obvious link between the desire to purchase more goods and the need to work more hours (or better-compensated hours) to pay for them. Many parents take second jobs, work overtime, or magnify their stress by extending their lines of credit. Yet the more hours they work, the fewer hours they have available for family time and especially for leisure time. Economists document that Americans have a lengthy history of working more hours per year than adults in other countries.[3] U.S. employers provide significantly fewer paid vacation days than in the European Union, for instance, and American workers often do not take all the vacation days available to them.

On the home front, heaps of prized possessions erode family time. Contributing mightily to the leisure deficits of U.S. adults are the great costs in labor and energy needed to *manage* all the furnishings and goods in a home, including cleaning, organizing, and maintaining them. Working parents certainly have some leisure hours—roughly 15 percent of their time at home—but much of it is experienced in front of the television or computer.[4] Not only is parents' leisure time indoors and sedentary, but it is fragmented into short segments, and mothers enjoy less leisure than fathers. It is striking how elusive outdoor leisure time has become for middle-class parents and children. This phenomenon—so much time spent indoors—is one of the more unfortunate end products of the intertwined elements in this self-perpetuating, complex story featuring escalating consumerism, increasing time spent at work, growing heaps of possessions at home, rising stress, and declining leisure.[5]

RECORDING LIFE AT HOME

Documenting the Material World

Recording the full, rich spectrum of the material culture inside middle-class Los Angeles houses has been fraught with practical challenges, among them how to cope with the tendency for certain objects to be shifted around the house and how to address the issue of objects tucked away in storage locales (dressers, closets, attics). The primary limiting factor in our documentation process is visibility: in the end, we can record only what we can see in our photographic archive. We photographed just about every square inch of wall and floor space, so in that sense the archive is quite comprehensive. Closet interiors were often but not always captured in photos; dresser contents were not visible. After untold hours of review and coding,[6] we are now armed with systematically recorded frequencies of all countable and visible objects in each room of each house, divided into categories such as furniture, media electronics, decoration, lighting, and toys. We provide estimates for aggregated, abundant items such as large collections of CDs or dense piles of toys on the floor. We have still barely tapped this rich data set, but a few examples illustrate what can be done and what we can learn.

Among our first investigations was an enumeration of possessions to illuminate the best means to measure clutter and densities of objects in these homes. At the first home we coded, the Roland-Santos house, the counts exceeded 2,000 visible possessions within just the first three rooms addressed (two bedrooms and the living room). This family purposefully acquired at least 2,260 artifacts—furniture, art, lamps, a book collection, a music collection, toys, decorative objects, photos,

Figure 4.1. Densely packed garages present challenges to the counting and coding of possessions. This is a typical garage with a wide array of household artifacts (tables, bed, couch, chairs, TV, books, art, over forty dolls/toys/games, sports gear, backpacks, sleeping bags, strollers, etc.) and dozens of yard/garden/automotive objects—but no car in sight.

and more—and placed them in these rooms somewhere *in sight* (on a table, cabinet, wall, etc.). This is certainly a robust figure, and in this portion (540 sq. ft.) of the modest house's (980 sq. ft.) cozy rooms, this corresponds to object densities of 4 per square foot. Tallies include all objects on floors, furniture surfaces, and walls as well as on shelves and hangers in open closets, but these counts *do not* include untold numbers of items tucked into closed dresser drawers, storage boxes, and cabinets or buried under piles of stuff. So our count is clearly a quite *conservative* measure of actual objects owned. Houses in our study average 1,750 square feet of living space, and many rooms in quite a few of the houses are similarly overstuffed and cluttered. Garages, which serve as the most popular relief valve for possession overflows from the house, are often so crammed with objects that they pose a serious challenge to our ability to arrive at reliable counts (Figure 4.1). The grand totals of possessions from the object-rich Roland-Santos household are clearly above average for the thirty-two-family sample but not by a large margin.

More than sixty parents in our study created self-recorded, videotaped home tour narratives, commenting individually on their home spaces and expressing thoughts about the artifacts these spaces hold. Such narratives are rich in information about the meaningfulness of our homes and possessions and provide a large sample of specific words and phrases that parents use to describe their homes. Analysis of word choices allows us to investigate, among other things, whether clutter and high densities of objects affect parents' enjoyment of their homes. For example, most mothers comment directly and with annoyance about messiness and clutter, and they typically highlight their central role in trying to keep household mess under control. Words such as *chaotic, messy, cramped,* and *clutter* pop up frequently—accompanied by *always, constantly,* and *usually* to characterize how often this state of affairs occurs.

But there is a much deeper layer embedded in this story. CELF researchers Darby Saxbe and Rena Repetti examined these linguistic data and discovered that a number of parents in the study experience measurable psychological stress associated with clutter and disarray.[7] Readings of the stress hormone cortisol, derived from participants' saliva samples, reveal a measurable physiological link to cluttered home environments. Mothers whose narratives say that the home feels messy, cluttered, or unfinished actually show elevated depressed mood as the day progresses, based on cortisol readings and self-reports. This suggests that living day-to-day in a home that is "stressful" due to ongoing struggles with clutter is a more serious problem than previously thought. The clutter crisis affects some women's long-term health. Mothers who use language indicating that the home is relaxing or pleasant, or who describe their outdoor spaces (and "nature") at some length, experience their home as a more "restorative" environment. These mothers have cortisol readings indicating less stress, and they report better mood during weekday evenings at home. The clear message is that intense consumerism and its primary manifestations—disorganization and a high density of objects and clutter in the home—present challenges to women's well-being. The effect on men's health is ambiguous, and men say little about clutter and mess in their home tours. Many of them appear to simply ignore the problem.

Why is this so? I suspect that the cumulative impact of thousands of visible objects on display in room after room of the high-density, cluttered home is much greater than once thought. This is particularly the case where objects are poorly organized. Disorder exacts a psychological toll because it so clearly taxes family labor. Dusting, cleaning, upkeep, repair, straightening, reorganization—all these chores consume parents' time and energy. Merely *anticipating* such work almost certainly generates anxiety and stress, and carrying it out is a measurable strain on the household time budget.

Documenting the Rhythm of Activities at Home

Several generations of scholars, albeit with different purposes than ours, have pondered how modern, Western families use their homes. One of the more interesting phases of study began during the 1880s, when home efficiency experts in the United States and northern Europe sought to understand how people used their kitchen facilities—the sink, the stove, the counters—so they could improve the efficiency of kitchen design. An engaging fictionalization of one of these studies is presented in the 2003 Norwegian film *Kitchen Stories*, which tells the tale of a paid observer who perched in the corner and traced, on paper, the pathways of movement in the kitchen of a Scandinavian bachelor for several months.

Our study of course has a far loftier goal: to capture a detailed record of all family members' activities in all spaces of the home throughout the day. We want to be able to address many current and future questions about American middle-class families' utilization of rooms (by gender, by age), uses of objects, frequency of multitasking, and intrafamily interactions. To systematically document complex sets of activities for four or five family members (and guests, if present) in real time, we introduced and adapted methods from other disciplines. Our main method is scan sampling (see Appendix), which has been used by scientists in various kinds of naturalistic observational studies. We conducted our research with a handheld computer in order to record all observations regularly and with precision. Every ten minutes, project ethnographers recorded what each at-home family member was doing, including the person, room or outdoor space, objects in use (computer, bike, cutting board), other people interacting, and secondary activity, if any, such as watching television while eating lunch.

The resulting 16,935 timed observations make it feasible to query the database with an array of complex questions. We can examine across all families or within any given family what fathers, mothers, or children of various ages do, and where they are doing it. We also can assess how much (or little) they are interacting, how much their behaviors vary across weekdays compared to weekends or mornings compared to evenings, and which possessions are most likely to be put to use. Moreover, we can assess important economic questions such as how much time mothers and fathers, respectively, devote to dinners, childcare, chores, and the like, and how much (or little) time they may have left over for leisure at home.

Among the questions we pursue, this chapter discusses findings about the vanishing outdoor leisure of middle-class parents and gender differences among parents in how they spend their limited indoor leisure time. We see a significant departure from the universal suburban ideal that emerged in the 1950s and 1960s that the backyard was a center for "outdoor living," meant to be used frequently for play and entertaining.[8] Families still articulate this ideal when talking about their lives at home, but more than 75 percent do not live this way.[9] Instead, the leisure of both parents and children is focused on the indoors, and mothers carve out considerably less free time than do fathers, with the most notable gender-based leisure deficit on weekdays.[10] Television, Internet use on computers, reading, and game playing indoors consume most of the open time of American families. Many of our findings regarding families and their time use find solid support when we compare the results from Los Angeles to those from a much larger-scale study on time use among five hundred middle-class families in eight regionally diverse U.S. cities.[11]

HAPPINESS IS (NOT) AN OVERSTUFFED HOME OFFICE

Our large archives of home tour narratives, videotaped naturalistic family interactions, and photographs of rooms demonstrate clearly that many parents in our study find the thousands of things they have in their homes exhausting to contemplate, organize, clean, and maintain. When family members narrating home tours comment on their possessions as they move through their homes, they frequently voice frustrations over an inability to contain or reduce the clutter that surrounds them. This widely felt frustration in the United States has spurred a whole industry of home organizing, devoted especially to closet organizing systems and garage overhauls. The problem of household clutter has also attracted considerable media attention, and during the 2000–2005 period we witnessed a flood of popular television shows on clutter clearing, home organizing, designing for better storage capacity, and house remodeling and expansion.

Garages and home offices appear anecdotally to be the most object-filled, impacted spaces in the majority of American middle-class houses, and this is true for most of the families in our study as well. Some children's bedrooms and family rooms are also viable contenders for clutter supremacy among the Los Angeles households. So many goods are flowing through these homes—and often ending up in garages and attics—that only one quarter of garages retain enough room for a car. When we code and count all visible objects in the garages in our sample, we find an average of about 225. This figure is *significantly* limited by the chaotic arrangement of goods in most garages, which hampers our ability to precisely count boxes, tools, soccer balls, bikes, clothes, cleaning products, furniture, and stockpiled food lurking underneath or behind the visible, counted items.

Plotting in a bar graph all objects that could be spotted and enumerated, we see three distinct peaks, suggesting that these garages fall into three emergent organizational types. Average garage size across the whole L.A. sample is 362 square feet. The very low density, neat garage, represented by five examples in the study, has an average count of 48 objects—including one or two vehicles regularly parked in the space! These garages, which average 340 square feet, contain fewer than 0.14 objects per square foot.

The prototypical garage (nineteen in the L.A. sample) is densely packed and/or chaotic in its distribution of items and averages 190 countable artifacts (range is 125 to 300 objects per garage) in a mean of about 350 square feet. These garages have object densities of roughly 0.5 per square foot. The six exceptionally overstuffed garages in the study are larger than average (mean = 528 sq. ft.) and average 435 visible artifacts (range of 320 to 625). The density is roughly 0.9 objects per square foot, or about six times the density in the tidy garages, and I must emphasize that far more objects are present that we cannot count due to piling and stacking. This is a problem that is exacerbated as object density rises; true densities in some of these garages likely exceed 2 to 3 items per square foot. In these packed and typically disorderly garages, the entire floor space is given over to a more or less solid block of stored or tossed items. Not surprisingly, since garages are now primarily storage loci for possessions that no longer fit in the house, they exhibit a high diversity of objects such as televisions, furniture, holiday items, clothes, boxes of paper documents, file cabinets, art, and food alongside scattered yard and

Figure 4.2. One corner of a high-density home office space.

car paraphernalia. Two households no longer have a garage space as such; their garages are now physically converted to bedroom or cabinet-lined computer/recreation room spaces.

Home offices, present in well over half the houses, reveal comparably high—if not higher—densities of objects, which are typically positioned on walls, shelves, desktops, and floor corners since the spaces must accommodate foot traffic. Six of the houses have small home offices (averaging about 60 sq. ft.) in various corners or cubbyholes, and another three families have established two home offices, the second of which is small. One third of the L.A. families have larger home offices, normally full rooms such as former bedrooms and measuring more than twice the size, or 120 square feet (Figure 4.2). Most observers would agree that they are visually stress-inducing rather than "restorative" or restful spaces, and home tour narratives verify that parents experience them this way (see discussion below).

These are spaces where job-related work, schoolwork, or record keeping mixes with recreational uses. Not counting loose papers, magazines, and newspapers, which we treated as ephemera not amenable to accurate counts, the average number of visible objects is 313. Densities in the home office spaces are fairly consistent across the range of room sizes. In the small offices, if we exclude the large music collection in the home office at one household (> 1,600 CDs and 350 vinyl albums), we find a mean number of 137 objects, or 2.3 per square foot. (If we were to include that case, the mean count jumps to 380, and the density rises to a whopping 6.3 objects per square foot. It is clearly an outlier in this sample, but an argument can be made that it is not unusual.) The larger office spaces yield a mean of 257 objects, or 2.1 per square foot. All these figures significantly underrepresent objects actually in home office locations since such spaces are burdened with a complex mix of (uncountable) papers (homework, bills, mail, schoolwork, etc.) as well as dense assemblages of family photos, sports memorabilia, books, binders, videos, computing gear, and furniture. A sense of clutter prevails.

The historian Peter Thornton uses density in a similar way when comparing visually "busy" interior design periods—such as Queen Anne Victorian—to the material signatures of other eras. Victorians filled every available inch of home space with furniture, mirrors, art, decorative items, dark woods, and floral fabrics, the classic high-density look.[12] At the other end of the density spectrum, a midcentury modern living room is simple, spare, and often but not always low density. Neat built-in wood shelving units filled with organized sets of books or record albums could transform it into a high-density but still uncluttered space.

Psychologists who study compulsive hoarding behaviors have developed sets of photographs of rooms in successive stages of clutter accumulation to help clinicians gauge the severity of hoarding.[13] These sequences of images culminate in extraordinary levels of density and clutter: kitchens or living rooms with stacks of newspapers, boxes, dishes, and clothes towering over a maze of dangerous, twisting paths, the floors totally covered. Such images of course represent pathological behaviors and are far more extreme than the simple shifting clutter situations of ordinary households. But they help to bring these terms and patterns to life. We might think of density as how many objects we see in a space and clutter as (largely) the neatness and arrangement of those objects. Thus higher densities make clutter increasingly and proportionally harder to control, but they do not always go hand in hand.

Turning back to our house inventories, we know from scan sampling data that kitchens and living rooms are the most heavily used spaces in the thirty-two L.A. homes (kitchens on weekdays, living rooms on weekends). Not surprisingly, they also reveal clutter. Whereas kitchen tables and other kitchen surfaces attract mostly shifting panoplies of foods, dishes, photos, schedules, newspapers, mail, backpacks, and the paraphernalia associated with schoolwork and bill-paying tasks, far more is hidden away (and thus uncountable) inside cabinets, pantries, and drawers. Clutter in the kitchen is common, but assemblages of objects are usually transitory. We do not count papers and magazines or the transitory food items and plates that are set out for meals. Thus densities of more or less permanently on-display objects such as magnets and photos on the refrigerator or dish racks, plants, cookbooks, and toasters on the counters are moderate in the kitchen. Counts average about 80, and the mean densities are well under one per square foot. Just seven households maintain more than 100 visible objects in the kitchen.

In family room and living room spaces, on the other hand, large furnishings create entertainment-friendly locales surrounded by a more stable set of decorative objects that reveal a great deal about family taste and identity. Common here are family photos, art, TV sets, game stations, music systems, remote controls, plants, books, DVDs, videos, decorative objects such as ceramics and mementos from travel, and of course toys of many varieties. The average number of visible objects in living rooms is 196, but the range is wide: from 30 to 1,282. The mean density is about 2 per square foot, but a few approach 5 per square foot. Eleven families have both living rooms and family rooms, with the latter adding just over 205 visible artifacts on average to those houses' assemblages. Although at least two-thirds of living rooms and family rooms are densely packed with goods, those of a handful of the families are far more spartan and tidy, each with well under 100 objects.

What is most important about these sets of numbers is how they translate into family experiences. Clutter demands the energy and attention of the households that are burdened by it. The majority of homes in our thirty-two-family sample harbor high counts of consumer goods and would be classified as cluttered by objective observers (Figure 4.3). A number of parents find the situation personally stressful, as our cortisol data and some of the home tour narratives show. Some parents try to direct their attention away from the mess, accepting that while the kids are young the situation is not going to resolve itself, and the ever-shifting masses of objects just need to be herded occasionally into closets and bins. In their narratives, about half the mothers comment on various concentrations of mess (piles of toys, mounds of books and mail) around the house. While several of these moms temper their frustration and view clutter as inevitable, others are clearly irritated—even bitter—about it.

Karita (mother, school aide) during her home tour:

Figure 4.3. A two-child bedroom displaying clutter and a high density of objects.

> This is the office. It's a place that we turned into from part of the garage. It's a total mess. . . . We probably should, you know, organize it better. But it works out well. Here is where the computers are and the kids do homework. We are all on the computers here from time to time. . . . And here we have the garage, with everything. This is usually a total mess, and it's a total mess today again. This is where we have bikes and all the old furniture, sofas, and things that we don't use. It's—how can I say it, it's a mess. It's not fun. It should be cleaned up, and we should probably get rid of a whole bunch of stuff.

Susannah (mother, administrator) during her home tour:

> This is the everyday mess I see when I walk into my house. I've chosen to video my house on a day that it's very messy because this is what it looks like every day, so why pretend it's clean. This is the kitchen where I spend a lot of my evenings cooking dinner, feeding the baby. The baby eats pretty much while I cook dinner because she's so impatient to eat dinner. And this is the mess that I have to clean up every day. Probably five, six times a day I am cleaning up after people. So beside my full-time job as a parent, this is my other

full-time job in the kitchen. And this is my hang-drying right there. Normally I'd be embarrassed to have anybody over but . . . I figured it would be better to have my real everyday life. This dining area is for, as you can see, junk. This is where junk piles up. I won't name names of who leaves junk on the table, but as you can see it's a newspaper. I don't read the newspaper.

A number of fathers in the study seem oblivious or unconcerned and make no comment as they pass untidy areas in their homes. Fathers are more likely to describe cluttered rooms as simply cozy or in need of remodeling or expansion, and they may muse about various artifacts without saying anything about messiness or crowding. But fathers such as Thomas, a marketing director, are exceptions. Showing his master bedroom, he says:

> Anyway, suffice to say that we cram an awful lot into this bedroom. In fact about six months ago we repainted and redecorated and took out an amazing amount of stuff. We really quite like it in here except for this area here which is a mess again [points to wife's items on floor]. And here's my little pile on the floor where I throw my day clothes.

Despite parents' best efforts to maintain order and keep their houses neat, disruptive material elements infiltrate just about every room, led by toys, mail, and paper from school and work. Keys, phones, books, computers, shoes, and newspapers add to the chorus of stuff that is moved around every day and often fails to find a good, out-of-sight resting spot. American families also have multiples of so many categories of possessions such as DVDs, CDs, books, digital games, toys, and magazines that it is inevitable that things are routinely strewn around in an untidy fashion, often leading, we now know, to measurable stress.

Turning to one last space in the public parts of the house, as we examined the kitchens in the study, I identified an interesting parallel between high total numbers of objects *in the house as a whole* and high counts of objects affixed to refrigerators. The typical American family places quite a few items on the front (and sometimes side) panel of refrigerators. For the 32 L.A. households, the greatest number of items on a single refrigerator is 166, the mean is about 52, and the lowest is 2 (Figure 4.4). Common objects are magnets, snapshots of family and pets, phone numbers, memos, calendars, kids' art, bills, and menus.[14] I assessed how many objects are typically placed there, what kinds of artifacts are considered appropriate, and how these patterns vary across families. Middle-class Angelenos consistently display decorative magnets as well as unframed

Figure 4.4. A prototypical "refrigerator display" featuring decorative magnets, informal snapshots, phone numbers, schedules, lists, and more.

family snapshots from various informal moments of family history. But we also find a dozen or more kinds of reminders such as school menus, plumbers' phone numbers, and invitations that are hardly added for their aesthetic value. Many refrigerator postings clearly serve a scheduling and organizing function for the family. Altogether, about 12 percent of households use their refrigerator panels sparingly (9 or fewer items), and these are rather neat by default. Every other kitchen fridge has at least 16 to 20 affixed objects; about 10 percent of these are well-organized spatially, with tidy rows of magnets and snapshots. The rest of the refrigerators have quite high object densities and appear from the outsider's perspective to be palimpsests of randomly placed objects, producing a rather untidy look.

My analysis suggests that a family's tolerance for a busy, untidy refrigerator surface appears to be a good predictor of a relaxed attitude about high object density and clutter in public rooms of the house: family room, living room, dining room, and office. To examine this phenomenon more closely, we had coders tally everything on the refrigerators, and then I grouped the six households with the highest refrigerator display counts (all with at least 80 artifacts on the panels) and grouped the seven households with the lowest counts (all with fewer than 20 affixed objects). Next, I aggregated the object count data from a set of the main rooms of each of those houses. The rooms I used for this analysis are the living room, dining room, kitchen, family room, and home office. I calculated the average artifact counts for the two groupings. The six houses in the first group (high-density refrigerator display) yield an average aggregate count of 1,448 objects in these rooms. The seven houses in the low-density refrigerator display group have far lower total object counts in these sets of rooms—just 322, on average. By any measure, this is a striking difference, and one consistent with my conjecture that there is a relationship. But I had to explore further whether the first group simply consisted of much larger houses, where we might expect more total objects.

To judge whether house size shaped the results, I turned once more to the density figures. I pulled in house square footage for the two subgroups and found that the houses with the highest raw counts of household artifacts and the visually busy refrigerators are *smaller* on average (1,336 sq. ft.), not larger, than the latter group (1,744 sq. ft.). This surprising finding means the homes with high-density refrigerator assemblages have exceptionally high household object densities. The houses with tidy refrigerator panels contain lower raw counts of stuff overall, even though they are more spacious. Thus these houses exhibit very low object densities. So there is some support for the idea that a family's tolerance for crowded, artifact-laden refrigerator surfaces mirrors high densities of possessions in the main rooms of the house and that families that keep tidy and minimally decorated refrigerators tend to have more modest assemblages of objects elsewhere in the home.

When we extended the analysis to include all thirty-two households simultaneously and ran simple significance tests, however, we did not identify a statistically significant correlation. This outcome may stem from the very basic approach we have taken to the question to date. We have not yet incorporated other variables that could be relevant, such as the effects of major "spring" cleanings and the number of years families have occupied their current residence. I believe there is an important pattern here, but it must be tested with a larger sample drawn from other middle-class U.S. homes.

It is nonetheless intriguing is that one iconic place in the home—the refrigerator panel—at least in part anticipates overall family tendencies regarding materialism (predilection to buy; intensive consumerism; accumulations over lifetimes) and tidiness and object organization in the house (dense vs. spartan, chaotic vs. orderly). The cases at the two ends of the spectrum (the very spartan and tidy panels and the very high density panels), at the very least, seem to mirror behaviors in the rest of the house. If this idea ultimately finds broader confirmation, we should be able to go to a house and make reasonable projections about the household material assemblage just by documenting characteristics of the refrigerator display.

PERSONAL IDENTITY: THE LABELING OF SPACE

Compared to other historical times and other societies around the world, the extent to which contemporary American household spaces display family members' personal identity and taste is striking. Given the array of elaborated goods of all imaginable kinds available to purchase, it is no surprise that parents, teens, and even younger children find objects to arrange in their homes that announce, "This is who I am." Our objects are our biographers. Middle-class Americans typically select two or three main classes of objects as suitable to embody chosen self-identities. One is iconic images or symbols from popular culture with which they feel a strong affinity. This part of our family biography we purchase or inherit. Many kinds of entities are available, including posters of rock stars and sports heroes, Disney motifs, national flags, sports pennants, paintings by prominent artists, and the like. Display of these artifacts in our homes assigns them considerable implicit value: we feel a strong attachment, we admire them, they entertain us, they are part of our heritage, or they reflect core interests and values. Preteens and teens most frequently identify with musicians, film and television stars, and sports heroes, materialized by means of posters on their bedroom walls. Such images are close to universal among the L.A. families.

Another class of objects dominating walls, doors, and desktops in many bedrooms and home offices includes markers of our accomplishments and other paraphernalia trumpeting our existence such as blue ribbons, diplomas, engraved trophies, and commercially made or homemade signs with personal names ("Marcus," "Giselle") that effectively lay claim to that space. These represent a more overt announcement of the identity of room "owners." They say, I am an important member of this family, and this is my name and my room! Or, I am a middle-school graduate, a soccer player, a ballet pupil, an Honors student, or a champion dog breeder, and these are my accomplishments. Honors are materialized and projected; space is carved out. Achievement- and name-related artifacts are ubiquitous in the L.A. households. One child's room has no fewer than six name emblems. This seems more prevalent for girls than for boys. Children use these material markers alongside social networks materialized in displays of photos of friends and family to carve out emerging identities and justify control of their own spaces and artifacts. Parents do this, too, in places such as home offices, where they might post a diploma or a photo of themselves with a famous public figure.

And third, family photographs are everywhere, numbering in the triple digits in many Los Angeles homes. Informal snapshots plaster surfaces such as refrigerators and kitchen cabinets, and framed photographs are ubiquitous in living rooms, family rooms, bedrooms, offices, and hallways. Recent family histories are captured in photos that preserve memories of weddings, school days, vacations, and other happy times. Although such displays are both commonplace—averaging 85 photos per household—and highly visible in the U.S. home (sets of photos are almost always visible from the front door), they are not mirrored in the homes of the Swedish and Italian families studied by our sister research centers. A few formal photos of family ancestors may be present in the typical Roman home, but displays do not spread throughout the house or extend to other object types. This pattern is distinctively American.

Although it seems grounded in recent consumerism as much as anything, the personalization phenomenon actually has deep historical roots. Clifford Clark's analysis of American homes shows that even the earliest emergence of suburbia during the late 1800s was framed by a set of new expectations about what the American house should be.[15] The thinking was that houses for the middle-class family must become far more than simply shelters or places of refuge. The house needed to support and nurture the family and encourage "the growth of each family member's talents, capabilities, and health"; moreover, it was expected to enhance "individual self-expression and creativity."[16]

As if wives and mothers were not burdened enough with child-raising and house upkeep, they were also then saddled with the responsibility of developing an attractive home design that announced who they were to neighbors and visitors. The house was strongly identified as the women's sphere as early as 1880—and artistic and musical activities and training of children in the arts were expected to take place there—and it was particularly true starting in the 1900s that women needed to imbue the house interior with *things* that creatively conveyed family tastes and personal identities. The house became a place for artistic expression and the projection of family ideals through the careful selection of furnishings, china sets, front porch decorations, paintings, and the like. The house form itself—both the style (Queen Anne, bungalow, colonial, Greek revival) and the room layout—was also considered an embodiment of personal expression, materially reflecting the owner's ideas about family, comfort, and social standing.

Such strong encouragement to express individuality naturally led to a rather competitive approach to home furnishing and upkeep. Although people sought a distinctive look for their own homes, most yearned more than anything to conform with the highest-ranking arbiters of taste in the neighborhood, those most well-off or admired. Widespread emulation in turn led to much duplication of house styles and furnishings. Strong tensions arose between imitation and creativity in the home.

Social critics of the early 1900s labeled the increasingly prevalent middle-class need to show off the home and possessions a form of exhibitionism.[17] This thrust toward personal, individualistic display of objects has persisted unabated in the American ethos for more than 120 years, and the zeal to personalize home spaces is clearly still with us.

Considering the house as an instrument of display, a "museum" for preserving family memories and histories, and an arena of self-expression helps to frame our understanding of the intense personalization evident in American homes. Specific places such as the fireplace mantel and the front parlor or foyer have evolved into standard locations for family photos, art objects, and sophisticated or expensive artifacts suggesting worldliness. As early as 1880, material possessions became signs of refinement, achievement, and status, and thus the home became the place for family display.[18] Since we could hardly carry all these things around, we brought people to see them in our homes.

The pressure to decorate escalated significantly with the birth of advertising in magazines and newspapers in the 1880s, creating a culture of consumption fully accessible to the common woman and man. Values shaped by media depictions of house-decorating ideals contributed significantly to what people wanted. Commodities multiplied, and women were encouraged to furnish their homes with everything new. The emergence of glittering, fantastic, museum-like department stores with sumptuous choices (Macy's, Marshall Field's) was seductive,[19] and it placed Americans of modest to substantial means on a path of consumer frenzy from which we have rarely swayed. It was not long afterward that Thorstein Veblen made his renowned, scornful comments about conspicuous consumption and waste in American society.[20] So the house as an unusually expansive canvas of personal expression is a true American legacy, materialized by as many dazzling and identity-projecting possessions as can be afforded.[21]

Intergenerational transitions—the ways in which each new generation of householders perpetuates this legacy—are underexamined in studies of material culture and modern life. Little is known about the process by which young couples, who have been socialized by the distinct family traditions of their respective childhood homes, may struggle to articulate what they identify with as they create new material surroundings. Couples must negotiate and ultimately develop a strategy to furnish and personalize their home as they build inventories of goods through purchases and inheritance. In cultures with deeper and stronger material heritage (Italy, for example), young couples might inherit a few valued heirlooms around which to build the new household. Twenty-first-century American couples are more likely to purchase their new household identities at Ikea and Target.

Among the families in our sample, a few decorating choices appear nearly universal, and these cases tell us something important about U.S. culture. Nothing puts the stamp of "this is ours" on a home and celebrates the unity of the family more than depictions of the family itself, and almost all the thirty-two Los Angeles families make a strong effort to portray family history through the display of photographs in multiple rooms of the home. While numbers of visible photos of family members (and pets) vary from as few as 10 to as many as 210, most families display at least 70 person-centered photos, and the average per household is a robust 85 (Figure 4.5). Some families maintain veritable shrines of family member images.

Photos range from formal (weddings, annual school pictures) to casual snapshots from family vacations, and they may be found in living rooms (often on mantels, walls, and special tables), hallways, bedrooms, kitchens, home offices, and even garages and bathrooms. Favorite locations for informal, unframed snapshots are the children's bedrooms and the refrigerator. On average, families include about 9 or 10 photos among the many items they attach to the refrigerator door. Framed photos and images from formal occasions like studio portraits or weddings usually

Figure 4.5. A living room wall featuring family photos in a highly visible locus immediately inside the front door. These are part of a large assemblage of photographs of family members located throughout the house.

are matched to spaces that are the most formal in the house (e.g., living rooms) and rest on the nicest tables or mantels. Middle-class families clearly share certain values regarding the appropriate placement of photos and the formality of framing.

Also on display in 97 percent of the homes are diplomas, certificates, awards, trophies, and other insignia of personal accomplishments of the children. We see less emphasis on markers of personal accomplishment among parents (found in about one quarter of the homes). But quite a few sets of parents in the study strongly identify with a specific cultural group, ethnicity, religion, or sexual identity, and they make an effort to display one or more important material markers in the home that signal their membership in or affiliations with those groups. These can be of fundamental importance to family self-identity. A Swedish-born mom displays a Swedish flag over the front door and has a large framed painting of a seascape from Sweden in her living room. Japanese American parents show off delicate decorative figurines from Japan in a living room display case. One of the two-father families in our study has rainbow artwork and other art pieces that celebrate the gay rights movement.

Another way in which American families commonly express identity and announce their values and interests is through the display of school and professional sports teams logos. Allegiance to teams takes the form of pennants, caps, and other items. In our study, the storied franchises of the Los Angeles Lakers basketball team and the Dodgers baseball team, represented by flags, foam fingers, posters, and helmets (about 18 percent of households), clearly predominate over lesser franchises and more distant teams. These are important ways that families announce their support and participation as members of a locally significant community.

Beyond these materializations that help to express in very central ways who the families *are*, we see their attempts to reveal a sense of style, cultural refinement, or "taste." Families adopt aesthetic preferences pertaining to certain styles of furniture, paint colors, and art from formative life experiences (parents, college friends, neighbors, high-end hotels) or overt emulation of cultural icons (the rich and famous). However, most young middle-class families with limited means are more likely to acquire furniture and framed posters from big-box stores than gilded bath fixtures and original paintings like the ones their cultural heroes have. Emulation can go only so far. There is also the issue of a new household needing to blend and accommodate the disparate tastes of the couple. The results in middle-class U.S. homes are, as we would expect, not always coherent. Mixed styles, little formal art, vacation mementos, knickknacks, and clutter are more prevalent than clean, recognizable furnishing styles.

Some homes in our study are dominated by juvenile iconography, including large, framed Disney icons in living room spaces. Others eschew Disney art but cannot wrestle free of children's materials in every room of the house. To say the least, it is challenging to have a stylish living room with blankets, Barbies, and Legos all over the tables and floor. Some families buy low-end furniture that can handle spills and tears until children get a bit older. Investments in stylistic expression may be thoughtfully postponed until the family gets farther along in the life cycle.

THE DECLINE OF OUTDOOR LEISURE

The home also exhibits clear material residues of busy families' vanishing leisure time. With so much of life focused on jobs and school activities, parents often convert areas such as bedrooms and corners of garages into home offices. Formal, dedicated office spaces and computer rooms (found in eighteen of the thirty-two households in our sample) are common, and almost every house has multiple computers and multiple desktops covered with work-related materials that take space from other home activities. And while families devote considerable money, effort, and sentiment to beautifying their front and back yards, they are rarely observed spending time in these leisure-oriented spaces. For example, Karita (mother) reported during her home tour:[22]

> I'm going to go outside now to the backyard. This is the outside patio. We sometimes eat here and things like that. We have a nice fireplace and barbecue, so we can, you know, use that. It's a big yard. We did get gardeners about two years ago because it took way too much time to do the yard. We were never home . . . doing baseball and softball every weekend. So we felt the yard started to kind of look kind of bad so . . . We have lots of side space, and again, it could be used better. It's more just putting stuff there that we don't use, I guess. I finally cleaned up a few days ago. We have this big pool, but we don't use it anymore, so I would like to get rid of it.

When we recorded how everyone spends time at home, we found that parents have moderate amounts of leisure—about 15 percent of their time at home. But virtually all their leisure moments happen inside, they occur in fragmented episodes, and they are most often associated with television watching (50 percent), followed by reading (21 percent) and playing games or playing with kids (18 percent).[23] Certain families prove to be exceptions to these trends, but even for them leisure at home is mainly devoted to sedentary indoor activities. Frequent interruptions arise from children, cell phones, and the need to attend to household chores.

Important gender differences exist as well. Mothers have less leisure time overall (roughly 13 percent of time at home), and the average duration of their leisure episodes is about ten to twenty minutes. Looking at all the mothers collectively, only 2 percent (one in fifty) of their leisure events lasted more than one hour. Fathers do better, enjoying an average of 21 percent of their time at home in leisure, and the episodes are slightly more likely to last longer: collectively, 5 percent (one in twenty) represents more than one hour. Leisure time experiences vary by gender across hours of the day as well. During busy meal preparation and cleanup time blocks, from 4:00 P.M. to 6:00 P.M., mothers have notably less leisure than their spouses. Mothers do chores or tasks on average 94 percent of the time between these hours (6 percent leisure), whereas fathers typically manage to enjoy leisure for about 18 percent of this time span.[24] The disparity lessens in the 6:00 to 8:00 P.M. block, but mothers are still investing more time in nonleisure tasks (mothers spend 86 percent of this time span doing chores; fathers, 81 percent).

One of the most striking discoveries of our study is the inability of busy L.A. parents to find time for outdoor leisure. Less than 3 percent of parents' hours at the house are enjoyed in leisure activities in their back-yards. Fully three-fourths of parents have no outdoor leisure moments at all during a typical week (including weekends), and 58 percent of fami-lies—children included—spend *no time* in these spaces, for fun or even for yard work.[25] The children in just one-fourth of the families used their backyards for leisure activities one or more hours during the record-ing period. These minuscule usages of outdoor spaces occur despite the draws provided by southern California's famously good weather and the families' significant investments in their backyards in the form of swim-ming pools, slides, play sets, baseball cages, trampolines, skateboard ramps, large expanses of grass, brick fireplaces, barbecues, patios, decks, outdoor dining sets, lounge chairs, and hot tubs. Parents' and children's home tour narrations for a good number of the study households verify these minimal uses of outdoor spaces as the family norm.

CONCLUSION

This chapter describes the consequences of the sheer numbers of pos-sessions American families have in their homes. We can see that many parents point with pride during their home tours to objects of special meaning and value in their homes, including art, heirloom furniture, and artifacts from their travels or their home countries. Attachments to mate-rial culture are a nearly universal fixture of our modern cultural heritage and can give us pleasure and a strong sense of our family's history. Most furnishings and decorations in the study sample appear newer and may be valued simply for their monetary value, whereas others may be largely sentimental and related to family connections (children's art, grandma's sewing machine, an old wedding dress). Regardless, their importance to most people makes it clear that possessions have a powerful impact on our general well-being. Behavioral archaeologists have long understood this deep connection between people and their material culture.[26]

But taken to an extreme, great mountains of things in our homes cost us considerable money, drain our labor and energy, and detract from the attractiveness of our homes. For some adults, women more than men, persistent clutter exacts a psychological toll and causes unhealthful stress. The mania to accumulate prized goods prompts us to work harder, take less vacation time, enjoy less leisure at home, and savor startlingly little leisure outdoors. Many families in Los Angeles, as well as across much of the United States, take part in an unremitting work-and-spend

cycle, engaging in competitive purchasing and spending fragmented leisure time in sedentary indoor pursuits. Still, as other chapters in this
book reveal, many of these families absorb or deflect experiences of
time stress, material abundance, and other pressures in ways that allow
them to enjoy happy, energetic daily lives. Ultimately, the tale of the
middle-class family at the opening of the twenty-first century is a story
of remarkable resiliency.

NOTES

1. *Consuming Kids: The Commercialization of Childhood.* DVD. Media
Education Foundation, 2008.

2. The archaeology/material culture researchers are Jeanne Arnold,
Anthony P. Graesch, Margaret Beck, and Angela Orlando. See Appendix for
a more detailed description of methods.

3. Bianchi, Robinson, and Milkie 2006.

4. Beck and Arnold 2009.

5. Schor 2004; Whybrow 2005.

6. When we set out to document the material culture of modern middle-
class Los Angeles, we designed procedures that allowed us to count and clas-
sify the visible objects in each room of each house. Because so many objects
are present, this proved a monumental task. Undaunted, our trained coders
spent more than a thousand hours carrying out this project using our large
digital photo archive. Coders assign every photographed object to an over-
arching category (e.g., furniture, media electronic, decorative item, lighting,
toy) and then directly count (for most categories) or estimate (for abundant or
piled items) the number of such items present, room by room.

7. Saxbe and Repetti 2010.

8. Clark 1986, 179.

9. Arnold and Lang 2007.

10. Beck and Arnold 2009.

11. This study included five cities in the Midwest, one in the Northeast,
one in the Southeast, and one on the West Coast. Suburban, urban, and rural
localities are represented. The 500-family study was conducted by the Sloan
Center at the University of Chicago, and the comparative analysis was done
by members of the Chicago and UCLA Sloan Centers (Broege et al. 2007).

12. Thornton 1984.

13. Tolin, Frost, and Steketee 2007.

14. Objects affixed to refrigerator panels comprise these categories, in
descending order of frequency: Magnets, Photos, Magnetic Photo Frames,
Children's Artwork, Calendars, Assorted Papers, Children's Schoolwork,
Achievement Awards, Emergency Contact Numbers, School Notices, School
Menus, Schedules, Lists, Magnetic Bins, Coupons, Receipts, Save-The-Date,

Magazine/Newspaper Cutouts, Post-Its, Business Cards, Holiday Cards, Invitations, Postcards, Rosters, White Boards, and Charts.

15. Clark 1986.

16. Ibid., 102.

17. Ibid., 112.

18. Ibid., 120.

19. Belk 2001.

20. Veblen 1899.

21. The visual record of home lives of the 32 Los Angeles families is provided in the book *Life at Home in the Twenty-First Century: 32 Families Open Their Doors* (Arnold et al. 2012).

22. This family did not use its 3,600-square-foot backyard space (with pool, batting cage, brick BBQ, tiled patio, and dining set) at all during the study.

23. Beck and Arnold 2009.

24. Ibid.

25. Arnold and Lang 2007.

26. Schiffer and Miller 1999.

5 Housework

WENDY KLEIN, CAROLINA IZQUIERDO,
AND THOMAS N. BRADBURY

After working all day at their respective jobs, how did the couples in the CELF study manage and divide household chores? In the United States, ambiguity in division of household responsibilities between working couples often results in ongoing negotiations, resentment, and tension between them. According to a 2007 Pew Research Poll, sharing household chores was in the top three highest-ranking issues associated with a successful marriage—third only to faithfulness and good sex. In this poll, 62 percent of adults said that sharing household chores is very important to marital success. There were no differences of opinion reported between men and women, between older adults and younger adults, or between married people and singles.

Mirroring trends in industrialized nations around the world,[1] men's participation in housework in U.S. families has nearly doubled in the past forty years, and their amount of time spent on childcare has tripled.[2] Yet in the United States women still perform the majority of household tasks,[3] and most of the couples in our study reported having no clear models for achieving a mutually satisfying arrangement. Determining who was responsible for various household tasks was a particularly contentious process for couples who tended to bicker about housework on a regular basis. Other couples, however, appeared to carry out tasks separately or in collaboration without much tension or discussion. Studying how couples divide their many household chores is important on its own terms, as the results of the Pew Poll suggest. More important, close examination of how husbands and wives collaborate on or fail to coordinate their household activities allows us to contemplate more encompassing phenomena such as gender roles, issues of power, respect, intimacy, and attempts to broker an equitable or fair partnership. What are couples' perceptions of their roles in the division of labor in the home? How do spouses coordinate and enact different patterns of household labor? How do family systems operate to sustain particular distributions of labor? This chapter looks at these issues in the CELF families.

The current dual-earner arrangement that typifies the couples we studied certainly reflects a major shift in the roles that women take both inside and outside the home over the past several generations. The traditional 1950s model of marriage—men as breadwinners, women as bread makers—gave way to the social activism and upheaval of the 1960s and 1970s and the dramatic influx of women into the workforce. While gender roles have since become more egalitarian, many couples still struggle to achieve a workable division of household labor. The sociologist Arlie Hochschild, who has written extensively on gender roles in working families, refers to this phenomenon as the "stalled revolution."[4] Although women have met with some success in achieving a more egalitarian status in the workplace, their expectations for a parallel status regarding the division of labor at home have generally remained unfulfilled. Another prominent sociologist, Andrew Cherlin,[5] in reflecting on the historical development of marriage, notes that while men's participation in housework has increased, there is no longer a shared set of conventions that couples and families can turn to for running a household. This situation has the potential to create opportunities for conflict, on the one hand, and for more equitable and satisfying arrangements, on the other, as couples work out ways of dividing responsibilities. Cherlin attributes this situation in part to new expectations of marriage as a source of personal fulfillment and an arena for self-development in which individual needs are given priority over social obligations.

Another spin on a contemporary model of marriage is set forth in Pepper Schwartz's discussion of "peer marriage."[6] Schwartz uses this term to describe an egalitarian relationship in which both spouses share decision making, household work, and childcare, with the mutual goals of equality and collaboration. She acknowledges that it may not be possible to consistently divide responsibilities equally and that the actual number of peer marriages may be quite small. Indeed, studies of contemporary couples indicate that while this model is not prevalent, sharing domestic responsibilities is one of the keys to success in working family life. According to Cooke,[7] couples with more equitable division of labor are less likely to divorce than couples in which one partner is the breadwinner and the other manages housework. The distribution of household labor, however, becomes a much more complex issue when both partners work full time outside the home.

WORKING COUPLES AND THE DIVISION OF LABOR AT HOME

Among CELF couples, on average, men worked longer hours outside the home,[8] yet even in families where women worked equivalent or longer hours and earned higher salaries they still took on more household responsibilities.[9] When our data were merged with the Chicago Sloan Study of five hundred working families, we learned that men spent 18 percent of their time doing housework and took on 33 percent of household tasks, whereas women spent 22 percent of their time on housework and carried out 67 percent of household tasks.[10] Women performed over twice the number of tasks and assumed the burden of "mental labor" or "invisible work," that is, planning and coordination of tasks.[11] Moreover, leisure was most frequent for fathers (30 percent) and children (39 percent) and least frequent for mothers (22 percent).[12]

In our study we categorized household work into three activities: (1) household maintenance (e.g., organizing objects and managing storage issues); (2) household chores (e.g., meal preparation, cleaning, outdoor work); and (3) childcare (e.g., bathing, dressing, grooming, feeding, putting to bed). The distribution of these tasks among the couples in our study is captured in Figure 5.1. While men spent slightly more of their time on household maintenance tasks (4 vs. 3 percent), women spent more time on chores (26 vs. 14 percent) and childcare (9.1 vs. 5.6 percent, respectively). Women on average spent 39 percent of their time on these activities, compared to 23 percent for men. Women prepared 91 percent of weekday and 81 percent of weekend dinners, even though fathers were present at 80 percent of weekday and 88 percent of weekend dinners. Overall, women spent much more of their time cooking, cleaning, and taking care of children, compared to their husbands. Women also spent more time multitasking, often juggling meal preparation with cleaning tasks and childcare.[13]

Although our quantitative findings replicate the well-documented disparity in the division of labor between men and women, we also found that the nuanced ways couples interact with one another about and during these tasks were linked to the couples' relationship satisfaction and sense of well-being. More than constituting a series of simple instrumental tasks, household work represents a complex set of interpersonal exchanges that enable family members to achieve (or fail to achieve) solidarity and cohesiveness.[14] Direct observation of middle-class dual-career couples as they engage in their everyday activities is rare. Studies in psychol-

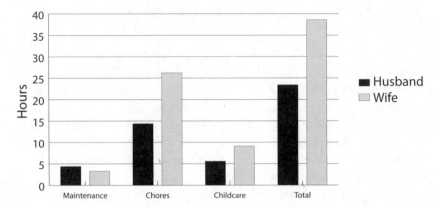

Figure 5.1. Percentage of participants' time spent on household maintenance, household chores, and childcare.

ogy have yielded quantitatively rigorous descriptions of marital interaction,[15] yet most of this work has been conducted in laboratory settings or, in rare instances, has studied enactments of couples' interactions.[16] Below we examine couples' subjective perspectives on their roles at home as expressed in interviews, along with interactional patterns between spouses revealed through the analysis of our video recordings. Finally, we provide insights into partnership, respect, and marital well-being.

COUPLES' PERCEPTIONS OF THEIR ROLES AT HOME

While watching television on a Saturday morning, John kicks back in a lounge chair as his wife, Susannah, sits on the couch folding laundry and talks on the telephone to arrange a play date for their eight-year-old son. At one point, their one-year-old daughter cries for Susannah's attention, and she puts down the clothes to pick her up. Hanging up the telephone, she goes into the kitchen to start preparing a meal. Previously in an interview Susannah described how she holds down a full-time job while also handling most of the household work and the childcare—even when John is home:

> Personally, I don't have a life. My life is my family because whatever their needs are they always come first before mine and I can honestly

> say that. He—and I think it's great—he does his golfing, he does his
> bike riding, and it doesn't take a long time and he needs that. I don't
> get that yet. I don't have that yet. I don't have the time or the luxury.
> That for me is like a huge luxury that I don't see happening in any
> time in the near future.

According to Susannah, while her husband has time to pursue his own
interests, she views herself as the only member of the family who must
continually sacrifice her well-being for the needs of others. Having time
for oneself is equated with "having a life," and not only does this mother
feel that she has neither, but she does not foresee any changes on the
horizon. The strong sense of being burdened that Susannah expressed
was not unusual among the women in our study.

Although working women's feelings of being overwhelmed is well
documented, in some cases men are also often highly stressed by managing everyday household decisions and prioritizing the needs of family
members. Travis, the father of two boys ages two and a half and eight,
laments the constant demand of "managing someone else's needs," specifically, being unable to fulfill the "demands" of his wife, which often
comes at the expense of his own health. He talks about his concerns as he
spontaneously interviews himself in front of a video camera, which we
provided to him for conducting a self-guided home tour:

> You'll notice when I'm walking around the house that, um, there's
> basically very little respite for me. It's all about, um, managing some-
> one else's needs most of the time, and admittedly, I'm not as strong
> and caring of my own needs, but I see that my own physical health is
> being compromised by not doing that, so, um, I'm starting to do more
> of that, which of course leads to aggravation from my demanding
> wife, um, by not paying attention to her and not fulfilling her needs.
> So I think my house kind of represents, um, work. And my workplace
> kind of represents rest in a certain way.

Travis's home is a source of stress, a place where he finds "little respite."
Rather than use the home tour video to describe physical spaces in his
house, Travis explores the psychological dimensions of his home life
and vents about the frustrations he encounters when he returns from
work. He feels that he has been neglecting his own needs in order to
attend to his family members, and, in contrast, he often finds solace in
his workplace. This perspective on the workplace as a sanctuary reflects
the phenomenon discussed by Hochschild,[17] who found that for working
parents one's job offered a less stressful environment than life at home.

Travis and his wife, Alice, discussed their perspectives on their domestic lives in an interview. Alice explained that she and Travis have different orientations to handling household tasks: she recognizes that she is an "accomplisher" who can be "domineering" and less "easygoing" than Travis. Alice then elaborated on the consequences of these differences:

> I have to, like, I manage the household, and, like, I delegate what needs to be done, 'cause basically I'm the one in charge of seeing that—everything needs to get done. That's how I look at it. Anyway, so that's a real source of tension between both of us, I think. It's not like the trust thing. It's just that—that, um, it wouldn't be like Travis would walk into the room and go, gee, my underwear's on the floor; I guess I'd better pick it up. It'll be, like, Travis, pick up your underwear off the floor. I mean, it's like, basically for me, it's like having three kids in the house. Sorry, no offense. I love you very much.

From Alice's perspective, the need to push Travis stems from her belief that it is the only way to make sure that chores will get done. Alice and Travis expressed having divergent needs and expectations of what is necessary for running a household successfully. They have different ideas about how to organize their everyday lives, and they debate these approaches throughout the interview.

TRAVIS: I mean, she's no—she's not a saint in terms of keeping the place clean and, uh, fixing stuff or—she doesn't fix anything.

ALICE: No, but I cook meals. I just can't do it all. I don't. But I made you dinner tonight.

TRAVIS: That's good.

ALICE: There you go. I'm no saint, but I just can't do everything. I can't buy all the groceries, cook the dinner—

TRAVIS: I know, but just for the—don't you think that there's— you know that little board we have on the refrigerator?

ALICE: Mm hmm.

TRAVIS: Why don't you use that and, like, say, like, um, write me notes?

ALICE: [I don't want to.

TRAVIS: [Number one, dishwasher. Number two, rain gutter.

ALICE: To be honest with you, I don't want to have to tell you to do stuff. I want you to figure out that the—that the dishwasher needs to be—that you need to figure it out that the dishwasher needs to be—

> TRAVIS: I did. Did you ask me to fix the dishwasher, or did I?
>
> ALICE: No, you ordered a part, and then six months went by and we don't know what happened to it. I don't want to be, like, micro-managing you. Anyway, that's a whole other story.

Alice's frustration is evident in the content of her utterances and in her demeanor during the interview. Her tone of voice is tense and defiant as she expresses her exasperation. In the first several lines, she emphasizes that she "can't do it all," repeating the words *can't* and *don't want to* throughout the excerpt. During this exchange it becomes clear that Alice does not wish to constantly remind Travis what to do around the house. Perhaps as a way to distance himself from the nagging he experiences, Travis suggests that Alice post notes on the refrigerator, listing tasks that need to be done. She responds that she would prefer that he "figure it out," indicating, once again, her desire for him to take initiative without her constant input, or as she refers to it, "micro-managing," an approach that does not work for either of them. For Travis, Alice's micro-managing is problematic because it does not occur only when something needs to be done; it permeates almost every moment of his waking life. He comments on his wife's continual negative appraisals and states that there is a great deal of "punitive language coming my direction."

Research on marriage has examined the significance of the division of labor in the home and its link to relationship well-being, especially in regard to the issue of intimacy and marital satisfaction. Coltrane found that when chores were shared more equitably, women's marital satisfaction increased, less marital conflict ensued, and women were less depressed.[18] Gottman's study indicates that women expressing a greater interest in sex tended to be married to men who did more housework.[19] In an interview on health and well-being, Karita discusses the consequences of what she perceives as her husband's lack of involvement in household work.

> KARITA: Sometimes I feel I don't get any help from Derrick— with, you know, dinner or cleaning up or things like that, and I think that that's such a typical female reaction, you know, you don't get help, you get nothing.
>
> INTERVIEWER: Hm[mm.
>
> KARITA: [You know? No sex—I didn't get any help, you know?
>
> INTERVIEWER: Hm[mm
>
> KARITA: [And the men they don't get that part so,
>
> INTERVIEWER: You mean they don't get?

> KARITA: That they need to kind of do something, you know?
> ((*Derrick remains silent*))

Karita's analysis of the situation is presented as a causal equation ("No sex—I didn't get any help"), or what Capps and Ochs call a "breach of expectations" in which her lack of physical intimacy with her husband is the consequence of his inaction.[20] She views her predicament as a common phenomenon among couples, indicating that her response is a "typical female reaction" and adding that "the men they don't get that part," referring to her husband's failure to understand her feelings. Karita frames household work as an arena in which issues such as mutual care and fair exchange surface and shape spousal attitudes toward the marriage. Derrick's silence displays his unwillingness to engage in this discussion. At the same time, Karita refers to her husband in the third person ("I don't get any help from Derrick") and does not include him as a participant. She addresses her statements to the interviewer rather than to him.

Derrick eventually enters the discussion by offering an account of his long commute to work and his dedication to coaching his children's sports activities. He feels Karita should take these issues into consideration when evaluating his contribution to the household. Derrick emphasizes that the amount of time required to manage his sons' teams precludes him from doing more work around the house.

> DERRICK: I'm just not doing the *lau:*ndry. So.
> KARITA: O:r (.) cooking or cleaning or (xxx). W[ell =
> DERRICK: [So—
> KARITA: = we can fight about that all night. ((*she laughs*))
> DERRICK: *Good* (so) you go coach the kids and I'll cook a dinner (big deal).

Derrick's annoyance with Karita's complaints is apparent. He equates coaching his children's teams with household chores, which is a view that Karita does not share. It is clear that this is an area of ongoing disagreement and that the resentment stemming from this issue has contributed to mutual feelings of dissatisfaction in their marriage at this point in their lives.

Several findings stand out from the above excerpts. First, the burden spouses experience managing household responsibilities interferes with individual well-being and expressions of intimacy. Spouses spontaneously mention the struggles they experience in their relationship over the allocation and completion of chores, and when they reflect on the division of labor in their families they sometimes couch their arrangement in terms of trust (e.g., Does my partner trust me to do what I am expected to do?) and authority and subordination (e.g., I want my partner to recognize what to do and do it vs. I want my partner to prompt me when tasks need attention).

Housework appears to be far more than the mere completion of tasks needed to keep the family running smoothly. It also colors individuals' daily experiences and appears to affect how couples characterize their partnership.

INTERACTIONAL PATTERNS BETWEEN COUPLES

While several of the spouses in our sample expressed frustration regarding household division of labor, some couples seemed to be particularly skilled at smoothly accomplishing domestic tasks. A study of the CELF couples preparing dinner together revealed a variety of interactional styles, including (1) "silent collaboration," in which both partners worked in the same space and went about the task at hand; (2) "one partner as expert," in which one spouse was considered an expert or authority in a particular task, either humorously or with genuine respect; (3) "coordinating together," in which partners verbally organized the activity in concert; and (4) "collaborating apart," in which partners carried out their share of the labor in separate locations.[21]

"Silent collaboration" refers more specifically to the smooth coordination of tasks in which both partners contributed to the household activity of meal preparation and cleanup without needing to clarify information or monitor one another's tasks. We expect that these couples have worked this way for a while; both know their way around the kitchen and feel at ease with their responsibilities. In the second category, one partner routinely takes on a particular task and is considered "the expert." This arrangement usually involved a shared understanding that one spouse was not only highly competent to carry out the task, but was also willing to do so with or without assistance. The third pattern, "coordinating together," provided the setting for the highest degree of positive interaction as well as the most potential for conflict. For example, on some occasions spouses may have collaborated harmoniously and anticipated each other's needs, while on other occasions one partner might have interfered and monitored the way the other partner carried out the task. In the final category, spouses collaborated apart, or attended to a task individually (e.g., father barbecued outside while mother made a salad in the kitchen).

When coordinating together, couples displayed how they related to and treated one another in the midst of carrying out domestic tasks. In the following example, one couple collaborates harmoniously as they unwind after work one evening. As the dinner preparation begins, Adam has just put on a jazz CD and offers his wife, Cheryl, something to drink (he uses her nickname, "Sweeps").

ADAM: Sweeps, you want any wine?

CHERYL: Sure.

ADAM: I bought you zinfandel that you *love*.

Adam displays his attentiveness to his wife as he uses a term of endearment and pours her a glass of wine. This couple often made dinner together, alternating who took the lead. At one point while Adam is out on the patio barbecuing chicken, Cheryl comes out to offer to help.

CHERYL: Adam, what do you want me to do? Rice? Salad?

ADAM: I'm doing rice already.

CHERYL: Okay, You got (.) broccoli?

ADAM: I have mixed vegetables steamed.

CHERYL: You want that paper out here, or can I bring it in?

ADAM: Yeah, that's all done, I'm done with all that.

CHERYL: Okay.

In these exchanges we see that each spouse is trying to anticipate each other's needs regarding the task at hand, as well as attending to other features of the setting and concurrent activities. Adam opens a bottle of his wife's favorite wine and turns on music they enjoy; Cheryl asks about helping with the food preparation and checks with her husband on where he would prefer her to put the newspaper he had been reading.

When couples coordinate together, however, there is also the potential for counter-collaborative communication, which may produce tension and lead to conflict. In the following example, David is preparing dinner, which is particularly challenging for him since he only recently began to take on cooking responsibilities. He attempts to appease his wife, Julie's, numerous queries, demands, and requests, which target him repeatedly throughout the dinner-making activity.

DAVID: I'm making such a mess.

> JULIE: You always make a mess, David.
>
> DAVID: I know.
>
> JULIE: It's like you don't know how to cook.
>
> JULIE: (This is going)—look at what you've done!
>
> DAVID: ((*laughs*))

When David acknowledges that he is "making such a mess," Julie confirms and generalizes his assessment to all the occasions on which he takes on meal preparation. Her next comment, "It's like you don't know how to cook," is a further critique of his poor performance. David calmly accepts her condemnation and even finds his performance humorous. Instead of joining her husband in laughing about the situation, Julie continues to adopt a critical supervisory role.

> JULIE: First of all, you don't do this *on* the stove. You do it over on the counter. Ugh. You're going to have to clean up, too. So sorry to inform you.
>
> DAVID: I know that. I'll clean it up.

As Julie watches over and evaluates her husband's actions, her tone is authoritative and her imperatives are unmitigated. She makes no attempt to soften her stance or to couch her talk as suggestions rather than orders. She does not respond to David's humor and instead maintains a monitoring role in the interaction. This pattern of participation also surfaces on a subsequent evening in the couple's kitchen.

> JULIE: (Did you put) these in there? ((*referring to soy meatballs*))
>
> DAVID: What?
>
> JULIE: (Here).
>
> DAVID: Yeah, they're in there.
>
> JULIE: Why didn't you put them in?
>
> DAVID: Oh, because there were like more than twice as many as that.
>
> JULIE: Oh.
>
> DAVID: There's a good ten, twelve in there. I think.
>
> JULIE: I thought you were changing (xxx)?
>
> DAVID: ((*Laughing*)) I changed my shirt and my shoes.
>
> JULIE: This is probably just about done.

DAVID: Yes, I was just checking it, and it wasn't quite—it was a little *al dente.*

JULIE: Stir it though.

DAVID: I have been. ((*A few moments later*))

DAVID: The sauce is—no, the sauce is controlling *me* as opposed to me controlling the sauce. Yeah, feta's great.

JULIE: Why are you using this lime?

DAVID: I squeezed a little on that salad.

David fields Julie's interrogations and comments without hesitation, and he appears to be doing his best to meet her expectations of how the meal should be prepared. He attempts to inject humor into the situation on more than one occasion. When Julie critiques his clothes, as she wonders why he has not changed, David laughs as he responds that he *has* changed certain articles of clothing. While he chooses here to handle his wife's close scrutiny of his behavior and appearance with humor, Julie does not adopt his tone of playfulness. David again takes a humorous stance when he comments that the pasta sauce is controlling him when it should be the other way around, but even this self-deprecating bid for understanding fails to elicit a friendly response.

Julie continues to monitor the activity and notes that the CELF researchers are videotaping his missteps. She then refers to a news story about police videotaping interviews with suspected criminals. David's manner then shifts. He makes no more attempts at humor and self-deprecation; instead, his tone becomes curt and his words more adversarial.

JULIE: You know what, I heard this morning on NPR that police departments are going to start taping their interviews with um ((*pause*)) you know, suspects.

DAVID: You don't say.

JULIE: Well, they haven't been doing it before.

DAVID: Genius idea. Yeah.

JULIE: You know what? I don't need your sarcasm.

DAVID: Yeah you do.

David's response to Julie's comment is received as antagonistic. David criticizes the idea behind the news story she is relaying rather than anything about Julie personally, yet she chooses to defend the idea and appears to feel slighted personally by his comment. Her annoyance is apparent in her hostile response ("I don't need your sarcasm"). We can only speculate about the longer-term implications these exchanges have for future conversations between these spouses, yet psychological analyses of family interaction would suggest that David might respond more negatively to Julie's incursions (by avoiding her more or criticizing her), perhaps leading her to escalate her requests even further.[22]

While working women often complain that men engage less in accomplishing multiple and simultaneous family-related tasks, men express dissatisfaction about consistently being "nagged" by their wives, giving rise to the "henpecked" husband. Several studies have identified a pattern called *demand-withdraw* as a reliable marker of maladaptive communication and future relationship distress. In this pattern, "one member (the demander) criticizes, nags, and makes a demand on the other, while the partner (the withdrawer) avoids confrontation, withdraws, and becomes defensive."[23] Withdrawing responses can take many forms and can serve specific functions, including avoiding intimacy, avoiding conflict, and angry withdrawal.[24]

The tension that arises in everyday interactions concerning household management can influence the quality and nature of communication between couples as they broach other domains of discussion. As some psychological studies note,[25] humor and positive affect in marital interactions foreshadows marital success and can neutralize the effects of poor communication skills. Interactional patterns of conflict in marriage are complex and are often the symptom of underlying tension concerning other issues related to professional work status and differing rights, obligations, and expectations. For example, in the excerpt above David was temporarily unemployed and seeking work, which may have contributed to Julie's frustration, to David's willingness to adopt a subordinate and subservient role, and to the apparent tension in their interactions.

PARTNERSHIP AND SHARED UNDERSTANDINGS

The couples in our study who lacked clarity on *what, when,* and *how* household tasks and responsibilities would be carried out often said that they felt drained and rushed and had difficulty communicating their dissatisfaction in their lives. Spouses who appeared to have a clear and respectful understanding of one another's roles and tasks, in contrast, did not spend as much time negotiating responsibilities; their daily lives seemed to flow more smoothly. For example, in one family the couple emphasized the importance of establishing a mutual perspective on managing household chores.

INTERVIEWER:	How do you divide the chores between you two?
RAYA:	He does outside chores, and I do inside chores; that's very clear.
INTERVIEWER:	That's how it works?
RAYA:	Yeah, very clear distinction. We both have professions, we both are strong minded so we make it clear— this is what you do, this is what I do, and I don't go out and do, you know, his outside chores and he doesn't do the inside chores.
SAM:	Like, like, you know, groceries, most of the times I do it. If it's things like— we need to get for the house I do it; things of that nature, but the thing—the way that we do it is if she does it, I don't interfere; if I do it, she doesn't interfere, so you know one person ((*pause*))
INTERVIEWER:	Like for example for cooking.
SAM:	Then she does it.
INTERVIEWER:	And you know that.
SAM:	I know that it's clear, it's very clear.

Above Raya explains the need for clarity. "Outside chores" for this couple does not refer to the typical inside/outside distinction of the woman taking on the housework while the husband mows the lawn. The "outside" chores include doing all the shopping and often shepherding the children to various activities. What we ended up observing, however, was that each spouse frequently assisted the other with whatever needed to be done in each domain. On the weekend, for example, Sam cooked a rice and vegetable dish for lunch. The following morning, it was Raya who took the boys to their soccer games. While they appeared to have a clear division of labor, the underlying principle expressed through their actions was that they were a team, working together to keep their lives running smoothly. The frequent use of the second-person plural "we" by both parties indicates the management of the household as a joint project.

Sam stressed that one aspect of the clarity the couple shares involves not interfering in each other's activities: "If she does it, I don't interfere; if I do it, she doesn't interfere." This statement displays the respect that each spouse has for the way they carry out their respective tasks. Interference, evident among several couples in our study, is tantamount to the demanding behaviors psychologists have studied previously in laboratory settings. When a spouse feels encroached upon, the interaction often leads to conflict or avoidance.

In the interview above, Sam's realization that interference is a potential problem—one that can be avoided by a clear and consensual division of labor—is a critical insight. Couples that established a shared understanding of their respective responsibilities were less likely to monitor and critique each other's behavior. These spouses were also more likely to spontaneously chip in when their partners were sick, away, or otherwise unavailable to carry out a task. These findings upend conventional wisdom about the value of communication between working partners: the *absence* of communication in certain domains may be an indicator of a healthy and efficient partnership in which spouses display mutual respect.

Comparison of dinner preparation in the CELF families and iCelf families (Rome) revealed marked differences in the quality of affect and collaborative features of interactions. These differences appeared to reflect couples' strategies regarding household management in working family life. Strikingly, couples in Rome did not express any overt complaints regarding household chores. During meal preparation, there was more humor and laughter in their interactions. Compared to middle-class families in the United States, Italian families spend more time at home with each other and in closer physical proximity, in part due to their smaller and more compact living spaces. Since most families own only one car, they also arrive home together at the end of the workday, which offers more of a chance for collaboration since they are on the same time schedule. The more important point is that data from both locations provide glimpses into the patterns of collaboration that *can* occur in families and that family members actively create the settings—to their benefit or to their detriment.[26]

CONCLUSION

Couples are composed of individuals who coordinate their behaviors in relation to one another. In working families—where both adults work outside the home and raise school-aged children—the challenge of coordinating behaviors to meet family needs is especially great. A central premise of this chapter is that the emotional tone of family life pivots to a significant degree on the extent to which family members negotiate and enact effective strategies for contending with the numerous tasks encountered in their daily lives. More generally, observing family members as they go about their everyday routines reveals important insights into family dynamics and communication. Although we have noted some salient exceptions here, our global impression is that expectations and roles are not yet clear and that satisfying domestic routines for many working couples have yet to be established.

Among CELF couples, mutually shared understandings of responsibilities minimized the need for spouses to evaluate and manage one another's task-related behaviors. These understandings enabled partners to fulfill their household duties with the knowledge that established boundaries would be not be crossed. Demands were few, disengagement in the face of demands was unnecessary, and partners were more likely to feel respected for the contributions they made. Conflict was more prevalent when couples had not worked out a clear division of labor in the home and had to renegotiate responsibilities from one day to the next. Ambiguous models appeared to provide ample opportunity for partners to express displeasure toward one another as they completed their chores, such that various attempts at controlling these exchanges—for example, through requests and avoidance of these requests—revealed the ongoing and occasionally tense negotiation of power and influence between partners.

Underlying our discussion in this chapter is the assumption that only the mother and the father are equipped and capable of tackling the daily demands of family life. Do children step into the breach and help? As the next chapter shows, although the couples in our study desperately needed help around the house, their children typically did not do chores on a consistent basis. In at least some families, the failure of children to pitch in reflected a tendency on the part of the parents themselves to resist implementing a systematic way to manage household responsibilities.

Interactions around everyday chores are often tinged with strong emotional reactions that may go unacknowledged in relationships: partners may feel unappreciated because other family members fail to contribute to meal preparation, express dissatisfaction at how family members go about their chores, or convey frustration at the seemingly endless list of tasks that must be completed by a certain time. Conversely, in some of the families the management of tasks presented opportunities for genuine humor, irony, and warmth. Families appear most successful in contending with the routine tasks of everyday life when (a) family members are active contributors rather than passive or entitled recipients of others' contributions; (b) family members acknowledge the contributions that others make, if only by overlooking their missteps; (c) there is mutual respect for autonomy and limited interference or "micro-managing" of one another while carrying out household work; (d) a consensually established arrangement precludes the need to renegotiate the allocation of tasks anew each day; and (e) there is flexibility rather than rigidity in the arrangement so that one family member can pick up the slack if another is unable to fulfill his or her usual responsibilities. These conditions seem most likely to promote positive engagement in families, and to encourage the view that everyday chores are a vehicle for connection rather than a threat to individual well-being. Though household work and family responsibilities are a burden and a source of tension for many working parents, for some couples, these same tasks can be a crucial domain in which partners can express solidarity, respect, and intimacy.

NOTES

1. Hook 2006.
2. Bianchi 2011.
3. Bianchi 2011; Bianchi, Robinson, and Milkie 2006; Lee 2005.
4. Hochschild and Machung [1989] 2003.
5. Cherlin 2004, 2005.
6. Schwartz 1994.
7. Cooke 2006.
8. Campos et al. 2009.
9. Klein and Kremer-Sadlik 2009.
10. Broege et al. 2007, 141.
11. Lee 2005, 241.
12. Arnold and Lang 2007; Broege et al. 2007.
13. Good 2009.
14. Folbre 2001; Wilk 1996.
15. Bradbury 1998; Bradbury and Karney 2010.
16. Burman, Mangolin, and John 1993.
17. Hochschild 1997.
18. Coltrane 2000.
19. Gottman 1994.
20. Capps and Ochs 2001.
21. Klein et al. 2005.
22. See Eldridge and Christensen 2002.
23. Ibid., 295.
24. Roberts 2000.
25. Johnson et al. 2005; Roberts 2000.
26. Klein et al. 2005.

6 Chores

WENDY KLEIN AND MARJORIE HARNESS GOODWIN

Children in societies around the world acquire skills through their routine participation in household work activities, and mastering these tasks prepares them to become competent members of their communities.[1] Not long ago, American family life was organized in a similar manner, with all family members, even small children, taking on a set of domestic responsibilities. According to the sociologist Viviana Zelizer,[2] the shift in attitudes to children's work in the United States began toward the end of the nineteenth century and continued into the twentieth. Historical examinations of children's lives emphasize the changes that occurred along with industrialization and the institutionalization of schooling. As the locus of economic production moved from the home to outside spheres of employment such as factories and the marketplace, laws regulating children's work in the labor force limited their involvement. These policies, in turn, curtailed children's economic contributions, and people began to have smaller families.[3] Children went from being considered an economic asset to the family to becoming emotionally "priceless."[4] The concept of childhood as a distinct and critical time period for development and cultivation, a notion once restricted to the upper class, was recognized and embraced by society as a whole.[5] Among the middle class in particular, children's time became increasingly occupied with schoolwork and preparation for their professional futures.

In recent years, the routine inclusion of chores in children's schedules has generally fallen by the wayside in middle-class family life. Most children are still expected to take on a few domestic tasks, but the amount of time they spend on household work has gradually decreased.[6] The decline in children's contributions can be linked, in part, to shifts in parents' priorities and parenting approaches. Parents typically enroll their children in a number of after-school activities and academic preparatory courses geared to their future success.[7] These outside commitments may not leave sufficient time for establishing routines that require children to consistently perform domestic tasks. More significantly, the ways parents and children relate to one another interactionally have also shifted, influencing children's understandings of their roles in the household. Starting in the mid-twentieth century, a more egalitarian relationship between parents and children began to overtake former structures of hierarchy that involved strict adherence to respecting and obeying parents' demands. As the ethos of questioning authority infiltrated the home, several domains of family life no longer conformed to a dominant model, and patterns of child socialization began to vary widely.

Previous studies of middle-class American families indicate that children's routine participation in household work is not necessarily a prevailing practice, and socialization into domestic responsibilities is not a high priority.[8] While a few popular books on parenting in the United States published in the past decade argue against overscheduling and overprotecting children,[9] others, for example, *Battle Hymn of the Tiger Mother,* by the Yale law professor Amy Chua, recommend a highly structured schedule of activities and a strong emphasis on academic achievement, leaving little or no time for chores. Yet we show that the consistent effort to involve children in housework may be *crucial* to their development of life skills, independence, and responsibility. In addition, analyses of the physical and spatial organization of parent-child exchanges reveal that these interactional dimensions play an important role in establishing and sustaining a shared understanding of household routines.

THE ANDERSON FAMILY: "THEY HAVE TO EARN THEIR PRIVILEGES EVERY DAY"

"This is something Sandra is supposed to do," Ed Anderson tells his wife on a Saturday morning as he takes a full bag of trash out from under the sink. Ed has just finished washing the breakfast dishes, and Sandra, his ten-year-old daughter, is in her bathrobe and pajamas watching a video in the living room when she overhears her name. "What'd you say?" she asks. Her father summons her into the kitchen: "Sandy, could you come here please? You have a chore I want you to do." Sandra responds with a long, exasperated sigh, "Uhhhhh," which displays her great displeasure at being asked to interrupt the video to take on a chore. Her father adds, "I'll go out with you," but his offer is met with Sandra's emphatic refusal:

"*No:!*" Ed immediately counters with "*Yup!,*" matching his daughter's insistent tone, and the struggle between father and daughter begins.

In the CELF study, children in many of the families regularly attempted to negotiate, resist, or refuse to carry out tasks.[10] Variation across families appears to be tied to a history of inconsistent and unfocused socialization practices for recruiting children to take on responsibilities. In general, the lack of routine expectations and the inconsistency in parental directives promoted extended discussions about children accomplishing self-care such as grooming and household tasks. In contrast, routine task assignment and close parental monitoring of children as they carried out tasks encouraged their awareness of and willingness to assume household responsibilities. Aronsson and Cekaite use the term *activity contract* to refer to mutual agreements about tasks and when they are to be carried out in Swedish parent-child interactions.[11] While children may be aware of their responsibilities for specific chores, they may nonetheless initiate extended negotiations of a particular "contract" by means of stalling or refusal. In Aronsson and Cekaite's study children's subversive responses constituted attempts to enact egalitarian intergenerational relationships. These moves were followed by mild threats about withdrawing favored activities such as watching television or moral justifications for parents' directives. In the end, the authors propose, these negotiation processes teach children accountability for their actions as well as for their future commitments.

Returning to the battle of wills in the Anderson household, Ed is determined to recruit his daughter Sandra's help and insists that she pause her video. After some hesitation, Sandra complies and enters the kitchen to find out what her father would like her to do.

Anderson Family: Saturday Morning

SANDRA: O:h my (hh). ((*she eyes the bag of trash*))

FATHER: You take this bag,

SANDRA: *Outsi:::de?*

FATHER: I'm gonna go with you.

SANDRA: In the co::ld?

FATHER: Sandra, list—do you want—do you like your cell phone?
This is called earning your cell phone.

Sandra takes one look at the garbage bag and expresses her displeasure in increasingly high-pitched, elongated tones throughout this exchange. Her father's second offer to help her does not dissuade her resistance.

Finally, in the last lines above, Ed issues an ultimatum. By tying the domestic task to Sandra's cell phone use, Ed invokes an economic model of household work in which rights and benefits are to be extended in return for labor. In an interview, Ed told us, "I bought her a cell phone the day before yesterday, but she has to earn that. Well, they have to earn everything, including the computer ((*pause*)) Everything is a privilege . . . They have to earn their privileges every day" in order to learn "how things work in the world." He added, "And by the way, I'm making it sound like it's easy, it's not," revealing his awareness of the interactional work required to maintain this ethos in his household. Ed reflects on his own upper-middle-class childhood and discusses how his upbringing has shaped his parenting style: "I think that I was so isolated from lots of the world that, that—that was not a good thing growing up. So, I don't want them to grow up ignorant about how things work in the world, and I want them to know how privileged they are . . . I think that's real important."

Michael Osit suggests in *Generation Text: How to Raise Kids in an Age of Instant Everything* that treating chores as a means to earning privileges socializes children into a healthy work ethic and discourages a sense of entitlement.[12] Yet across the CELF families there was no positive correlation attributed to receiving an allowance for tasks and the quantity of household work children performed. In the Anderson family, this approach to earning privileges might have faltered in that it was applied to very few tasks and, possibly as a consequence, needed to be continually reinforced. The Anderson children fell on the middle to low end of the scale regarding both the quantity of household tasks they carried out and their likelihood to cooperate with parents' requests. When children's participation is tied to avoiding occasional parental threats or to personal benefits such as monetary or material rewards, children may be less likely to become intrinsically motivated to help others. At the same time, emphasizing the ethos of earning privileges may be an effective way to cultivate an understanding of the material benefits of work and to counter feelings of entitlement.

CHILDREN'S CONTRIBUTIONS AND PARENTAL "INVESTMENT"

Although parents who work full-time may need their children's help with domestic tasks, recent studies have found that in two-parent families, parental work status (full- or part-time) is not correlated with higher rates of children's participation in household work.[13] Thus it is not surprising that children in the CELF study did not take on a large number of household responsibilities. In fact, only 2.8 percent of the CELF children's activities were devoted to household work, compared to 27.1 percent of mothers' activities and 14.8 percent of fathers' activities. Parents' household work does not include childcare and household management tasks such as planning and paying bills. The tasks we counted as household work were tidying one's bedroom, meal preparation, cleaning tasks, folding laundry, taking out the trash, outside chores, and pet care. When children carried out these activities, they often did so with a parent or sibling. The types of housework that children carried out most often were related to meal preparation, keeping one's bedroom in order, and assorted cleaning activities. In general, parents initiated children's involvement in these household tasks.

Children volunteered to help most often with meal preparation, which included making and serving food as well as setting the table. Food preparation, such as cooking and baking, provided opportunities for parents to apprentice children into tasks they enjoyed, and we observed a great deal of positive displays of emotion, such as laughter, affection, and pride, during these activities.[14] As expected, older children engaged in household work activities more frequently than did younger children, reflecting family expectations that older siblings are expected to make greater contributions than their younger counterparts.[15] Girls performed a greater range of household care tasks and took on tasks more frequently than did boys in all age groups. Previous studies on children's household work also reflect this imbalance, and not surprisingly, this often mirrors the gendered division of labor between parents within these families.[16]

There were clear asymmetries in the distribution of household work across CELF family members. Mothers' chores accounted for 60 percent of the total household workload, while fathers' chores totaled 27 percent, and children's chores constituted 13.3 percent of all scan sampling observations of household chores. Children's relatively low contributions parallel Blair's findings based on questionnaire data.[17] In our study, however, the 13.3 percent figure masks a wide range of participation. In some families, children were never observed carrying out a household task, while in others, children were recorded performing as much as 28 percent of the family's household tasks observed.

In general, school-related activities such as doing homework and studying for tests were given higher priority than helping out with household tasks. A few children in our study stated that their primary responsibility in their families was to attend school and complete their homework assignments, as captured by six-year-old Becky's response to a question about chores: "Well, the job is to go to school . . . that's my job." Getting homework done on one's own was, indeed, a help to parents. Children who could manage their school assignments saved their parents the daily trials of overseeing this activity. Yet socialization into getting homework done and taking on household tasks promoted somewhat different senses of moral responsibility and attention to the needs of others.

The sociologist Annette Lareau proposes that middle-class parents exercise "concerted cultivation" of children's futures by prioritizing their academic work and scheduling families' lives around children's extracurricular commitments.[18] These parents place a high premium on children acquiring skills entailing social and cultural capital that will ultimately increase their educational opportunities and professional advancement. Lareau illustrates that middle-class parents tend to negotiate with their children and include them in decision making in order to promote more egalitarian relationships. Many of the parents in our study reflect this ideology in the way they structure their lives and interact with their children. Lareau contrasts concerted cultivation with the "natural growth" approach, which she ascribes to working-class and lower-class parents in her study. In these families, partially due to possessing fewer economic resources, parents do not enroll children in many extracurricular activities and allow them to have long periods of unstructured time. These parents tend to use unmitigated directives (imperatives) with their children and to be much less open to negotiation, reflecting a more hierarchical structure regarding rights and obligations in the family. In these families, children appear to be more independent and take on household work and self-care tasks without parental prodding.

The prevalence of inconsistent socialization into taking on household tasks across CELF families resembles the concerted cultivation parenting approach documented by Lareau. Our findings also align with Kusserow's observations of upper-middle-class parents' emphasis on children's self-expression of feelings and their equal status.[19] In Kusserow's study parents felt that asserting power over the child inhibits the child's development. The fallout of such parenting styles, as viewed in the CELF video recordings of family life from morning to nightfall, is that parents often struggled on a daily basis to recruit their children's assistance. This was especially true in families in which parents were more open to negotiation (and whose lives resembled some of the middle-class families in Lareau's study and the upper-middle-class families in Kusserow's study). An examination of interactions in these families sheds light on some of the difficulties that arise and how these issues may be connected to spe- cific child-rearing practices.

THE NEUMAN FAMILY: "I'M *NOT* GONNA DO IT!"

When parental directives and justifications are open to negotiation on a regular basis and parents often give in, children will be less likely to perform tasks requested of them. One evening after dinner Brian (age eight) is getting ready to play checkers with his mother, Elsie, when his father, Benny, enters the room.

> *Neuman Family: Sunday Evening*
>
> FATHER: Let's not play. Son, come here, (you're) gonna help me
> out with the dishes. C'mon.
>
> BRIAN: No:::
>
> FATHER: Yes. Now. C'mon. Then you play. Let's go.
>
> BRIAN: No uhhh ((*sniffs and tears up*))

Benny attempts to enlist his son's assistance with washing the dinner dishes but is met with Brian's loud, defiant refusal. In a second attempt, his father prioritizes doing chores over playing.[20] After a brief discussion about why Brian's older brother is exempt from helping with this chore (he is doing his homework), the conflict continues.

> BRIAN: Why do *I* gotta go do the *dishes*. ((*crying*))
>
> FATHER: We'll do it together.
>
> BRIAN: *No:::.*
>
> FATHER: You can either put it in the sink—
> (0.2)
> I—I—I mean put it in the dishwasher,
> (0.4)
> or you can rinse it
> or you can pass it to me,
> You can choose any job you want.
>
> BRIAN: No—okay I'll choose a job,
>
> FATHER: Yeah,
>
> BRIAN: Me and Mom play checkers—that's a job.
>
> FATHER: That's not a job, that's a—that's playing.
>
> BRIAN: I'm *not* gonna *do:* it.

When Brian demands justification for his participation in washing the dishes his father tries to accommodate him by suggesting that the chore would be a joint project; he then offers Brian his choice of tasks. This strategy fails when Brian proposes his own option, which involves continuing to play checkers with his mother. Even though his father makes a logical distinction between a job and playing, Brian refuses to help. His mother then makes an appeal for his help.

MOTHER: It would help *me* out.

FATHER: Don't you want to help Ma? She *cooked*.

The mother's emphasis on her son helping her rather than her husband points to another possible dimension to this interaction. We observed that Brian was often more compliant with his mother than with his father. He and his father had frequent conflicts, and the mother's appeal here references her closer bond with Brian. Yet after this exchange Brian continues to refuse to help with the dishes. His father ends up extracting a promise from him that he will help "next time" and allows him to continue playing the game with his mother.

Brian's father was not alone in inadvertently rewarding a child's resistant behavior.[21] As M. H. Goodwin notes, "In situations where children are successful at bargaining . . . children may not gear into the projects their parents propose, and even run away from responsibilities . . . leading to escalations of assertions of authority through threats . . . or a parent's giving up in defeat."[22] As discussed earlier, providing options to children may give them a chance to actively exercise their own preferences and take up an agentive stance;[23] however, this strategy also indicates that the task is open to negotiation.[24]

UNPACKING THE INCONSISTENCY PREDICAMENT

One of the biggest obstacles to getting children to help regularly with household tasks was lack of mutually agreed upon routines in everyday family life. When family members shared an understanding of who was responsible for certain tasks, the undertaking of the chore was less likely to be open to negotiation on a daily basis. Similar to the couples discussed in the previous chapter, the lack of a clear family "model" of the division of responsibilities often promoted conflict about household work.

To avoid extended altercations some CELF parents opted to carry out most tasks without their children's assistance. As Jeff, the father in the Marsden family, told us, enforcing chores actually took more time and effort than doing the tasks himself. His approach was to assign chores when he or his wife had time. The result was that on certain occasions the parents took care of the tasks themselves, even when their children were available, and on others these parents either requested or demanded that a child take on the task. The children (ages eight, eleven, and thirteen) appeared to treat the inconsistency as license to refuse, since they did not necessarily view these chores as being their responsibilities.

We observed the same situation in the Beringer-Potts family, in which the parents were just beginning to assign chores to their older child who had just turned eight. When the boy resisted taking on a task, the mother often yelled at him in response and pushed him to get it done. At other times, she took an anything goes attitude, in which she either displayed amusement when her son refused to take on a task or simply ignored his refusals and took care of it herself. Such disparate interactional styles may account, in part, for why her son disregarded most of her requests to carry out a task and did not appear to understand why his mother became upset when he did not comply.

The significance of employing consistent socialization approaches when engaging children in practical tasks is evident when comparing observations of middle-class children growing up in Los Angeles to young children growing up elsewhere in the world. For example, caregivers in Samoa (Polynesia) and Matsigenka (Peruvian Amazon) hold consistent expectations for children's high participation in practical tasks, in contrast to middle-class parents in Los Angeles.[25] Similar to the Samoans and Matsigenka, Mayan children in Mexico coordinate their attention to ongoing family activities with little direction from adults to engage them in taking on tasks.[26] In these communities socialization into helping others is integral to the development of respect and a moral sense of responsibility. Respect is embodied through children's active attention to learning from and assisting others who are more experienced than they. In contrast, in many of the CELF families school-aged children appeared helpless, with parents assisting them in simple activities such as getting dressed. Cross-cultural studies provide perspective on the variation in socialization practices that have an impact on children's development and household functioning.

THE POLLEN FAMILY: "IS ANYONE LISTENING?"

Despite the prevailing tendency of children in the CELF study to contribute little to household work, they were expected to carry out certain self-care tasks (e.g., bathing, brushing their teeth, grooming). Parents often monitored these straightforward tasks even when children were old enough to carry them out by themselves. For example, on a weekday morning, nine-year-old Linda and seven-year-old Daniel were in the kitchen eating breakfast and watching television before going to school. Their mother, Kelly, called out to them from upstairs.

Pollen Family: Weekday Morning

MOTHER:	Daniel and Linda?
DANIEL AND LINDA:	((*no response*))
MOTHER:	Daniel and Linda?
DANIEL AND LINDA:	((*no response*))
MOTHER:	EXCUSE ME.
	I'M *talk*ing to you.
LINDA:	What?
MOTHER:	You should brush your teeth and go to the bathroom when you're done. Okay?
DANIEL AND LINDA:	((*no response*))
MOTHER:	Alright?
DANIEL AND LINDA:	((*no response*))
MOTHER:	HELLO:.
LINDA:	What.
MOTHER:	Brush your teeth and go to the bathroom when you're done.
LINDA:	Alright.
MOTHER:	Thank you.

Kelly had to make numerous bids for her children's attention before her daughter finally acknowledged her. Nonetheless, she ended the exchange with a "thank you," signaling that the self-care task was a favor that the children were requested to carry out for their mother rather than something they were responsible for without being asked.

MUTUAL ATTENTION AND PHYSICAL ALIGNMENT

Our study of the many ways in which children are socialized into doing practical household or self-care tasks has led us to appreciate the importance of how parents' and children's bodies are aligned with respect to one another.[27] It is not only the consistency of parental expectations or how parents ask for practical help that is consequential for children's performance of a task but also where parents' and children's bodies are physically located and aligned. Are parent and child facing each other or otherwise engaged when a practical task needs to be performed? Are they in the same room or communicating at a distance? Different kinds of routine interactional body alignments have consequences for how parents and children coordinate joint attention and collaborate together in everyday household activities.[28] As Goodwin notes, "Successful trajectories of directive sequences entail vigilant work on the part of parents—their full engagement in pursuing a response from children in the midst of the multiple competing activities that occupy their lives and demand their attention."[29]

Kelly, for example, often issued recycled directives to her children about self-care tasks when she was not in the same room as her children. Kelly and her husband Tommy's requests tended to be successful only when they were in face-to-face proximity with their children. Yet their children spent a great deal of time playing video games and watching television. As a result these parents often competed with various media and on-line activities for their attention, a situation we observed in several other families. When parents attempted to recruit their children's help while the children were "plugged in" conflicts often ensued.[30] These tensions were more likely to escalate into extended altercations if media or on-line activities were not brought to an end before parents made their expectations clear. Children who were more frequent media users, however, did not necessarily help less with household work. Children's assistance appeared to depend on how effective parents were at gaining and sustaining their children's attention as well as how clearly parents articulated their expectations and monitored their children's follow-through.

Tulbert and Goodwin,[31] in their study of how children were asked to brush their teeth, found an array of disparate bodily alignments. As in Kelly's exchange with her children above, when a parent was in another room or was competing with a distraction such as television, children were much less likely to disengage from their current activity to acknowledge or carry out the parent's request. Establishing a boundary between activities appeared to be consequential. For example, turning off the television before asking children to take on a task allowed parents to harness and refocus their children's full attention. Moreover, monitoring the activity by providing guidance to the child when necessary was also important in overseeing the follow-through of the task.

This point is related to the cross-cultural observations of adult-child interactions in communities such as the Matsigenka and Samoa, where very young children are socialized to attend to what other people are doing in their surroundings.[32] Early repeated orientation into social attention promotes children's learning of activities and their competent assistance in household routines at a young age. Similarly, children in highland Peru develop a heightened sense of self-esteem, independence, and responsibility through their involvement at an early age in sibling caregiving, textile work, horticulture, herding, and cleaning.[33] This is not simply a phenomenon observed in small-scale or developing societies. In Japan, for example, children are socialized into notions of respect and responsibility through tending to their environments. Although Japanese children are not expected to assist much in the home, they are responsible for *soji* (cleaning chores) at school, including mopping floors, cleaning bathrooms, and dusting. Participating in soji is viewed as an important aspect of students' moral education.[34]

While parents in Los Angeles tended to be highly accommodating to their children, a few did regularly engage them in household work. Researchers in our study closely examined the daily activities of one of these families, the Randolphs, to whom we now turn.

THE RANDOLPH FAMILY: "WE HAVE *A LOT* TO DO TODAY!"

On a Saturday morning, the Randolph children wake up and sleepily make their way into the living room where their mother, Paula, opens the window shades, allowing light to fill up the room. Her husband, Vincent, who holds down two jobs and often works on Saturdays, has already left the house. Paula greets and kisses her children affectionately before announcing, "Don't everybody congregate in here. We have a lot to do today. I want to be out of here by 12 o'clock!," alluding to the picnic scheduled for later that day. Paula starts opening the blinds in the bedrooms and, along with her children, begins cleaning. She periodically checks in with each of her three children (Stefan, 11; Michelle, 10; and Cynthia, 6) to gauge what has been accomplished.

Randolph Family: Saturday Morning

MOTHER:	Are you guys done with your room?
	Dusted? Vacuumed?
MICHELLE:	No.
CYNTHIA:	No.

MOTHER:	Well get it—Get
	[it together.
CYNTHIA:	[I'm dusting al[ready. I (xxx).
STEFAN:	[I did. I put the vacuum in their room.
MOTHER:	Thank you. You dusted?
STEFAN:	Yes.
MOTHER:	Hey can you empty the trash in the house please?
MOTHER:	Who's gonna vacuum the den and *my* room.
CYNTHIA:	*I* AM!
STEFAN:	She dusted—(too loud to say) "I am."
MOTHER:	Alright.
(MICHELLE):	(We're sorry)
CYNTHIA:	(xx[x).
MOTHER:	[Come *on* guys.
MOTHER:	You know—it's almost ten thirty.

As Paula choreographs her children's household work activities, she also monitors their progress and holds them accountable for the final outcome. She keeps her children moving by checking on the tasks she enumerated for them (such as dusting and vacuuming) and having additional jobs ready. When Stefan confirms that he has finished dusting, she instructs him to take out the garbage. She calls out, "Who's gonna vacuum the den and *my* room?," asking her children to take responsibility for another task. Cynthia, the youngest child, responds, "*I* AM," displaying her enthusiastic cooperation. Paula's subsequent announcement about the time adds a sense of urgency regarding their need to finish so that they could make it to the picnic. While she might appear to be a taskmaster, Paula did take a few moments to appreciate one of her children's drawings, which she picked up while helping to straighten their room. She also joked around with her daughters about the pet hamster, and music played in the background as her children continued with their tasks. Paula and her children spent a few hours cleaning, dusting, and putting the house in order before going out to meet friends.

CLEAR EXPECTATIONS AND CONSISTENT MONITORING

We asked CELF children to tell us about the types of tasks they did at home to help their parents and siblings. A few children admitted without hesitation that they did not participate in household work. Linda, the eight year-old daughter in the Pollen family, quickly responded, "Nothing. I don't do anything around the house." Some, like Mark, the nine-year-old son in the Moore family, even seemed surprised by the question: "I—never. Why do you think that? I never have to do chores." In the Castillo family, in which the children helped out periodically, they joked that their mother called herself "the maid."

Although most children in our study did mention occasionally taking on at least one task, such as cleaning their room and setting the table, none responded in the way that Stefan Randolph did: "We all clean our rooms, we dust, we have Swiffers we dust with, and you know, when we're done with that, we vacuum and we'll clean everything—the whole house on weekends—'cause it gets dusty and dirty." Stefan's ten-year-old sister, Michelle, also referred to this activity: "We clean the house. And then, um, after that, we do something fun." Their mother, Paula, often made her expectations explicit when she evaluated her children's work. After Stefan told her that he had completed dusting his room, she entered to conduct an inspection. She stopped at one piece of furniture and declared, "I see dust back there. Come on now you can't just du—you have to move stuff and get back in the corner. Okay?," indicating that he had not been thorough enough. Later Paula walked into her daughters' room and shouted, "*Woo:-hoo:! A:lright!* We're off to a good start. Looks grea::t!," which was high praise considering her strict standards. Paula did not hesitate to critique her children's work; however, she was also quick to show enthusiasm when they carried out a task well. This type of careful monitoring was unusual among the parents in our study.

A team of researchers at CELF and iCELF examined a subset of the families in the CELF project along with families in Rome and found that parents in Rome placed more emphasis on the specificity and difficulty of tasks when engaging children in housework.[35] Parents in Rome tended to monitor tasks more closely and recognized the need for a degree of expertise to successfully carry out certain tasks, as compared to the subset of Los Angeles parents. The Randolph family, however, was an exception that clearly stood out in the CELF study.

The children in the Randolph family often took on tasks on their own and recruited one another to help in household activities. One morning before school Cynthia observed as her older sister, Michelle, wrote down a list of objectives for the day. After summarizing their morning activities, Michelle asked, "What else did we accomplish?," a question that oriented Cynthia to conceptualizing their time as goal-directed. Her subsequent question, "What do we have to do tonight?," asked Cynthia to prioritize their evening activities. The siblings also socialized one another into new tasks. One evening when Michelle and Stefan were rinsing their dinner dishes and putting them in the dishwasher, Stefan told Michelle that he thought Cynthia was now old enough to clear her own dishes. He then ordered Cynthia to clean off her plate and put it in the dishwasher and stood next to her as he apprenticed her to the task. As Cynthia scraped her plate into the trash, he told her, "Make sure to clean off all—all the rice," then pointed out that there was still grease on the dish. Cynthia rinsed the dish and was about to leave it in the sink when Stefan instructed her to place it in the dishwasher. He then told her, "You're old enough to do that yourself. Okay? Put the juice away 'cause you took it out." Stefan then left the kitchen, and Cynthia returned the juice and other items to the refrigerator, cleared the table, and rinsed her glass and put it into the dishwasher. Stefan equated responsibility with age and positioned Cynthia as having reached a level of development at which she could competently carry out some of the tasks she saw her siblings perform every evening. As the CELF researchers Gonerko, Goodwin, and Tulbert note,[36] Stefan's directives and care-taking displayed a style of oversee-ing tasks similar to that of his mother, who expected a thorough job and a high degree of accountability, whether the task be dusting, brushing teeth, or completing a homework assignment.

The Randolph family interactions reflected aspects of both the natural growth and the concerted cultivation approaches discussed by Lareau.[37] Paula Randolph made use of bald imperatives, a no-nonsense tone of voice, followed up on her directives, and made clear what was appropriate and inappropriate behavior. She did not tolerate distractions when the children were told to take on a task. Paula also maintained a wide reper-toire of diverse types of interactions with her children. She interspersed her commands with playful and highly attuned empathetic responses. She praised them when they did their job well and placed a high degree of importance on homework *and* children's household tasks. Despite the periodic use of what could be termed a "controlling" parenting style, deemed by Grolnick and her collaborators to inhibit a child's sense of independence and self-sufficiency,[38] there was no evidence of any serious blunting of the creativity or development of the Randolph children, as many loving and engaging interactions occurred as the siblings played together. The development of hierarchical relationships in this family provided clear structures of authority; this is an approach that counters perspectives in some of the recent popular parenting books discussed above, as well as the work of psychological theorists who polarize "controlling" and "autonomy supporting" parenting. In fact, the mother in the Randolph family displays aspects of an authoritative, hierarchical parenting style while also supporting her children's autonomy as active, responsible members of the family.

CONCLUSION

A popular parenting book, *Raising Our Children, Raising Ourselves*, written by Naomi Aldort, a family counselor, encourages parents to allow their children free rein in the home. Aldort notes that children "occasionally feel empowered by helping in the home, but only when it is not required or expected." "When a child offers help," she advises, "express your gratitude and don't expect more."[39] In the CELF study, however, parents who appeared to take the child-centered approach described by Aldort or the "autonomy-supportive" perspective advocated by Grolnick and her colleagues,[40] did not have much success at getting their children's attention or assistance. These perspectives also neglect the social, moral, and developmental value of children's contributions to the household. Jean I. Clarke, Connie Dawson, and David Bredehoft, in their book, *How Much Is Enough? Everything You Need to Know to Steer Clear of Overindulgence and Raise Likeable, Responsible, and Respectful Children*, insist that assigning chores to children beginning at a young age (three to four years old) instills responsibility, perseverance, and an awareness of the importance of contributing to the family.[41] This type of socialization routine is illustrated in the Randolph family: the parents regularly assigned chores and held their children accountable for contributing to the household economy. At the same time, the resistance that children displayed in many families in our study is not necessarily a wholly negative phenomenon. As Aronsson and Cekaite demonstrate,[42] the negotiations that ensue as a result of children's challenges end up calling into question prescribed family roles and responsibilities. These exchanges also involve children in creating activity contracts and in enacting their negotiated contributions. Parents may use these interactions as opportunities to engage children in social reasoning and moral accountability.

The psychologist G. R. Patterson argues that one of the major skills for effective parenting is the monitoring of a child's behavior.[43] Goodwin and Tulbert and Goodwin examined parental monitoring of children's tasks in the CELF study and found that multiple modalities in these interactions contribute to the coordinated achievement of the activity:

language and tone of voice, eye gaze, the alignment of family members' bodies, and their shared orientation to relevant aspects of the material environment.[44] When parents and children have shared understandings of family routines that are enacted and acknowledged on a consistent basis, they establish a framework for collaboration. At the same time, excessive monitoring can be counterproductive and ultimately backfire in children's socialization into responsibility. When children display competence in a task and their participation no longer requires guidance and reinforcement, ongoing monitoring may not be necessary. In a few CELF families in which children's participation in household tasks was on the high end, children carried out some tasks on their own, without parental initiation.[45]

Everyday family interactions serve as a central context for children's socialization. The analyses of the physical and spatial organization of parent-child exchanges have revealed insights into how family members succeed or fail to establish mutual attention and develop understanding of household routines. In addition, in interactions about household work most children displayed resistance to parents' directives to engage in household tasks and often required reasons for their participation. The justifications that parents provided served to socialize their children into economic and moral understandings of what it means to be a member of a family. Children have grown increasingly dependent on their parents to maintain the household, and parents now bear the burden of these responsibilities. Children's involvement in domestic activities offers necessary training for becoming a self-reliant adult and may be consequential for the way children develop and contribute to their families and communities.

Parenting ideologies and practices, along with children's local social and physical environments, mediate children's socialization and constitute a developmental niche for understanding how culture organizes children's lives.[46] Returning to Ochs and Izquierdo's analysis of children's socialization into responsibility in three cultures, child-rearing practices among Samoans and the Matsigenka include the cultivation of attention to surrounding persons and activities and enacting consistent expectations that result in the habituation of tasks performed by children. In these cultures as well as in the Mayan community studied by de León, such practices lead to children's self-reliance, increased competence in domestic skills, and engaged, respectful orientations to others. Among the CELF families, the competing demands of work outside the home and children's schooling, academic, and extracurricular activities present a challenge to establishing consistent socialization routines in the home. Yet investing time and energy in engaging and sustaining children's involvement in household work both cognitively and corporeally orients children to helping others, which benefits children's moral development and contributes to family well-being.

NOTES

1. Bolin 2006; Ochs and Izquierdo 2009; Whiting and Whiting 1975.
2. Zelizer 1994.
3. Mintz and Kellogg 1988; Stearns 2003.
4. Zelizer 1994.
5. As Ariès (1962) notes, in Europe the institution of childhood emerged earlier among the elite, who organized an extended formal stage of education for their children, but this practice did not permeate all strata of society until the late nineteenth to early twentieth century.
6. Hofferth and Sandberg 2001b.
7. Kremer-Sadlik, Izquierdo, and Fatigante 2010; Kremer-Sadlik and Gutiérrez, this volume; Lareau 2003.
8. Coltrane 2000; Stearns 2003.
9. E.g., Levine 2008.
10. Klein, Graesch, and Izquierdo 2009.
11. Aronsson and Cekaite 2011.
12. Osit 2008.
13. Cheal 2003; Bianchi, Robinson, and Milkie 2006.
14. See Goodwin and Goodwin, this volume.
15. Goodnow 1988.
16. Antill et al. 1996; Blair 1992b.
17. Blair 1992a.
18. Lareau 2003.
19. Kusserow 2004.
20. See Wingard 2007 for a discussion of parents' prioritization of their children's activities.
21. Patterson 1982.
22. Goodwin 2006, 538.
23. Aronsson and Cekaite 2011.
24. Fasulo, Loyd, and Padiglione 2007.
25. Ochs and Izquierdo 2009.
26. de León 2011.
27. Goodwin 2006.
28. See Kendon 1990.
29. Goodwin 2006, 538.
30. Pigeron 2008.
31. Tulbert and Goodwin 2011.

32. Ochs and Izquierdo 2009.
33. Bolin 2006.
34. King 1999.
35. Fasulo, Loyd, and Padiglione 2007.
36. Gonerko, Goodwin, and Tulbert 2008.
37. Lareau 2003.
38. Grolnick et al. 2007.
39. Aldort 2006, 208–9.
40. Grolnick et al. 2007.
41. Clarke, Dawson, and Bredehoft 2004.
42. Aronsson and Cekaite 2011.
43. Patterson 1982.
44. Goodwin 2006; Tulbert and Goodwin 2011.
45. Klein, Graesch, and Izquierdo 2009.
46. Super and Harkness 1986.

7 Homework and Recreation

TAMAR KREMER-SADLIK AND KRIS GUTIÉRREZ

The afternoons and evenings of all the CELF families were filled with children's homework and extracurricular and other activities that dominated parents' after-work schedules and lives. Parents could not help but be heavily involved in their children's lives. Most of the children had to be driven to extracurricular activities several afternoons a week. They also needed help completing homework assignments due the following day. Children needed a "parent-manager" who kept tabs on where they had to be, when they had to be there, what they needed to bring with them, what homework assignment to prioritize, and how to pace one's progress on a long-term school project.[1] In addition, parents needed to make sure that their kids got a snack to keep them going, did their homework correctly, and performed to the best of their abilities during their extracurricular activities.

Consider the following description of a Wednesday afternoon at the Goodson family. As soon as Anita Goodson picks up her eight-year-old daughter, Hailey, from school at 2:30 P.M., she reminds her that she needs to "start that book report." Upon arriving home, Anita oversees Hailey's homework and checks that it is done properly. An hour later they leave for swimming practice, which Hailey attends three to four times a week. On the way, Anita gives her daughter a pep talk expressing a desire to see Hailey swim hard in the lanes where the good swimmers are. At practice Mom discusses Hailey's swimming goals with the coach and asks if Hailey could prepare for a more demanding five-hundred-meter race. Later Anita discusses this with Hailey and persuades her to try it, even though she is reluctant. The topic of the race comes up during Anita's phone conversation with her husband, Chad, and again later when he returns home from work. They both agree that training for the race is a good challenge for Hailey. During the evening Anita and Chad continuously monitor and urge Hailey to finish her homework, work on her book report, and complete the assignments she received at Kumon, a tutoring center she attends once a week. As bedtime draws near, Chad goes over Hailey's work with her, providing comments and corrections.

This level of parental involvement in children's lives and high expectations of children's performance have led to a growing unease about the way middle-class parents raise their children. Academics, journalists, and social commentators are expressing concerns regarding the welfare of children and question middle-class American child-rearing ideologies. Bookshelves are exploding with books such as *Reclaiming Childhood: Letting Children be Children in Our Achievement-Oriented Society* and *Pressured Parents, Stressed Out Kids: Dealing with Competition While Raising a Successful Child*,[2] which call for parents to find a balance between their child-centered approach to parenting and the push for children's achievement. In addition there are books such as *The Everything Parents Guide to Raising a Successful Child: All You Need to Encourage Your Child to Excel at Home and School* and *Raising a Successful Child: Discover and Nurture Your Child's Talents* that focus on ways parents can maximize their children's potential and guarantee their success.[3] Magazine, newspaper, and academic articles barrage parents with these contradictory messages: on the one hand, they tell parents to ease off of their kids and let them experience autonomy, free time, and other pleasures of childhood; on the other, they signal to parents that children's future success is heavily dependent on their participation in academic and extracurricular activities and on parents' involvement and dedication.

The authors of these documents level accusations at different parties. Some blame parents, whom they accuse of indulging their children or of pushing them hard to achieve.[4] Some suggest that schools are responsible for pressuring parents and children by assigning too much homework and subjecting children to an excessive amount of testing.[5] Finally, others accuse society in general for its competitive marketplace culture, whose every facet has become rife with the pressure to achieve.[6] No matter where the source of the problem lies, parents find themselves at the center of the problem as they experience angst and uncertainty about the best ways to raise their children to succeed and become all that they can be.

In this chapter we examine the phenomenon of parental involvement in children's activities, exploring what children are doing and how and why parents often spend much time and effort taking part in these activities. We hope to increase our understanding of what these practices intimate about contemporary middle-class parenting, childhood, and family life. We begin by looking at children's school-related activities and then move on to extracurricular activities.

DAILY INVOLVEMENT IN EDUCATION

The centrality of children's homework in family life is evidenced by the common occurrence of parents asking children about the "homework situation" shortly after they reunite with them after school and work. This question can be understood as a way of determining what the family's afternoon is going to look like, how time is going to be spent, and how to fit homework into the rest of the afternoon's plans. Leah Wingard called this practice "first mention."[7] She found that parents' first mention of homework most frequently occurred within five minutes of greeting their child. She suggested that this common behavior indicates a parental sense of obligation and responsibility for the accomplishment of homework, in addition to being a tool for socializing and monitoring children's time management, prioritization of homework activities, and supervising appropriate behavior in general.

Most afternoons at the Rosa family reflect this kind of parental involvement; they are all about education. This is true especially for Macy, who invests a great deal of time and effort in being involved in the education and schooling of her two children, Nancy, eight, and Peter, ten. Macy is a member of the PTA and of the Learned Council and attends all their meetings. When asked if she helps Nancy and Peter with homework, Macy admits that she does it "all the time" and goes on to elaborate: "We have flash cards, we have lots of books, I mean I have every book for resources, I have the homework helper for spelling, I have the homework helper for reading, I have the homework helper for math, for history." In fact, Macy spends hours daily assisting, monitoring, checking, and correcting her children's homework. She explains, "I feel that they need encouragement, they need a little push." Our observations reveal just how involved she is. After spending a whole afternoon monitoring Peter's and Nancy's progress with their homework, Macy sits down after dinner to go over Nancy's work. She demands that Nancy redo her work when there are mistakes, using "nice writing" or she'll have to do it again, and threatens that Nancy will stay at the table until she is done. Macy also encourages her daughter to come up with new ideas to make her work less repetitive and to do some extra credit work. This activity lasts until bedtime.

Parental involvement in children's education and homework is invoked and expected by the education system. Elementary and secondary schools often ask parents to become involved in their children's homework and make sure that it is complete.[8] Certain policies, such as No Child Left Behind, and government websites, such as Partnership for Family Involvement in Education, encourage schools to assign daily homework starting in first grade and call for parents to be involved in their children's education and schoolwork.[9] Research has shown that parental involvement has a positive effect on children's academic achievement and good study habits, providing support for the institutional approach.[10] Schneider and Stevenson, in a study examining teenagers' ambitions and pursuit of college education, argue that the direction these adolescents take is very much dependent on parents' ability to get involved in their children's school life and college application process.[11] Moreover, it has been shown that parents view their involvement in children's homework as a common responsibility of parenting.[12] They express their desire to help, assume that their involvement results in positive changes, and feel that teachers and their children expect them to be involved.

CELF parents' sense of responsibility for their children's schoolwork led at times to their initiating additional work for their children. Consider the following excerpt taken from an interview with Paula, mother of an eleven-year-old boy and two girls, ten and eight.

> MOTHER: Okay, you asked me one thing I don't like about Stefan's school—and that is—the one thing that I don't like is that the teacher—his teachers don't give them a lot of homework.
>
> INTERVIEWER: About how often during the week does he have homework?
>
> MOTHER: He may have homework three to four times a week. But usually about the time he gets home he's already done it on the bus. And the bus ride is about an hour. It's not very much. So I have things that I give him to do. I have him read. I have workbooks he can do, just to kind of keep stimulating him.

Video recordings in her household reveal that this mother was continuously involved in her children's assignments, spending much of her after-work time overseeing the quality and accuracy of her three children's schoolwork, assisting them when they had difficulties, and disciplining them when she perceived them as being lazy or producing sloppy work.

In spite of Paula's opinion that her son does not get enough homework, there has been a dramatic increase in homework assignments over the past two decades.[13] Research indicates that on average children 6 to 8 years old spend 2 hours and 8 minutes on homework per week and children 9 to 12 years old spend 3 hours and 41 minutes. Adolescents spend much more time on schoolwork, starting at 6 and a half hours for children grades 5–9 and 10 hours of homework per week for older teenagers.[14]

CELF parents' reports indicate that homework was the most prevalent activity their children engaged in at home after they returned from school.[15] In the charts that parents filled out describing their children's daily schedule on a typical week, homework was the dominant activity. Video-recorded observations in the home not only confirm this but also suggest that all the children in the study aged five and older had to do homework on a daily basis. Further, our scan sampling data indicate that children were doing homework as their primary activity in 14 percent of the weekday observations.

The frequency of homework activities in our study appears greater than that which was reported in other studies.[16] This difference may stem in part from a difference in perception of what counts as homework. We suggest that our parents viewed homework as an activity involving more than just the time children work directly on their assignments. Homework began with parents inquiring about the assignments that needed to be completed and concluded just before bedtime when parents did a final check of their children's work. It included parents' repeated reminders to do homework, parents' assistance (sometimes doing part of the homework themselves), parents' checking that assignments were completed and to a satisfactory level, and parents' clashes with their children when they did not comply or produced poor quality work. Thus in many of our homes homework began shortly after parents reunited with their children in the afternoon and lasted well into the evening. And it was treated as a chore that often affected other family activities as well as the atmosphere in the household.[17]

Parents' participation in their children's education went beyond assistance in daily assignments. It is not unusual for teachers in elementary and secondary schools to ask parents during "Back-to-School" nights at the beginning of the school year to volunteer. A sheet broken down into the days of the week and school hours was made available so that parents could note exactly when they could regularly be in the classroom assisting their child's teacher. An additional sheet asked parents to sign up to volunteer at various school events. The expectation was that parents, especially mothers, were available to be on school grounds during working hours. Not surprisingly, this expectation is hard to meet for our working parents, as the following CELF mother, Cheryl, confessed: "Seeing the moms, you know, go to class with their kids during the school year, I wish I could do that more, and I can't. I think this would be beneficial for the kids. Even Dana said to me, 'How come so-and-so's mom can come and you can't.' 'Or you won't' is her perception. And it makes me feel bad."

Cheryl revealed that the pressure to volunteer in the classroom came not only from the teacher and the school but also from her young daughter, who could not understand why her working mom was not like other mothers. For Cheryl, being in the classroom would offer time with her child that she cannot afford. All these made Cheryl feel guilty.[18]

Some of our CELF parents were able to rearrange their work schedules so that they could volunteer at their children's schools. Luisa Richardson was one of them; she was able to reduce her work hours on Fridays to volunteer in her children's school. She explains that this has a very specific benefit.

> MOTHER: Since I volunteer Fridays I get to know the teachers very well. And so every year I actually file a request for a teacher.
>
> INTERVIEWER: How long have you been volunteering?
>
> MOTHER: Since—I guess since my son started kindergarten, so about four years. It really helps to be there. Even though it's, you know, it's a lot of work. ((*laughs*))

Luisa told us that volunteering allows her to get to know the different teachers in the school and gives her enough leverage to select those that would be best for her children. In this way, she can have a certain degree of control and enhance her children's educational experience. This is taking the meaning of "benefit for the kids" that Cheryl mentioned to a tangible level.

HOMEWORK AS A SOURCE OF TENSION

Above we described Anita and Brad Goodson threatening their daughter, Hailey, with additional tutoring classes when she did not comply with their repeated requests to do her homework. In the Rosa household, Macy warned Nancy that she would repeat her work and stay at the table for a long time if she did not do her homework well. The incidents in these families are not unusual. In their analysis of parents' and teenagers' interviews, Solomon, Warin, and Lewis found that both groups perceive homework activities as a source of considerable tension.[19] Similarly, a 1998 parental survey revealed that homework activities were often a source of stress and conflict for both parents and children.[20] Fifty percent of parents reported serious arguments, including yelling and crying over homework; 49 percent got so fed up with their child's stalling that they walked away, letting the child suffer the consequences of not doing his or her work; and 22 percent admitted to doing part of their child's homework.

Unfortunately, we witnessed the strain that homework can put on parents' and children's relationships in some of our families as well. Scenes like the one described below were not frequent, yet the few occurrences captured on videotape suggest that these were not extraordinary events in those households. This incident unfolds in the Beringer-Potts family. Eight-year-old Jonah has been postponing doing his homework all afternoon. Alice, his mom, has acquiesced and allowed him to begin homework after dinner and even let him watch a little bit of a movie on the computer before starting his assignment. When Alice decides that Jonah should finally begin his homework, she walks into the den and instructs Jonah to stop watching the movie and get going with his work. When Jonah attempts to postpone it further, Alice reacts by taking the computer mouse and turning off the movie. Jonah is outraged that Alice did not pause the DVD. At this point a shouting match ensues.

MOTHER: GO DO YOUR HOMEWORK!

JONAH: ((*whining*)) I have to get it to the part ((*referring to queuing the DVD to the point where he stopped watching*)). You wasted time. (xxx). THIS IS YOUR FAULT THAT I HAVE TO DO THIS!

MOTHER: If you continue to talk to me this way I'm going to take—you're not going to be watching this vi- this video at all. I'm going to count to three and you're going to go do your homework. ((*pause*)) One.

JONAH: ((*whining*)) I HAVE TO GET IT TO THE PART AND THEN PAUSE IT!

MOTHER: NO, YOU DO THAT AFTER YOU DO YOUR HOMEWORK!

After two minutes of arguing Alice has enough and tries to pull Jonah away from the computer.

MOTHER: You're *not* watching it. ((*pulling Jonah and dragging him away from the chair by holding him under his arms*))

JONAH: YES I AM! ((*trying to resist mom by pulling away from his and moving toward the computer*))

MOTHER: No, you're NOT! ((*dragging Jonah away from the desk*)) You're going to do your homework now. ((*continuing to pull Jonah forcefully away from the computer*))

JONAH: Yes I AM! ((*trying to push his way to the computer*))

MOTHER: No, you're not! ((*blocking Jonah's path to the computer*))

The conflict escalates from a battle of wills to a contest of strength, where the winner is the one who prevails both physically and mentally. After five minutes the conflict ends with Alice taking away Jonah's TV privileges for the next day and threatening that she'll speak to his teacher. This loud and stressful episode reveals how sometimes parents' sense of responsibility for their child's homework and consequent involvement can result in an emotional and physical clash with their children, who may not be ready or willing to collaborate with the parents' goals at that moment.

What causes parents like Alice to get into such tense, even physical conflicts with their children? Why do parents like Macy and Paula find themselves overseeing homework very closely and parents like Luisa volunteering in schools? It is important to note that in parents' education interviews we found that our parents typically did not complain about the amount of homework and other school demands or acknowledge the negative effects these could have on their relationships with their children or on their home lives. We wondered why this was the case.

MIDDLE-CLASS ANXIETY

One possible reason for parents' heightened concern with and investment in their children's academic success may be found in Barbara Ehrenreich's book *Fear of Falling: The Inner Life of the Middle Class*.[21] Ehrenreich argues that there is an inherent anxiety in being middle class that centers on the ability to reproduce their social standing and secure one's children's place in it. She explains that in other social classes membership is transmitted by inheritance. If you are born into the upper or the lower class, you can expect that you will remain there all your life. Of course, there are exceptional cases of wealthy people who lose their riches or poor people who are able to attain wealth, but in most cases people's class membership remains relatively stable. In contrast, Eherenreich argues, if you are born into the middle class you need to earn membership in that class through years of educational success. The lack of cross-generational class stability is translated into parental anxiety regarding their children's futures. Sherry Ortner explains, "Middle class parents can only pass on to their children the means—economic, educational, and psychological—with which to (try to) reproduce their status. But ultimately the children must do it themselves."[22] Thus, we propose, CELF parents, like many other parents, try to do the best they can to prepare their children and give them a head start on their path to the middle class. They supervise and help their children with homework and volunteer in classrooms and school organizations. They enroll their children in expensive tutoring centers and provide them with private tutoring services. They purchase many educational materials, such as computers, software, books, and games, to make sure that their children have continuous access to valuable resources.

For some of our families, the attempts to give their children an edge involved greater effort. Nothing seems to ensure a secure future and the potential to sustain middle-class life more than a "good" education. Decisions about schools and schooling were strategic and shaped middle-class family life in unprecedented ways. We found that many CELF parents were willing to relocate the family to provide their children with the greatest academic advantage by attending award-winning schools with high-achieving student bodies. Let us return to the Rosa family, which, despite limited resources, relocated several blocks away from their previous home so that their elementary school children would be eligible to enroll in a school with better test scores. Here, planning for success required becoming familiar with the local schools' standards and achievement trends and making strategic decisions about where to live based on goals they had for their children's future. For this family, such planning involved both current and future educational considerations. Macy Rosa explained that they had two more years before "hopefully we will move to Santa Monica," where the children could attend a blue ribbon junior high. Similarly, the Neumans explained that they were living in a rental home instead of the one they owned in order to be in an area with a better school.

Planning for their children's academic success was a hallmark characteristic of many of our families. All CELF parents perceived college as an obvious path for their children, as illustrated by Debra, mother of a twelve-year-old boy and an eight-year-old girl: "Um, well, I—I think to them, it's a given that they're going to go to college. I don't think they—they don't know that they have a choice. That some people don't go to college."

Anxiety about going to the best colleges was evident in a few of our families. For example, Elsie Neuman admitted that her thirteen-year-old son was taking Japanese as a foreign language instead of a more common language like Spanish for the sole purpose of making his application stand out when he applied to colleges. And Tim Broadwell-Lewis, father of twelve-year-old twins, confessed with a degree of self-criticism that they had sent their very academic-oriented son to a college prep SAT review course when he was quite young:

> And I think Edward had to take, well basically, an SAT review course in fifth grade. And I mean, you know, while I think that's nutty, it says something about us. We talked to enough people who said you're making a mistake for that kid if you don't. As much as he whines, it will be good for him and he'll do better on the test and feel better about himself. And so we have a kid who gives up his entire Sunday morning every week to take an SAT review course in fifth grade—that's got to be, it's kind of sick.

While strategies such as selecting idiosyncratic foreign languages or participating in college prep courses at age ten may seem extreme, these cases evidence the need that parents feel to provide their children with the best opportunities to excel and increase their chances for a place in the middle class.

CHILDHOOD AS A PERIOD OF PREPARATION

The pressure to provide children with the best opportunities and prepare them for the long haul toward middle-class status is viewed by historians as a new approach to childhood. Steve Mintz, for example, has suggested that in the 1970s parents "turned away from an older ideal of a 'protected' childhood and began to emphasize a 'prepared' childhood."[23] Linking this change further, to class, Halldén has identified two approaches to child development.[24] The first, which was more commonly found among working-class parents, views the *child as a being*, referring to child development as a natural process driven by inner forces, and the second was a middle-class child-rearing preference in which parents view the *child as a project*. Perceiving the child as a project requires that parents have direct responsibility through planning, directing, and controlling the child's development and preparation for adult life.

The sociologist Annette Lareau, who examined the lives of children in middle- and working-class families, has also suggested that the phenomenon of parental involvement has to do with class.[25] She found that middle-class parents she observed engaged in a particular approach to child-rearing, which she termed *concerted cultivation*. In this perspective, parents "deliberately try to stimulate their children's development and foster their cognitive and social skills,"[26] by offering them environments that enhance their verbal and reasoning competence and their sense of entitlement and individuation, as well as by organizing numerous extracurricular activities to build personal skills.

The view of childhood as a period of preparation coincides with another contemporary change in the perception of what constitutes children's work. This approach has advanced the idea that in today's world, where children spend over thirty-five hours a week at school and on homework, their work (and responsibility) has changed from paid work to school.[27] Jens Qvortrup has rejected the proposition that children's usefulness has decreased with compulsory schooling and changes in child's labor laws, arguing that children's manual labor has been replaced with school activities.[28] Given the economic need for an educated workforce, children's educational work has become valuable and essential.[29] Indeed, children's education work can be viewed as a contemporary way of accumulating social and cultural capital, not only for children themselves, but also for their families. Viviana Zelizer,[30] revisiting her original argument of the decreased usefulness of children,[31] agrees that not only can children produce capital they can use later in life, but that it is beneficial for their social relations and families in particular. For example, a child's stellar academic performance not only enhances a child's professional future, but his or her family status as well.

Hilary Levey, who has studied children's participation in beauty pageants and accelerated after-school tutoring programs and chess clubs, has expanded Qvortrup's argument that school is the new work of children by suggesting that extracurricular activities are also part of the new responsibility of children.[32] She contends that children's participation in these activities constitute work since they "increase transferable use value and /or produce human capital that will later be available for the production of use value."[33] That is, extracurricular activities, like school, offer a way of accumulating skills and knowledge that will be translated into material value in the future as the children become adults.

INVESTING IN EXTRACURRICULAR ACTIVITIES

To get a sense of how extracurricular activities may shape the parents' and family's day, we want to take a look at the Reis's Tuesday afternoon. As soon as Pam picks up her children, Allison, eight, and Mike, seven, from school at 3:00 P.M., they head to karate class, briefly stopping at a drive-in fast-food restaurant to grab a snack. While still in the car, Pam cajoles her son to begin his homework. She keeps a lapboard and a pencil box in the car, which she calls "our school kit—everything imaginable to do homework in the car." Once at karate, Pam stays to watch her children perform. When asked by the researcher if the kids participate in karate competitions, Pam explains that "we do plenty of competing," referring to the other sports Allison and Mike participate in: hockey, baseball, fencing, and tennis. When Jerry, Pam's husband, joins the family at the karate studio, she explains, "He comes to pick up Mike, takes him to hockey, and then I take Allison to Score, so we're all kind of converging here." Just before the class ends, Pam and Jerry watch Mike spar with his teacher and cheer him loudly as he makes a good move and wins. Later, in the parking lot, Jerry makes sure to transfer the hockey equipment from Pam's car to his, and as she says good-bye, she makes sure to instruct Mike to finish his homework on the way to hockey practice, an hour's drive. Then she gets in her car with Allison, and they head to Score, a tutoring center, where Allison spends the next hour while Pam quickly makes a run to the supermarket. As soon as Pam and Allison get home, at around 7:00 P.M., Pam begins preparing dinner. Mike and Jerry get home almost an hour later. There is still a little time for Pam to check the children's homework and read them a book before bedtime.

While not all our families were like the Reis family, the degree to which they engaged in extracurricular activities, as well as our parents' attitudes toward these activities, lends support to Levey's argument that participation in after-school sports, music and art and tutoring programs, and other activities constitute a kind of children's job. For a start, all but one of our families engaged in some after-school activities. The dominance of sports was evident among most of our families: forty-three of the sixty-four school-aged children participated in sports activities, most of them team sports like soccer and baseball. Such activities typically involve one or two practices a week and a game or match on the weekend. Participation in sports has always been important in American culture, and in the past two decades there has been an increase in girls' participation in what used to be considered primarily a boys' sphere. Today girls regularly join soccer teams, play basketball, and even join football teams.[34]

Not only is there a sense that children's participation in sports programs is encouraged, but there are also cultural, social, and historical messages that signal that children should participate in sports. Apportioning children's leisure time for use in sports activities provides a preferred alternative to leaving children's time entirely open for discretionary use.[35] Growing concerns regarding the rising rates of obesity in childhood have drawn attention to children's physical inactivity as a public health issue and have propelled calls for greater involvement in athletics.[36]

Other types of extracurricular activities were also found among our families. For example, of the 64 school-aged children, 18 were involved in some religious activities, attending classes and services at least twice a week. In addition, 15 children took music or art classes, 16 received tutoring either for remedial or accelerated purposes, and 11 participated in community-based activities such as Boy Scouts or Girl Scouts. These activities usually meant a commitment to at least one meeting a week.[37]

To better understand the level of family commitment to children's extracurricular activities, we counted the number of activities in which each family chose to enroll their children. If in a family with two children one child played violin and tennis and the other piano and soccer, the total of activities for this family was scored as 4. The results revealed great variability among families; some selected to have each child participate in only one activity, and some enrolled their children in a number of activities. We also had one extreme case of a family with two children who participated in a total of ten extracurricular activities. And as mentioned above, the children in one of the CELF families were not enrolled in any activities at the time of the study. The mother of this family explained that the children were between sports seasons, but at the same time she admitted that she didn't "really necessarily like them having commitments during the week, because it cuts into homework time." The median for CELF families, however, was three activities that children were engaged in each week, with at least one of them being sports.[38]

It is not surprising that our families committed themselves to participation in so many activities. Children's extracurricular activities have regularly been shown to have positive effects on many aspects of children's lives. Many researchers have found that participation in structured extracurricular programs is strongly associated with academic achievement and social adjustment and decreases the likelihood of engagement in delinquent behavior.[39] This information is available to parents in books and articles and on numerous websites. The Family, Youth and Consumer News site, for example, provided this information: "Extracurricular activities not only give children something to do in their free time, but involvement in these activities promotes a positive sense of self and decreases the chance a child will drop out of school."[40] And a parents' advice site reported, "Extracurricular activities also play a role in reducing drug and alcohol use and irresponsible sexual activity in older children and teens, especially those who otherwise would be on their own after school."[41]

Parents internalize this information, and when talking about reasons and motivation for committing their children to various organized activities, they reveal their beliefs that these activities foster qualities children need to be successful, well-adjusted people and respectable members of society.[42] CELF parents consistently described activities as opportunities for and arenas in which children can learn to master social and cognitive skills, as well as improve their psychological well-being.[43] For example, parents, as the quote below from one of CELF mothers illustrates, view engagement in certain sports activities not only as offering physical training, but as imparting a broader benefit.

> They do karate, for instance, which is so much more than just karate fighting. That class alone is a complete education in self-confidence and, you know, setting and achieving goals. Leadership roles that, you know, the kids have to learn in class. Respecting the authority figure.

This mother suggests that the martial arts class offers her children a "complete education" in valuable skills for adult life. Other parents see extracurricular activities as directly connected to improved school performance. One CELF mother said of her eight-year-old daughter:

> Her grades have really improved, not just from swimming, obviously, but the discipline of having to be in a set schedule. And she knows that she's got to do her homework at a certain time or that she won't have the time or the energy.

This mother suggests that being part of a swim team (with a set schedule of three to four practices on weekdays and one or two swim meets a month on weekends) has taught her daughter discipline, which in turn has helped her manage schoolwork. For this mother, time management appears to be at the core of her daughter's success; it is not the amount of time available for activities that matters but the ability to discipline oneself and manage whatever time one has that leads to successful performance at school.

Our parents tended to underscore the role of participation in formal extracurricular activities in children's socialization to important values and to underplay their own contribution to this learning. Yet our observations reveal that during activities parents regularly commented, evaluated, and displayed to their children their own attitude toward the unfolding events and socialized them to certain behaviors and moral stances.[44] For example, in the following segment, a mother who could not attend her eight-year-old daughter's basketball game, said this to her daughter in a telephone conversation after her team lost the game.

> I know you lost, but that's okay. You can't win them all. It's a—just the first game, right? You almost scored? How excellent! Well, next time you'll be much better at it. And the team is gonna gel as a team as they get better.

This mother's postgame pep talk reveals her stances on the issues of winning and losing, having an optimistic outlook, working as a team, and setting improvement as a goal. Underlining the importance of patience and perseverance, this mother was teaching her daughter that having these qualities will result in better outcomes in the future both for herself and for the team.

In another example, a father and a neighboring boy were playing a basketball game in the driveway against his two daughters (ages eight and ten) and a neighboring girl, Reagan. The game ended with the girls' team winning with a final basket, and the girls cried out an insulting cheer: "Girls rule! Boys drool!" The father interrupted the cheer, suggesting that it was an inappropriate way to end the game. Rather than reprimand the girls, he invited Reagan to find an acceptable cheer:

> Don't you say like— ((*pretends to high-five invisible players*)) welcome, welcome, welcome, welcome, and all that stuff? And then they say thanks for the good game? Or you s- you walk by and go like this ((*walks with palm out*)) and shake hands with everybody and walk by?

This father took the lesson a step beyond the practical (how one should end a friendly game) to the theoretical (why one should end the game that way).

> FATHER: Does anybody know what that's called?
>
> REAGAN: Yeah.
>
> FATHER: What?

REAGAN: Good game.

FATHER: Good.

FATHER: It's not only about—It's not always about winning. It's about being a good sport.

The father identified by name the value—being a good sport—he has been trying to instill through the cheering exercise, indicating that the cheer signifies more than a simple verbal routine, that is, an attitude toward playing sports. For this father, taking care to compliment the other team at the close of a game was a reflection of good sportsmanship. The father further defined the meaning of good sportsmanship, explaining that the objective of sports is not only winning but also playing right; "it's about being a good sport."

Parents' comments on their children's performance were not only gestures of support, but often also lessons in attitude and behavior. A father who thought his daughter had a defeated attitude while competing against her older brother for possession of a ball during an impromptu game at home urged her not to whine, signaling an expectation that she assert herself and play competitively. And a mother whose son had just fallen during a hockey game, after making sure that he was not hurt, instructed him to get up, aligning herself with the attitude that players have to be tough and recover swiftly.[45] Some parents who were particularly knowledgeable about their children's activities watched their kids' actions carefully and provided them with detailed feedback and analysis.[46] These assessments and comments are part of parents' forms of involvement in children's activities that serve to optimize and enhance the child's performance.

A study that compared children's participation in extracurricular activities and parents' attitudes toward it in both the CELF and iCELF families found that in both sites children tended to engage in a similar number and type of activities.[47] Parents in both sites expressed the belief that through this participation their children were acquiring important skills important for adulthood. Yet only in the American parents' discourse was the notion that children also needed to push themselves and excel in these activities present. CELF parents expressed their desire to see their kids put great effort into their performance; they highlighted their children's grades and ranking; they underscored their children's success and even suggested that they could go very far (e.g., national competitions). In contrast, the iCELF parents appeared conflicted when the issue of competition was raised, as if it did not belong in the children's worlds and underplayed the importance of performance. CELF parents' emphasis on success may be viewed as sensible since regularly assessing children's performance and rewarding achievement can help parents determine the level of their child's preparedness of the adult world.

Participation in extracurricular activities, especially certain sports, requires parents' involvement in different ways. In addition to paying fees, buying equipment, getting uniforms washed and ready, and driving children to and from activities, parents regularly attended their children's matches and meets, provided team snacks when it was their turn, cheered from the sidelines, comforted when it was needed, and provided evaluations and lessons for future performance. However, some parents did much more. Certain national recreational organizations, such as American Youth Soccer Organization (AYSO), National Junior Basketball (NJB), and Little League Baseball, rely completely on parents volunteering for the most essential roles of coaches, assistant coaches, and referees, as well as the less critical roles of team parent, snack bar duties, and more. This means that in order to have a team, parents must give of their time and volunteer. Of our thirty-two families, eight parents volunteered regularly for these tasks. And most of them expressed pleasure at being involved in such a way.

One self-employed father who particularly loved his coaching duties told us that, in addition to his business, he tried to run his boys' baseball team and sometimes also a basketball team (gesturing toward photos hanging on the wall in his office that portrayed himself as the coach standing proudly by his teams) and admitted that he was often more prepared for baseball than for business. He conceded that he should spend more time on his company but that he doesn't because "After twelve years [of running his own business] comes a point when I've had enough. Plus I really enjoy spending time with the kids doing the baseball stuff." Another father recounted how after volunteering as assistant coach and enjoying the time with his son, he decided to volunteer to coach, which he now did regularly.

Rather than spend after-work time and weekends at home engaged in must-do household activities, such as cooking meals, doing laundry, cleaning, and working in the yard at a more leisurely pace, parents often found themselves juggling these chores with driving kids to and from activities. Yet typically our parents did not complain. Only one set of parents complained about these demands and felt that their daily life was more hurried and stressed because of their children's schedules. Yet at the same time they expressed a desire to have their children participate in extracurricular activities and admitted that they had to push their non-athletic daughter to attend her weekly ice-skating lessons. Most parents expressed pleasure at their kids' level of participation and enjoyment at their ability to share these experiences with their children and spend time together.

CONCLUSION

CELF parents, like many other middle-class parents, invest much time and effort in their children's school and extracurricular activities. We suggest that this preference epitomizes the perception of childhood as a period dedicated to preparing children for adult life[48] and of middle-class parents as the ones responsible for maximizing their children's acquisition of skills and development of abilities valuable later in life.[49] Expanding on Erhenreich's argument that middle-class parents are inherently anxious because their children are not guaranteed a place in the same social class, we propose that parents' heightened involvement in their children's life reflects this angst. In other words, this anxiety drives parents to perceive their children's school performance, extracurricular achievements, and acquisition of "adult" skills (e.g., concentration, teamwork, competitiveness, discipline) as important for enhancing their children's chances later in life. Most important, parents see their own involvement as a crucial component that guarantees maximizing the benefits.

The perception of parental investment and involvement as increasing a child's well-being is rooted in the ecocultural idea that optimal parenting is achieved in routine activities. Though one might view a father's playing catch with his son as leisure activity, according to this approach this father invests time and effort in it because he views it as an investment in his child's and family's well-being.[50] According to the ecocultural perspective, a family's routine activities reflect a cultural understanding of how one should raise a child.[51] Answers to questions such as what would be considered good care and how one would prepare a child for adult life are embedded in cultural beliefs that shape the way everyday activities are organized. Activities, such as assisting with homework, driving children to dance or tennis class, or coaching one's child's soccer team, gain their meaning for participants as they map them onto goals, expectations, and values. In this view, the engagement in meaningful activities enhances participants' sense of well-being. Thus the construct of well-being is linked directly to families' organization of and engagement in routine practices.

The frequent parental involvement in children's school and extracurricular activities suggests that, indeed, parents' sense of well-being is associated with these routines. Some of the CELF parents reflected on the fact that when they were young their lives and the lives of their parents were very different. They described a childhood that was less busy, with fewer activities and less structure. And they depicted their parents as less involved with either schoolwork or extracurricular activities. Yet none of our parents complained about this new way of parenting. In fact, another type of dissatisfaction was conveyed. It came from some of our mothers who felt that they did not find a good balance between work and family life and expressed a desire to spend *more* time with their children. For instance, Cheryl, the same mother who wished she could volunteer in her children's classroom, in response to a question regarding whether there were things in her life that did not fit with her idea of well-being, intimated a wish that she "worked less because part of my well-being would be spending more time with my kids." This mother's frustration with her inability to dedicate time to her children during work hours reinforces the notion that one aspect of parental well-being is derived from parents' ability to invest time and effort in their children's lives and futures.

As we noted at the beginning of this chapter, today parents are often unsure about whether they are preparing their children adequately for adult life. They are confronted with contradictory messages that tell them, on the one hand, to let their children be free to experience childhood and, on the other, to provide them with as many opportunities to excel and achieve as possible. They are also bombarded with strong messages from schools, government agencies, psychologists, and child development specialists who repeatedly signal to them that, even though there might be other experts who may warn them that their overzealous engagement may damage their children, parental involvement is not really a choice. By examining in this chapter how this involvement unfolds on the ground and how it may shape parents' and children's experiences, we have shown that it is difficult for parents to find a balance between the broader cultural forces and their desire to achieve well-being for their families.

NOTES

1. Wingard 2007.
2. Crain 2003; Grolnick and Seal 2007.
3. Witmer 2004; Burt and Perlis 2006.

4. Elkind 2001.

5. Kralovec and Buell 2000; Orenstein 2009.

6. Grolnick and Seal 2007.

7. Wingard 2006a.

8. Cooper 1989, 1994; Hoover-Dumpsey et al. 2001.

9. U.S. Department of Education 2009a, 2009b, 2009c.

10. Balli, Demo, and Wedman 1998; Bempechat 2004.

11. Schneider and Stevenson 1999.

12. Forsberg 2007, 2009; Hoover-Dumpsey, Bassler, and Burow 1995.

13. Hofferth and Sandberg 2001a; Nocon and Cole 2006.

14. Hofferth and Curtin 2005.

15. Gutiérrez, Izquierdo, and Kremer-Sadlik 2010.

16. E.g., Hofferth and Curtin 2005.

17. Wingard and Forsberg 2008.

18. Chapter 11 in this volume examines parents' experience of work-family conflict and the ensuing guilt.

19. Solomon, Warin, and Lewis 2002.

20. Farkas et al. 1999.

21. Ehrenreich 1989.

22. Ortner 1998a, 428.

23. Mintz 2004, 343.

24. Halldén 1991; see also Forsberg 2009.

25. Lareau 2003.

26. Ibid., 5.

27. Qvortrup 2001, 2005; Miller 2005.

28. Qvortrup 2005.

29. Qvortrup 2001.

30. Zelizer 2005.

31. Zelizer 1994.

32. Levey 2009.

33. Ibid., 198.

34. Redekop 1984; Coakley 2006; Messner 2009.

35. Larson and Verma 1999.

36. Andersen et al. 1998; Goran, Reynolds, and Linquist 1999; Odgen et al. 2002.

37. Kremer-Sadlik, Izquierdo, and Fatigante 2010.

38. Ibid.

39. Eccles et al. 2003; Larson 2001; Zaff et al. 2003.

40. Alexander 2003.

41. Needleman 2001.

42. Alwin 2001; Arendell 2000; Dukes and Coakley 2002; Dunn, Kinney, and Hofferth 2003; Lareau 2003.

43. Gutiérrez, Izquierdo, and Kremer-Sadlik 2010.

44. Kremer-Sadlik and Kim 2007.

45. Ibid.

46. Van Hamersveld and Goodwin 2007.

47. Gutiérrez, Izquierdo, and Kremer-Sadlik 2010.

48. Mintz 2004.

49. Halldén 1991; Lareau 2003.

50. Bradley and Corwyn 2004.

51. Weisner 1998, 2002, 2009.

8 Nurturing

MARJORIE HARNESS GOODWIN
AND CHARLES GOODWIN

Despite the busyness[1] of the Los Angeles families we studied, the interactions many family members experienced during shared leisure activities as well as while doing everyday chores and children's work (homework) were characterized by caring, supportiveness, playfulness, and pleasure, just the sorts of experiences psychologists[2] and psychological anthropologists[3] have said are necessary in order for individuals to thrive. In the midst of mundane, largely unstructured activity such as taking a walk, riding in the car, or cleaning a piano keyboard, children and parents could cultivate active and joyful engagement in imaginative inquiry about the world, often colored by language play during forms of "occasioned knowledge exploration"[4] during "quality moments."[5]

This chapter demonstrates ways in which forms of love were manifested among family members in everyday life situations and activities in four families. When children received outstanding grades on report cards or demonstrated superior talent in sports, parents displayed considerable enthusiasm for their accomplishments. Parents actively responded to children's desires to learn new skills (e.g., making waffles for family breakfast) by apprenticing them into the activity. Love was also expressed through building opportunities for children to discover new ways of encountering the world or solve problems during unstructured activities such as an evening walk in the neighborhood or while cuddling in bed on a Saturday morning. Through the tactics of tough love parents taught forms of responsibility and perseverance in the midst of conflict. While caring for children was primarily in the hands of parents, siblings in some households were also important partners in nurturing young children, teaching self-care activities, and reading with them, providing moments of relief for parents and opportunities for learning and rich emotional exchange.

Our methodology of videotaping everyday interactions provides a unique lens for examining how moments of intense caring and apprenticeship unfolded in real time and through embodied practice; rarely has it been possible for researchers to document the in situ experience of family members building a life with one another in the intimate spaces of the home in the way we did. This chapter differs from others in this book in that we examine displays of family affection as if looking through a microscope; we investigate how feelings and relationships unfold moment by moment in daily activities. Specifically, we explore how the choreographing of routine events (linked to family cultural values and aspirations) highlight forms of caring and empathy in four different families.

THE REIS FAMILY: SOCIALIZING FOR SUCCESS IN SPORTS AND ACADEMICS

The Reis family devoted considerable energy to preparing their children for the "credentials crisis"[6] that twenty-first-century children experience when applying for college. The Reis parents wanted their children to excel in sports so they could get sports scholarships to attend college. Through "concerted cultivation,"[7] the parents directed children's development and attempted to stimulate children's cognitive and social skills, in projects designed to accumulate cultural capital.[8] The Reis parents expressed love through endless expenditures of time arranging for structured sports and academic preparation (Kumon) for their children. During the weekdays the Reis family, the busiest family in our study, was in high gear, often going from one after-school activity to another in the same afternoon before dinner.[9] The Reis children spent 56 percent of their activity time on sports;[10] approximately nineteen hours per week were allocated to children's out-of-school practices. Both children (Allison, age 8, and Mike, age 7) were enrolled in a number of sports simultaneously, such as baseball, basketball, ice hockey, fencing, and tennis. Life in this family was so hectic that a whiteboard used for doing homework en route from one activity to another was a permanent fixture to the backseat of the family van.

The parents encouraged sports because of what they felt was a lack of sports in their own upbringing. After dinner in the presence of Dad's mother the following conversation with two ethnographers about why the family encouraged sports took place.

DAD: Because my mother never encouraged it when I was
        growing up.

MOM: *Ou:::::.* passing blame here.

DAD: She wouldn't let me play football because she was afraid
        the other kids were too big. 'Cause I was big for my age.

MOM: So because of that ((*turning to grandma*)) We allow
        our daughter to play with weapons, and our son to get
        pucks shot at him.

The Reis parents collaborated in transporting their children to events on weekends. Their strategy was "divide to conquer"—for example, taking one child to Fresno and another to Bakersfield for competitions. Technology was crucial in this family and provided a material indicator of the family's busyness.[11] In order to keep track of the multiple activities (and ever-changing dates for activities such as Allison's baseball games), Mom relied on her Palm Pilot to keep everything organized; she commented it was what "keeps everyone all together." Cell phones were also important for this family; although family members often had to be in disparate places because of the busy schedules taking children to activities, they always felt connected because parents were constantly updated regarding the achievements of children, whether at the hockey rink, baseball field, or tennis court. In the midst of a Saturday morning hockey practice Mom phoned Dad to inform him of the superior playing that Mike was doing as goalie to propel his team to win. As in other American contexts,[12] winning and being the best player was important.

As Mom was present at her son's hockey activities on weekdays as well, she not only could fortify him during breaks with Gatorade but also could congratulate him on specific plays with exclamations such as, "Excellent game! That was great! That was great!" while patting him on the head. When Mike informed his mom that he had scored two goals, she gave him a high five while exclaiming, "No way! You scored two goals today? Dude! ((*undulating sound*))." This assessment showed heightened affect not only through the positive assessment "No way!" but also through undulating voice quality over the term "Dude" and a celebratory high-five handclap. Such forms of positive assessments contrasted dramatically with other parents' greetings on first reunions after sports activities,[13] as, for example, in "Bess sweetie? I'm gonna pack up the stuff and then I'll come back and get you. Okay?" Parents were frequently in such a hurry to collect belongings and move to the location of their next activity as expediently as possible that they did not make time for talking about their children's performances in sports at the time of the sports event itself, though commentaries might come later in the day on the way home or at dinner.

In order to make the hectic schedule of activities possible, Pam Reis found a job that allowed her to have time flexibility—director of financial aid at a high school. What started out as a part-time job became more permanent employment. In fact, she gave up a former job as a television producer so that she could dedicate herself to "producing a family." She explained that she really enjoyed being able to pick up her children from school and spend the afternoon with them. Pam Reis was fortunate that she could depend on her eighty-year old mother-in-law to take care of the children when she needed her. As she stated, "And I love the fact that she's here and that the kids have such a great relationship with her." The paternal grandmother went to all the games and special events that the children participated in. The Reis family had a human safety net, someone they can call on for childcare if they needed it.

Scholarship was important in the family. Allison had a perfect report card. Mike, the youngest child in his class, had excellent grades as well, with 100 percent every week in spelling. There is little wonder that this was the case, given the family's ever-vigilant attention to homework. Ethnographers observed that the entire drive from home to school each morning before a spelling test was occupied with Mom quizzing her children on the list of the day's spelling words.

Competition in sports was critical in this family: advice giving frequently contained assessments and rankings of players relative to one another. As Mike left the benches to go onto the hockey rink one afternoon, Mom told him, "I want you to beat Eric's butt today, okay?" When Mike described a classmate as faster than he was to his father, Dad responded, "But they don't play goalie better than you do." Family members talked about the comparison of Allison (eight) and a boy, age fourteen, who both came in eighth place in fencing in the Junior Olympics. Mom reported that the coach said, "Alex, it wasn't a big *deal* to come in eighth. For *you* [meaning Allison] to come in eighth was amazing!" Joking at dinner about how happy her mom would be should she be in the Olympics, Allison said, "Mommy, if I win a gold medal i(h)n the Olympi(hh)cs? You're gonna be stuck to the ceiling and I scrape—I'll have to scrape you o(hh)ff. With a spatula."

Informal coaching was a frequent activity in the Reis family. When Dad drove Mike home from hockey practice he critiqued him on the way he had played: "You need to make sure you focus a little more. And I'd—We're going to work on your left kick out. Your left right kick out. 'Cause what happens when you kick your left leg out? If your left foot stays in the same place, And your body goes to the right. The right." Even in the midst of individual activities such as Mike's bike riding on weekends Pam Reis assumed the role of coach, with talk such as, "Go slow. Uh oh. Use your brakes not your shoes. Push on your brakes until you stop." Simultaneously monitoring Allison's skating, she said, "You gotta get much better at the T stop. It's not real strong. It's a little wobbly. I want you to come to a complete stop doing the T."

One might predict that with such a tightly organized and managed schedule there would be little time for creative activities such as working collaboratively to solve everyday problems or ponder the mysteries of everyday life[14] outside of the more extended time together that eating a meal together affords. We did not expect playful talk to be occurring at 7:00 A.M. as family members were cuddling together in the parents' bed! As the family was discussing a neurosurgeon—"brain doctor"—who was also a reporter, Dad posed a question: "Is a brain doctor smarter than other doctors 'cause he has to work on the brain?" Allison replied to this with, "Yeah. 'Cause he takes all of the smartness out of them." As the conversation drifted to consideration of hypothetical dual careers (Allison as a zoologist and a fencer, Mike as a hockey playing drummer) the parents created a scene that would meld zoology and fencing.

> MOM: If your animal goes out of control,
>
> DAD: No no. I was thinking more like,
>
> You can watch the animals
>
> And then you have the perfect skewer for barbecuing them.

The topic next drifted to the possibility of Mike being a poor poet rather than any other profession, and the family together explored the economics of various professions and their implications for parents having to support their offspring. Countering the idea that poets are necessarily poor, Allison inserted her own idea that a poet celebrity such as Shel Silverstein need not imply a situation of abject poverty.

While in bed, Mom, commenting as informal coach, joked about seven-year-old Mike's plays as goalie the day before during hockey practice: "You let five get past you. But so did the other guy." Mike playfully disagreed with his mom about the scores in the previous night's game. The talk about competitive activities was all the while overlaid with playful touches, reciprocal nose taps and tickling, and sound play involving the terms *confuse you* and *confusable*.

Figure 8.1. Making waffles cooperatively.

MOM:	I was trying to confuse you.
MIKE:	I tried to confuse you too.
MOM:	Well you *al*most did. But not *real*ly. Not really. I was trying to confuse you too.
MIKE:	It's confusable.
MOM:	Are you confusable?
MIKE:	No.
MOM:	Well neither am I.
	((*tickles Mike*))
MIKE:	eh heh!
MIKE:	Hey Mom.
MOM:	What.
MIKE:	Beep! ((*taps her on the nose*))
MOM:	Hey Mike.
MIKE:	What.
MOM:	((*does a reciprocal play punch*))

As the family was cuddling, discussion of Mike's future as a hockey playing drummer was interspersed with wordplay, tickling, and gentle nose tapping to punctuate points. Across a range of circumstances the Reis children were socialized to view events in terms of rank ordering of positions in a game or monetary worth on a relative scale of professions. The Reis parents helped their children learn the embodied skills they would need in order to excel in sports (skating, riding bikes, hockey, shooting baskets, fencing, etc.) as well as the intellectual skills they needed to get perfect scores on tests. They assisted in children's activities

Figure 8.2. Pouring waffle batter.

such as Little League baseball; on the baseball field through helping to pitch or referee Mom demonstrated concern for their children's development through sports with her active engagement.

On occasion children in the Reis family initiated activities that benefited the entire family. In the midst of the Saturday morning cuddling Mike asked if he could make waffles for a family breakfast. Although he had never done so before his mom patiently worked with him in what could be viewed as a lesson in scientific practice. Ingold argues that a young apprentice is led to "develop a sophisticated perceptual awareness of the properties of his surroundings and of the possibilities they afford for action" as he is instructed in "what to look out for, and his attention is drawn to subtle clues that he might otherwise fail to notice."[15] Mom helped Mike to read the recipe; locate, assemble, and position the tools and ingredients for the task; and showed him how to hold and use a measuring spoon, understand the difference between teaspoons and tablespoons, figure out the arithmetic to make double the recipe, measure the flour in a glass cup, break up hardened brown sugar in a cup, place batter into a waffle iron—all the time carefully guiding his engagement with the task and warning what mishaps could occur. She physically encircled him, helping him hold a measuring spoon in his hand as she poured salt into it and ladling batter onto the waffle iron. In essence Mike as novice was being trained in the enskillment that is needed to be a cook. Mom taught when it is important to be precise in measurement (not adding too much salt) and when it is not as important (when adding sugar). (See Figures 8.1 and 8.2.)

Through his waffle making Mike contributed to the well-being of the family and received appreciative assessments; tasting one of his waffles, Mom commented, "Oh man. ((*hand slap*)) They're awesome! Excellent job." (See Figure 8.3.)

Figure 8.3. Mom congratulating child on making waffles with a high five.

Parents such as the Reises actively assisted their children in acquiring important skills they could use in navigating future problem-solving activities, in schoolwork, sports, or helpful activities such as cooking. They were also highly successful in getting their children to do self-care chores without extended argument,[16] as occurred while doing cleanup chores in some families.[17] When the Reis children mildly protested compliance with, for example, taking a bath, they were calmly told that following through with what a parent wants them to do was "non-negotiable."[18] Mom rarely raised her voice, and the protest ended. Parents demonstrated engagement in the lives of children through extended dialogue with them. Through playful and counterfactual talk that occurred in the midst of cuddling in bed on a Saturday morning or while being shepherded to brush teeth,[19] children learned to envision themselves as actors who had career trajectories and could construct hypothetical worlds and as agents who could playfully dispute ideas with their parents, yet eventually complied with what they were told to do.

THE TRACY FAMILY: CULTIVATING CREATIVITY AND JOYFUL EXPLORATION

In contrast to the Reis family, the lives of Miles (age five) and Gwen (age eight) Tracy were not organized with respect to tightly scheduled age-specific sports or academic activities, though Gwen did participate in weekly piano lessons. On weekends the family members enjoyed activities such as excursions to the downtown library, walking on the beach in Santa Monica and making sand castles, playing music together (Dad on keyboard and Gwen on the piano), or simply hanging out in the living room together. What was central to Tracy family life was that in the midst of family-centric activities children and parents engaged in a continuous stream of deeply involving interactions. Parents and children interspersed whatever activity they were undertaking with playful as well as joyful moments of exploration of possible ways the world could be understood, cultivating active engagement in imaginative inquiry about the world.

When the parents in the Tracy family came home, all office work was left behind, and the focus was on the children. Within minutes of when Dad came home he took the children for a half hour walk around the neighborhood. Mom felt this was a very important time of the day for the children to develop cognitive skills in talk with Dad. During neighborhood walks, in the midst of car noises and against the cityscape environment, Dad and children entered into a play world, taking on the characters of different animals (a zebra, a cobra, and a firefly) and elaborating dramas between these animals—chasing, scaring, and assisting one another—as they walked several blocks. In addition, Dad asked his children about their day at school and helped them think of ways of dealing with problems as strangers to a new school. After Gwen discussed her new school friend from Brazil, Dad empathized with his daughter's situation being a newcomer in a school; then, putting her situation into perspective, he commented on how hard it must be for her Brazilian friend to be both new to the school and from another country. The evening walk in the dark was therapeutic, as it provided a daily opportunity for eliciting talk about children's feelings, opinions, and thoughts about their day.

The walk provided the opportunity not only for the Tracy children to dramatically enact and collaboratively describe the habits of animals, but also to hypothesize various things about their natures. As Miles enacted a firefly, Dad became uncertain about how the firefly's "lighter" worked. In so doing he left open the possibility of one of his children resolving what for him was an unsolved mystery. In response Gwen connected the idea of a firefly's "lighter" with how a flashlight works and proposed, "They have some sort of charge." Repeating what Gwen said ("Some sort of charge"), Dad ratified her understanding while expanding on it, saying, "Or maybe electrical charge?" He then introduced another possible explanation for how the firefly produces light with "some kind of chemical process." In response Gwen provided a tentative biological model of how the "lighter" of a firefly could be passed down from one generation to the next, proposing, "maybe charges from *their* mother and their mother before that and their mother before that."

After talk about the properties of fireflies Dad began commentary on the animal he was enacting, the zebra. He pondered how it is that despite having stripes that "are very easy to see" (i.e., having little camouflage), zebras have nonetheless escaped being eaten. He then mentioned the animal that zebras would most have to fear, stating, "*But* the lions haven't got 'em all yet." At this point Gwen joined in the discussion, adding her own perspective on animal behavior: "The lionnesses—uh—hunt the most. The lion is actually (.) sleeping at home while the lio*ness* is doing all the work." To this Dad responded, "Right. That happens in a *lot* of societies where the women do most of the work." Father permitted his daughter to offer her own position about the roles of lions and lionesses. He subsequently added his own commentary on the social roles of women in society. Much like what has been discussed as "science at dinner"[20] or emergent "islands of expertise,"[21] here Dad socialized perspective taking and critical thinking in the midst of a very playful scene. Moments of "occasioned knowledge exploration"[22] occur when children and parents extemporaneously connect new knowledge to existing knowledge in collaborative endeavors, such as the talk about firefly "lighters" and lions' and lionesses' hunting habits during an evening walk. They thus differ from didactic "lessons" in which parents lecture children about science (e.g., discussing how rockets are launched by referring to encyclopedia entries) without a child's inviting them to do so.

Father was very attentive to any indication of his children's wanting to know more about how the world works. He responded to what his children were interested in learning about in age-appropriate ways. When Miles made a comment about lights that were blinking on a parked car,

talk was transformed into a lesson about hazard lights. Dad animated
the car lights talking as he explained what the lights were "saying": "I'm
just stopping here for a minute. Don't bother me, policeman." However,
when Gwen asked about the blinking car lights he provided an elaborated explanation of "hazard lights" for her, detailing their practical uses.
In explaining the meaning of the blinking lights, Dad waited until the
children displayed interest in the developing topic (when Gwen asked
the question, "Do you put that on sometimes?") before providing a more
elaborated discussion. Explanations were child-oriented and carefully fit-
ted to the level of understanding of each child.

A playful rendering of talk[23] was also characteristic of the way that
parents in this family interacted with their children. One Saturday morning in the living room area, Gwen was looking at encyclopedia entries
for parts of the body on the computer, and Dad and Miles were nearby
cleaning the keyboard for her to use. The computer voice stated, "Flexor
digitorum superficialis muscle." Immediately Dad responded playfully,
focusing on one part of the Latin nomenclature. He stated, "Superficialis,
that must not be very important." Gwen's next move was to provide a
further playful rendering, emphasizing "fish" in "Super *fish* ialis." Dad
laughingly responded and then using the sounds of the same words as
Gwen, interjected a line modified from *Mary Poppins*: "Superfishialic
cajifrigilistic exphiladosus?" In the midst of Dad's talk Miles chimed in
with his own further permutation of "superficialis," singing "Super fish!"
Then in his next move Miles provided his own fanciful explanation
about how fish might have evolved into land animals, stating, "But fishes
can't go on the ground. Just if they have—a ear muff . . . A:nd—a:nd—a
breathing lip- atector." Father and children made use of sound play, a
way of sequencing to talk that children delight in,[24] to transform what
the computer voice said. What emerged was a child's hypothesis on the
evolution of fishes. Much like a jazz composition,[25] participants carefully
attended to the sounds of others to produce their own playful elaboration
of ongoing talk.

Sequencing talk to the sound properties of language rather than literal
meaning occurred across multiple exchanges in the family. When Dad
said one night that he was reading a story based on a story by Octavio
Paz, Miles responded, "Paws?" Dad then answered with, "Not like kitten
paws." When Gwen added, "Octave paws. Like octaves on a piano and
paws like a kitten." Miles next riffed, "Pause like stop." Though Dad eventually provided his interpretation of what Octavio meant, he permitted
the children to elaborate their own meanings in the midst of his talk.

While some families in our study infused their directives with threats,[26] an alternative way of framing directives in the Tracy family was through teasing and wordplay. At mealtime one evening the family had been discussing a shy new Brazilian boy in Gwen's classroom. Mom and Dad told Gwen to ask him about the samba, a Brazilian dance, and they discussed their versions of what Brazilian Portuguese sounded like. As the conversation about Brazilian Portuguese wound down, Mom initiated talk about getting ready for bed: "Okay. *Time* to brush your teeth." This was playfully countered by Gwen with "Time to brush your teeth. *That* is not Brazilian." Answering Gwen, Mom then said, "*Samba. Samba* to the bathroom." Here, by tying her talk to Gwen's countermove, she issued a directive that entered a frame of play rather than seriousness. Yet she got results as well. Gwen started to literally dance her way to the bathroom. When Miles responded, "I don't *know* how to samba," in an attempt to stall the directive, Mom, tying her talk to the same form answered, "You'll *learn* how to samba." She then produced an explicit command: "Get in the *bath*room." Providing backup to Mom's directives, Dad then issued direct imperatives in rapid-fire form like a drill sergeant: "*Now. Go. Wash* face, *wash* hands, *brush* teeth." Such forms of bald commands were in fact more frequent in the Tracy family than in another family where there was little playful interaction.[27] While Mom infused her directives with features of playful negotiation, Dad demanded and expected compliance with his directives.

In the Tracy family, as in the Reis family, parents treated their children as capable of carrying out complex tasks and invited their coparticipation in matters of concern to the economics of the household (as in seven-year-old Mike cooking waffles in the Reis family). For example, on returning home from school Mom gave her eight-year-old daughter, Gwen, the task of ordering books from a school pamphlet. She asked Gwen to make up a list of the books she would like to order and their prices. Gwen then devised her own system for prioritizing the books.

Though Mom never mentioned prices as a constraint on the task, Gwen told her, "I bet it's gonna be more than twenty dollars—for all these books." "I don't think we can get them all, only a few." Rather than directly oppose her mother, Gwen instead used hesitations and questions ("Do you really want me to get that?" and "You really do?"), forms of disagreement associated with polite adult conversation.[28] Rather than counter that they already have a copy of the *Guiness Book of World Records*, Gwen asked if her mom knew where an earlier version of the book is in the house. Mom eventually came around to Gwen's position with, "Okay, if you don't want to get it this time that's fine." Gwen proved successful in negotiating the sequence so that she was able to get what she felt was appropriate in a highly mitigated way, using indirect strategies characteristic of adult speech. Miles as well was able to negotiate what he wanted because he has learned how to provide explanations justifying his perspectives in negotiations with parents.[29]

We see from our brief overview of these two families that loving and playful engagement with children, attending to and providing uptake to what they say, appears to have payoffs for socializing children to be responsible and respectful in carrying out activities that contribute to the well-being of the family (whether cooking or figuring out a budget), doing well in school and in extracurricular activities (whether sports or music), and maintaining peaceful relationships with siblings.

THE WALTERS FAMILY: NURTURING SIBLINGS

It is well known that in small, non-Western agrarian societies siblings are highly valued caregivers as well as socializing agents[30] and that sibling care promotes interdependence and prosocial behavior in children.[31] In studies of the Kwara'ae of the Solomon Islands Watson-Gegeo and Gegeo describe dialogues between siblings in which empathic attention by the caretaker is important and in which teaching and instruction occurs.[32] They note, "In nonserious contexts, which encompass most of everyday life, directives and repeating routines are used to teach infants and young children rights, obligations, roles and cultural expectations associated with birth order, gender, and kin relation; to develop their skills in work tasks and other activities; and to teach language and give them practice in interactional skills."[33]

Weisner, summarizing cross-cultural studies, notes, "Most children will rehearse, display and experiment with language capacities and cognitive skills with their siblings well before they will do so with other people."[34] Zukow, studying socialization of rural and urban Mexican children, found that interactive play with sibling caregivers was more advanced than play with adult caregivers.[35] Older siblings' use of both verbal instructions and nonverbal demonstrations help a younger child's transition to a more advanced level of functioning.[36] During communication breakdowns in play interactions with a twenty-one-month-old, Zukow observed that mothers did not adjust their verbal messages, but instead reiterated verbal directions not understood by the child that

Figure 8.4. Helping baby to get from bed to the bathroom.

interfered with completing the activity.[37] By way of contrast the child's three-and-a-half-year-old sibling was able to reframe the interaction and engage the younger child by providing nonverbal demonstrations of what to do as well as commentary. Older siblings differed from parents by at times providing very explicit correction of a younger sibling's activity, calling into question the younger sibling's competence,[38] while providing very explicit models of appropriate performance. While adult caregivers guide the child in subtle ways, "siblings in their own exuberance, impatience, or pride seemed intent on showing off their own competence."[39] Zukow has proposed that because siblings accommodate to young children less than adults, their participation with siblings could encourage infants' development of pragmatic skills.

In our study of videotaped interactions we found that children of dual-earner middle-class Los Angeles families could also act as critical socializing agents of younger siblings, freeing parents for engagement in other household tasks.[40] The forms of participation and engagement in families with toddlers vary quite a lot; they included momentary transactions of entertaining baby when Mom was fully occupied (the Slovenskis), extensive custodial care with a teenage sister (the Morrises), pretend and parallel play and helpful voluntary caretaking while Mom was busy (the Moss family), roughhousing (the Beringer-Potts family), assistance in self-care and in initiation of playful interactions (the Pattersons), and rich engagement, characterized by joint attention in mutually enjoyable activities (the Walterses). In this section we will look at the forms of participation through which ten-year-old sibling caretaker Leslie Walters and her eighteen-month-old sibling, Roxanne, organized involvement and the teaching of enskillment in a routine activity: tooth brushing.

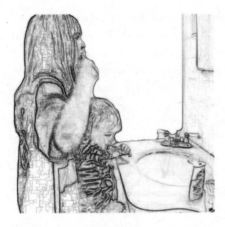

Figure 8.5. Apprenticeship by nesting baby's body.

Investigating a routine task important in the lives of American children, tooth brushing, Tulbert and Goodwin found that explanation and critique were interspersed in ten-year-old Leslie's mentoring of her younger sister into the activity.[41] Leslie's caretaking practices had close resemblances to the way in which Kwara'ae child caretakers go to great lengths to engage in dialogues with their charges during routine activities, naming objects, telling them stories, and so on.[42]

Narration about the steps involved in tooth brushing occurred as the activity unfolded. Directives (e.g., "Roxanne spit") were given as the child manager herself was accomplishing the activity requested (spitting). Demonstrations of how to perform a task resembled those of Kaluli mothers; they provide instructions for children on how to carry out an activity while embodying the activity (cupping the hands to drink water from a stream, peeling a hot cooked banana, or pulling weeds from a garden) as they say, "Do like that."[43]

We will examine in some detail a tooth brushing activity that was launched on a weekday morning, as Leslie and her younger sister, Roxanne, were sitting close together on their parents' bed watching television. Leslie turned to her sister and said, "Roxanne, just stay here. Okay? Roxanne, I need to—go—I need to brush my *teeth*." When subsequently Roxanne turned her body ever so slightly toward her older sister, Leslie quickly readjusted her course of action. She queried, "D'you wanna come and brush your teeth with me? Okay, let's go brush our teeth." Leslie got off the bed and offered her arms for Roxanne to climb into (Figure 8.4). As a highly attuned caregiver, Leslie responded to her sister's change in body orientation by finding ways to include her sister.

When they got to the bathroom, Leslie moved a small stool for Roxanne to stand on before positioning Roxanne on top of it and guiding her to face the sink. Leslie then requested that Roxanne give her the bottle she had in her mouth and put it on the shelf adjacent to the sink. She thus freed both her sister's hands and directed attention to the new task, closing one activity in order to begin another. Stepping on the edge of the bathtub, she retrieved the objects that the two would need for brushing teeth. Stating, "Okay, so," Leslie verbally demarcated the initiation of the actual brushing routine, turned on the water, and lifted Roxanne's toothbrush under the running water. As Leslie was uncapping the toothpaste, Roxanne extended her toothbrush to Leslie. Leslie then initiated a politeness routine, saying, "Thank you Roxanne. Could you say 'you're welcome'?" When no answer was forthcoming, Leslie repeated the request: "Roxanne, could you say 'you're welcome' for me?" Here, as at the onset of the activity, requests such as "could you" and questions were used to structure the activity.

After Leslie prepared her own toothbrush the two were positioned toward the mirror in a nesting formation (see Figure 8.5). As Leslie began brushing her own teeth she gave Roxanne a directive: "Now keep on brushing your teeth Roxanne." At the age of eighteen months, Roxanne was already able to show her familiarity with various steps of this routine through her production of the correct physical gestures. She held her toothbrush out toward her sister, waiting for the application of toothpaste.

After Leslie put her toothbrush on the sink and closed up the toothpaste, she provided closure to the activity: "We're all done." Simultaneously Roxanne took the toothbrush out of her mouth. Through talk and embodied actions and gestures, Leslie expertly turned her sister's physical attention toward the activity and then guided her to its completion.

This example allows a view to how small children's presence in the unfolding of their caregiver's activities affords a site for the socialization of carefully attuned attention to a physical activity. Roxanne knew some aspects of how to physically participate in the unfolding sequence of the routine (in holding out of the brush), though she did not yet know how to embody the rhythm of brushing. Leslie explicitly pointed out the action steps of the sequence as she performed them, providing a verbal narrative of the physical routine.

Across a range of different activities, from reading a book together to teaching Roxanne how to defend herself and kick, the ensemble of practices that were orchestrated in interaction between Leslie and Roxanne demonstrated a high degree of intersubjectivity,[44] supporting Zukow's argument that child caregivers can adjust or finely tune their input to a particular younger child's level of development.[45]

Often Western siblings' sophisticated knowledge of the social world has been largely ignored, Here, and across various dual earner families we have studied, we find, as Zukow has argued,[46] that older siblings can function as competent socializing agents of younger children, and not merely as monitors of the young child's most basic biological needs. Sibling caregiving provides infants with a great diversity of cognitive and social stimulation while older siblings practice nurturing roles. Children learn how to shift frame between moments of more egalitarian peerlike play and the serious business of self-care activities (changing diapers, putting on clothes, brushing teeth, etc.)—creating a rich social learning environment.[47]

THE ANDERSON FAMILY: AFFECT AND MORALITY IN HOMEWORK

The types of frameworks for participation that caretakers and children evolve in the midst of moment-to-moment interaction are consequential for how family members shape each other as moral, social, and cognitive actors. Not all participation entailed the sustained expressions of mutual affection we have seen in the previous examples. Participation frameworks for parent-child interaction can change dramatically over the course of time and be quite consequential for how important features of children's "work" (in the present case, homework) are achieved and relations in the family are maintained. The scene we will examine took place on a Monday evening as eleven-year-old Sandra Anderson, who was just coming down with a cold, was lying on her parents' bed doing her mathematics homework.

What is required for mutual engagement in a task activity? As we saw with Mike Reis making waffles and Roxanne Walters brushing her teeth, in order to carry out relevant courses of action participants must position themselves to see, feel, and in other ways perceive as clearly as possible. This needs to be achieved in ways that are relevant to the activities in progress, considering consequential structure in the environment that is the focus of their attention (e.g., pages of an arithmetic assignment) as well as the orientation of participants toward each other. Participants arrange their bodies precisely to accomplish such work-relevant perception. As Ingold has argued,[48] such arrangements are critical to the education of attention. When participants visibly orient to one another and the environment that is the focus of the work they are attempting to accomplish together, their embodied participation framework displays what we could call a cooperative stance. Not going along with what is being proposed in the present, however, is another possibility; it is what Goffman terms "role distance."[49] Given the possibility of noncooperation by children who have both autonomy and choice, frameworks of mutual engagement should be viewed as accomplishments, as frameworks for the organization of cognition and action that are sustained through the ongoing attentive work of people interacting together. How are such frameworks for mutual engagement achieved?

When Dad in the Anderson family initially began to help Sandra with her homework, she refused to fully cooperate. She did not address her father's question about the math problem. Instead of looking toward her Dad and showing coparticipation with respect to what he had said, she closed her eyes and put her head between her arms. She used whining, "put-upon" prosody that suggested that her father's requests interfered with her ability to watch television.

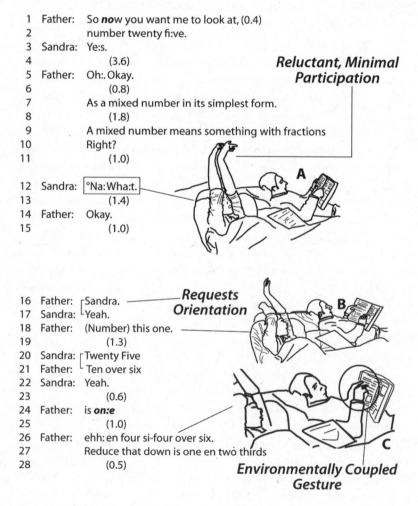

```
 1   Father:   So now you want me to look at, (0.4)
 2             number twenty fi:ve.
 3   Sandra:   Ye:s.
 4                 (3.6)
 5   Father:   Oh:. Okay.
 6                 (0.8)
 7             As a mixed number in its simplest form.
 8                 (1.8)
 9             A mixed number means something with fractions
10             Right?
11                 (1.0)

12   Sandra:   °Na: Wha:t.
13                 (1.4)
14   Father:   Okay.
15                 (1.0)
```

Reluctant, Minimal Participation

A

```
16   Father:  ⌈Sandra.
17   Sandra:  ⌊Yeah.
18   Father:   (Number) this one.
19                 (1.3)
20   Sandra:  ⌈Twenty Five
21   Father:  ⌊Ten over six
22   Sandra:   Yeah.
23                 (0.6)
24   Father:   is on:e
25                 (1.0)
26   Father:   ehh: en four si-four over six.
27             Reduce that down is one en two thirds
28                 (0.5)
```

Requests Orientation

B

Environmentally Coupled Gesture

C

Sandra's father did not get mad but a moment later summoned Sandra, and she answered and turned her head toward him. In line 26 the father further demanded that Sandra attend by producing an explanation that included an environmentally coupled gesture,[50] an action that requires that the listener not only see the speaker making the gesture but also take the gesture into account. However, Sandra made no move to more closely attend to the text that her father was pointing toward.

Both Sandra and her father maintained different ideas about how participation in the homework activity should be orchestrated: When Sandra asked her father how to do a problem, he responded by asking for a pencil. However, Sandra simply wanted her father to do the homework for her rather than figure it out herself. She said, "No. Just tell me. How do you do that." All the while she kept her hands positioned so that she was not looking. Dad then explicitly stated, "I can't just tell you."

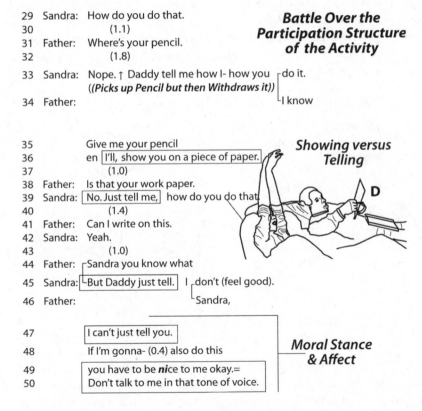

		Battle Over the
29	Sandra: How do you do that.	**Participation Structure**
30	(1.1)	**of the Activity**
31	Father: Where's your pencil.	
32	(1.8)	
33	Sandra: Nope. ↑ Daddy tell me how I- how you ⌐do it.	
	((*Picks up Pencil but then Withdraws it*))	
34	Father: ⌐I know	

35	Give me your pencil	***Showing versus***
36	en │I'll, show you on a piece of paper.│	***Telling***
37	(1.0)	
38	Father: Is that your work paper.	
39	Sandra: │No. Just tell me,│ how do you do that	D
40	(1.4)	
41	Father: Can I write on this.	
42	Sandra: Yeah.	
43	(1.0)	
44	Father: ⌐Sandra you know what	
45	Sandra:└But Daddy just tell.│ I ⌐don't (feel good).	
46	Father: └Sandra,	

47	│I can't just tell you.│	***Moral Stance***
48	If I'm gonna- (0.4) also do this	***& Affect***
49	│you have to be **ni**ce to me okay.=│	
50	│Don't talk to me in that tone of voice.│	

Thus two alternative ways of attending to the work in progress occurred. Sandra refused to move her body into alignment so that she could view the papers that were being worked on. She refused to take a cooperative stance toward the work in progress. An appropriate alignment toward others and the task in progress is crucial for the organization of mundane activities in the lived social world. Father characterized Sandra's actions and refusals to engage in the math task he was helping her with as moral failings.

ACTOR ADDRESSEE

49   you have to be *nice*—to me okay. =

50   (you) Don't talk to me in that tone of voice.

Father made explicit the responsibilities that his daughter had with respect to showing appropriate forms of affective engagement. With his complaint, "You have to be nice to me," he treated Sandra as an actor who was morally responsible for the types of stances she took up as well as the forms of actions she engaged in. However, rather than getting angry, Father refused to continue the activity unless Sandra displayed the appropriate alignment. He then walked out, offering as the reason for this move Sandra's refusal to coparticipate with him (lines 13–14 below) and her derogatory treatment of him (line 16).

1   Father: Do you want me to do this number twenty six
2   (0.8)
3   Sandra: mm hm=
4   Father: =So you understand it better.
5   Sandra: No.
6   (0.8)
7   Father: Okay. Forget it.
8   (1.9)
9   Here.
10   (1.3)
11   Do your homework.
12   (1.0)
13   If you change your mind
14   en you want some help
15   let me know
16   But if you gotta be nice to me.

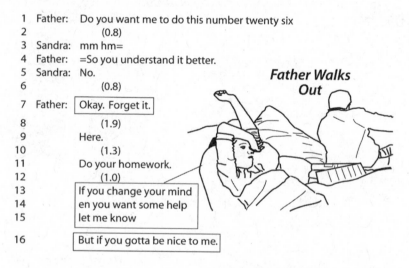

Father Walks Out

The successful completion of the homework session occurred only after Father came back seventeen minutes later, when the participation framework changed dramatically. At first there was tense negotiation about whether Father could show Sandra how to do homework.

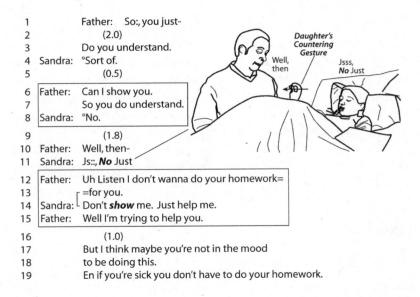

```
 1       Father:    So:, you just-
 2                  (2.0)
 3                  Do you understand.
 4       Sandra:    °Sort of.
 5                  (0.5)

 6  |  Father:    Can I show you.
 7  |             So you do understand.
 8  |  Sandra:    °No.

 9                  (1.8)
10       Father:    Well, then-
11       Sandra:    Js::, No Just

12  |  Father:    Uh Listen I don't wanna do your homework=
13  |           ⌐ =for you.
14  |  Sandra: └ Don't show me.  Just help me.
15  |  Father:    Well I'm trying to help you.

16                  (1.0)
17                  But I think maybe you're not in the mood
18                  to be doing this.
19                  En if you're sick you don't have to do your homework.
```

Father did not become angry and proposed that it was possibly because she was sick that she could not do her homework. He did, however, insist on a particular form of participation, one in which both arranged their bodies so that they were looking at the book. Sandra did dramatically change her orientation, so she could attend to what her father said as well as to anything he might do on the homework pages. The affective tone then changed, and both began laughing while working on the problems.

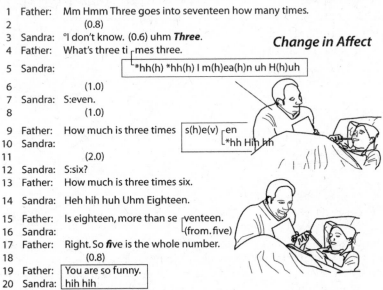

```
 1   Father:   Mm Hmm Three goes into seventeen how many times.
 2             (0.8)
 3   Sandra:   °I don't know. (0.6) uhm Three.
 4   Father:   What's three ti ⌐mes three.
 5   Sandra:             └ *hh(h) *hh(h) I m(h)ea(h)n uh H(h)uh
 6             (1.0)
 7   Sandra:   S:even.
 8             (1.0)
 9   Father:   How much is three times s(h)e(v) ⌐en
10   Sandra:                                └ *hh Hih hh
11             (2.0)
12   Sandra:   S:six?
13   Father:   How much is three times six.
14   Sandra:   Heh hih huh Uhm Eighteen.
15   Father:   Is eighteen, more than se ⌐venteen.
16   Sandra:                        └ (from. five)
17   Father:   Right. So five is the whole number.
18             (0.8)
19   Father:   You are so funny.
20   Sandra:   hih hih
```

Change in Affect

Here we can see how mundane interactive activities such as helping with homework constitute a key site where the work of parenting, with its accompanying cognitive, social, and emotional components, is achieved in the daily round of family life. This instance shows how forms of affect may change over time as a parent holds his ground regarding standards he expects to be upheld. At first when Sandra did not comply, her father made pejorative judgments about her character. He permitted a tense encounter, one he unilaterally walked away from, to change to a situation in which the participants were joyfully laughing with each other as they worked together on the homework problems.

CONCLUSION

Across a range of activities we thus find ways that family members can work together to build forms of cooperative engagement that produce moments of intense pleasure during everyday events of their lives. In the midst of both extracurricular and unstructured leisure activities, during help with homework, and during sibling child care, we find that parents and/or sibling caretakers provide warm, supportive interactions that help their family members explore known and possible meanings of how events in the world are structured, understand feelings of being new-comers or outsiders, congratulate them for successful accomplishments, apprentice them into new activities, and guide them into new ways of approaching difficult endeavors. These activities are often overlaid with heightened forms of affect, gentle touch and smiles. Through the ways in which family members organize participation, including talk and the body, in specific, constantly changing activities, parties shape each other as moral, social and cognitive actors.

NOTES

1. Darrah 2007; Graesch 2009.
2. Larson and Richards 1994.
3. Weisner 2009.
4. M. H. Goodwin 2007.
5. Kremer-Sadlik and Paugh 2007.
6. Levey 2009.
7. Lareau 2003.
8. Zelizer 2005. For an extensive review of theories about middle-class anxiety about parents' ability to secure their children's place in the middle class and the view of childhood as a "period of preparation" and parents' views of "the child as a project," see Kremer-Sadlik and Gutiérrez, this volume.

9. See Kremer-Sadlik and Gutiérrez, this volume, for a description of the series of events occurring one weekday afternoon.

10. Gutiérrez, Izquierdo, and Kremer-Sadlik 2005.

11. Graesch 2009.

12. Levey 2009.

13. Van Hamersveld and Goodwin 2007.

14. Getzels and Csikszentmihalyi 1976; Ochs, Smith, and Taylor 1989.

15. Ingold 2000, 37.

16. Klein, Graesch, and Izquierdo 2009.

17. Goodwin 2006; Klein, Graesch, and Izquierdo 2009.

18. Goodwin, Cekaite, and Goodwin forthcoming.

19. Tulbert and Goodwin 2011.

20. Ochs and Taylor 1992.

21. Crowley and Jacobs 2002.

22. M.H. Goodwin 2007.

23. Fasulo, Liberati, and Pontecorvo 2002.

24. Keenan 1977; Schieffelin 1983.

25. Black 2008.

26. Fasulo, Loyd, and Padiglione 2007; M.H. Goodwin 2006; Klein, Graesch, and Izquierdo 2009.

27. Press 2003.

28. Pomerantz 1984.

29. Goodwin 2005.

30. Maynard 2002; Ochs 1988; Rabain-Jamin, Maynard, and Greenfield 2003; Schieffelin 1990; Weisner and Gallimore 1977; Weisner 1989; Zukow 1989.

31. Watson-Gegeo and Gegeo 1989; Weisner and Gallimore 1977.

32. Watson-Gegeo and Gegeo 1989.

33. Ibid., 61.

34. Weisner 1989, 11.

35. Zukow 1989, 89.

36. Ibid., 91.

37. Ibid., 90.

38. Ibid., 92, 96.

39. Ibid., 98.

40. Goodwin 2010.

41. Tulbert and Goodwin 2011.

42. Watson-Gegeo and Gegeo 1989.

43. Schieffelin 1990, 76.

44. Goodwin 2010.

45. Zukow 1989, 97.

46. Ibid., 254.

47. Goodwin 2010.

48. Ingold 2000, 37.

49. Goffman 1961.

50. C. Goodwin 2007.

Stress

RENA REPETTI, DARBY SAXBE,
AND SHU-WEN WANG

We may all wonder how the ups and downs of life outside the home affect what goes on inside the family. Do stressful experiences permeate the domestic sphere? If a father has a bad day at work, will he treat his wife and children differently that evening? When we examined the behavior and physiology of CELF family members after work, we did find evidence that job stressors influenced life at home. However, the effects were not "one-size-fits-all." First, the nature of work-to-home spillover differed for mothers and fathers. Among fathers job stress appeared to have a visible effect on their outward social behavior at home, whereas among mothers the impact was more internal, with evidence of lingering stress hormones in the evening after work. Even within each gender, the consequences of job stress varied depending on characteristics of the parent and the family. The responses of fathers who had trouble regulating their negative emotional states or who were unsatisfied with their marriages differed from the responses of fathers who generally maintained an even emotional keel or were in happier marriages. Mothers who described their marriages as less satisfying or performed a highly disproportionate share of the household labor seemed to recover less readily from the physiological effects of a stressful day at work.

WHAT WE ALREADY KNEW

Our analysis of the CELF data was guided by previous research on how parents' experiences at work shape family life. One of the ways that psychologists have addressed those questions is by looking closely at the lives of people who hold different kinds of jobs. Employees who say they are satisfied with their jobs, or who describe greater autonomy at work, seem to have happier family lives. They show more warmth and responsiveness to their children and describe their marriages as more satisfying. Of course, correlation does not necessarily imply causation. But longitudinal studies follow the same group of people over months or years and are therefore able to tease out the effects of stable individual characteristics, such as personality traits, that shape life both at work and at home.[1] These studies indicate that experiences of achievement and fulfillment at work can, over time, carry over into the family and have a positive impact on relationships. On the flip side is chronic job stress, which can lead to signs of personal distress, including symptoms of depression, and can also impair marital and parent-child relations. Employees whose dealings with coworkers and supervisors are conflictual and unsupportive seem to have less affectionate and angrier interactions with their children and to experience more marital tension and arguments. Similarly, workers who face constant demands and time pressure on the job report more interpersonal tensions at home, get into more conflicts with family members, and know less about their children's daily activities and whereabouts.[2]

Some psychologists have considered how behavior and emotion in the same family differ from one day to the next. For example, prior to the CELF project, Rena Repetti and her students studied air traffic controllers in Southern California, mothers employed in white-collar jobs in New York City, and a different sample of dual-earner middle-class couples in Los Angeles.[3] In each study, we measured the stressfulness of each day at work for several consecutive days, asking our employed participants to rate their workload and the quality of their social interactions with coworkers and supervisors. We wanted to see if the family's interactions differed following a particularly jam-packed day at work or one marred by a tense exchange with a coworker. To assess how the employed person interacted with family members on each day after work, we sometimes used videotapes and we always asked family members to describe social interactions in their family each evening.

Across studies, when we compared these two sets of measures— daily job stress and daily family interactions—two interesting patterns emerged. On the one hand, more stressful days at work were often followed by more expressions of anger and irritability at home, compared to the same employed person's behavior after less stressful days. For instance, when describing marital interactions after the stressful workdays, both the employed person and his or her spouse were more likely to say that the employee was "impatient," or "sarcastic," or "a little touchy" that night, or that he or she started an argument or disagreed with something the spouse said. Interactions with a child were more likely to involve the use of disciplinary tactics such as reminding, yelling, or even punishing the child. This pattern is called "negative emotion spillover," based on the idea that the frustrations and pressures of the workday spilled over into the home, where they continued to be expressed in the mood and behavior of the employed parent or spouse.

The second observed pattern is social withdrawal: more stressful days at work followed by an overall decline in the employee's expression of all emotion, both positive and negative, and an overall decline in the amount and intensity of his or her social behavior. Compared to the slower, easier, or more socially serene workdays, after stressful days at work the employed person was more likely to say that he or she "wanted to be alone," "was too tired to interact," "didn't want to talk," "wanted some quiet time to be alone," or simply "ignored" the spouse. Spouses' ratings were in agreement with the description of a less involved, more distracted family member. When we looked at videotapes taken at a work site day care center of mother-child reunions, we saw that after fast-paced and demanding days at work mothers spoke less and their attention was less likely to be completely focused on their preschool-aged child.

How can we reconcile two such seemingly different responses to job stressors? One paints a picture of an employed person backing off from family members and the other suggests a more intense and more irritable person. We wondered how these patterns would appear without the filtering of individual perception and reporting; what would they look like in the raw? Would we find that some people respond to job stress with social withdrawal and that a different group responds with irritability? Alternatively, after a difficult day on the job might the same stressed-out and fatigued person try to avoid social interaction and then become impatient and disagreeable if a spouse's request for assistance or a child's question interferes with that goal? What does wanting to be alone or feeling too tired to interact with others look like to an outside observer who doesn't know what the individual is thinking or feeling?

CELF PARENTS' SOCIAL INTERACTIONS IN THE FIRST HOUR HOME

The CELF study was uniquely positioned to shed new light on this subject; it could show us how employed parents actually behaved at home after work. Researchers would finally see what husbands and wives, mothers and fathers, actually say and do when they are with their loved ones at home after work. When psychologists study social behavior, they quantify—often in minute detail—what they see. They rate qualities such as degree of responsiveness to another person, facial expressions, and emotional reactions to others; the codes they use often require a painstakingly detailed analysis of social behavior every few seconds. With this type of approach, it would be easy to get lost in the over 1,600 hours of video that CELF collected. We had to devise a unique strategy to describe social interaction in the CELF families. Belinda Campos, a researcher at CELF, hit upon the idea of systematically sampling and coding thin slices of video.

Working with another CELF researcher, Tatyana Plaksina, Repetti, and Campos devised a coding system that would be applied to thirty-second segments of videotape sampled every ten minutes from the continuous footage taken in the homes of the families in our study. The sampling started as soon as a parent returned home from work and ended when the cameras stopped rolling at night. Before long, a larger team, which included graduate students Shu-wen Wang and Jacqueline Sperling, and ten UCLA undergraduates, was assembled. We worked for a full year applying the detailed coding scheme to the mothers' and fathers' interactions captured on videotape on the two weekday afternoons and evenings. By examining video recordings of family interaction at home at ten-minute intervals and characterizing whom the parents were with and what they were saying and doing, we were able to sketch a picture of their social behavior after work. The result after a year of coding was an archive consisting of long strings of numbers that quantified the social and emotional qualities of each parent's interactions with family members on two weekday afternoons and evenings.

We can only put faith in these strings of numbers as reliably reflecting meaningful aspects of social behavior if the codes they represent were applied in an equivalent way by all coders. Recall that a rather large team, more than ten coders, was involved in the coding effort; how did we ensure that Coder A's coding was comparable to that of Coder B's . . . and Coder C's . . . and Coder D's? This is where inter-rater reliability comes in. Inter-rater reliability reflects the consistency with which the coding system was implemented. To ensure a high level of inter-rater reliability, all members of the CELF coding team were intensively trained on practice video clips and required to reach a high level of inter-rater reliability (we used the criterion of an intraclass correlation coefficient = .80) before being allowed to code. Afterwards, all coders overlapped on 10 percent of the video, and inter-rater reliability was computed regularly to ensure the quality of the coding (i.e., that intraclass correlation coefficients remained above .80). Crucial to this process were regular weekly meetings in which all members of the coding team gathered to discuss and resolve coding concerns and questions.[4]

CELF researchers, led by Wang, used the codes to see how experiences at work related to social behavior at home in the evening.[5] Reasoning that the effects of job stress would be most readily observed soon after leaving work, we decided to focus our analysis on the social interactions that occurred in the first hour after each parent arrived home. Based on prior research showing that job stress is associated with social withdrawal and negative emotion spillover, the analysis honed in on three of the codes. Two describe how vigorous the individual's social behavior was during each thirty-second slice of video. One of the "social vigor" codes, scored on a 0–3 scale, measures the intensity of response to another's initiation for interaction. For example, if a spouse asks, "How was your day?" the person whose behavior is being coded could simply ignore the question (and receive a 0 for being "not at all" responsive), grunt (and be assigned a score of 1 for low response intensity), or say, "Good, how was your day?" (which would be coded a 2 for moderate response intensity); an effusive and detailed response that included details of the day would get a high response intensity score of 3. The other social vigor code was talking, and it was also scored on a 0–3 scale. Complaining about work continuously at the dinner table would earn a score of 3, whereas complete silence would result in a score of 0 for that thirty-second clip. A few words would receive a score of 1 for minimal talking, and a conversation in which the target asks a couple of questions while also responding to another's questions would be rated a 2 for moderate talking.

Although the two social vigor codes might seem similar, they actually tapped different dimensions of social behavior. First, a response intensity rating could be assigned only if another person made some bid for attention during the thirty-second clip. The other social vigor code, talking, was scored regardless of any particular behavior on the part of others who were present. However, even when both codes were applied, the ratings could differ quite a bit. For example, a parent could do plenty of talking while ignoring an initiation from a child, which would earn a high score for talking and a low score for response intensity. Alternatively, a parent who said little but hugged her child when she described a bad day at school would merit a low score for talking and a high response intensity score.

Because the two social vigor codes reveal nothing about the emotional tone of an interaction, the other key variable was a measure of negative emotion displayed by the parent. The scores, which could range from 1 (none at all) to 7 (many), reflected both the effusiveness and the quantity of negative emotion behaviors, such as facial movements (e.g., frowns, raised eyebrows), body language (e.g., turning away), and voice quality (e.g., angry, stern). Taken together, the social vigor and negative emotion codes told us quite a bit about how active and intense, and how negative, the parent was during the first hour after returning home. This information allowed us to recognize social withdrawal and negative emotion spillover if they were present.

The sheer descriptive power of these codes—response intensity, talking, and negative emotion—paint a picture of how working parents interact with spouse and children during their first hour home after work. We observed that the men and women in our study showed similar amounts of talking (low to moderate), whether they were interacting with their spouse or with their school-aged child. Interestingly, although men and women generally expressed little negative emotion, women displayed more negative emotion in their first hour interactions with husband as well as school-aged child. Men, on the other hand, responded to their wives with greater intensity than wives did to their husbands; however, there was no difference between men and women in levels of response intensity to their children in their first hour interactions.

Of course, we were primarily interested in how experiences on the job would be linked with social behavior after work. In addition to video recordings of their family interactions, twice each day at work—once before lunch and once before leaving at the end of the day—CELF parents told us about their work experiences. One set of questions asked about the demands on their time and the pressure to perform tasks quickly. Another set of questions asked them to rate how they felt—resentful? tense? distant?—during interactions with coworkers and supervisors that day. The validity of both measures is documented in our prior work; there are significant correlations between these scales and objective measures of workload, social support at work, and satisfaction with work relationships.[6] Likewise, both measures demonstrate adequate internal consistency in prior research,[7] as well as in our CELF families. With only two weekdays of video, the CELF study was not well designed to compare the same person's social behavior on more stressful and less stressful days. After all, the chances were low that the two days that we happened to videotape would capture one high-stress workday and one low-stress workday from each member of a couple. Therefore, each individual's job ratings were averaged across the two days and then, given the high correlation between the two measures, aggregated to form a composite score, a single overall assessment of the stressfulness of each parent's job over the two days. The ratings that the coders made of each parent's social behavior during the first hour at home on the two weekdays were also averaged.

Armed with these two sets of ratings—the stressfulness of the parents' jobs and the parents' social behavior during their first hour at home after work—Wang tested correlations between them. The husbands' and wives' data were analyzed separately because of evidence from the research literature that the two sexes may respond differently to stressors. At first glance, there were no unambiguous and convincing patterns suggesting that parents with more stressful jobs behaved any differently when they got home from work than did the parents who described wonderful relationships with supervisors or said they worked at a relaxed pace. But then Wang dug a little deeper. Some earlier studies, including publications coming out of our own group (though not based on the sample of CELF families), suggested that patterns of negative emotion spillover or social withdrawal may differ according to individual differences in personality or differences in the quality of family relationships. In one of those earlier studies, both patterns—withdrawal and negative spillover—were more likely to be observed in families with higher levels of conflict and more expressions of anger.[8] In another previous study, individuals who experienced symptoms of anxiety and depression were more prone to carry their stress into the home; both withdrawal and negative spillover were observed in the portion of the sample that reported more symptoms of emotional distress.[9]

Parents in the CELF study had all completed standard measures of marital satisfaction and neuroticism, which is the tendency to experience negative emotional states. The neuroticism scale asks about feeling "worthless," "angry," "depressed," and "tense or jittery." Individuals who score high on neuroticism are thought to have trouble regulating negative emotional states like these and are perceived to be less emotionally stable. The scale we used has shown good internal consistency and has been well validated in other studies.[10] To assess marital satisfaction, couples told us about their feelings of closeness and happiness and agreements and disagreements in a variety of areas, such as friends, in-laws, and the handling of finances. This scale has been shown to discriminate well between satisfied and dissatisfied couples and demonstrates good internal consistency.[11]

Working from the clues in the earlier studies, Wang tested whether men and women in happier marriages, or those with lower neuroticism scores, responded to job stress differently than did the men and women who described their marriages as less satisfying, or those who scored at the higher end of the neuroticism scale. Bingo! Multiple regression statistical analyses revealed a very clear and consistent pattern in the men's data. Among these husbands, we could see evidence of both withdrawal and negative emotion spillover. The impact of job stress was there but depended on the husbands' levels of marital satisfaction and neuroticism.[12]

On the one hand, among the husbands in happier marriages and among the men who scored lower on the neuroticism scale, job stress was associated with something that looks very much like social withdrawal at home. Among these men, as the scores on the indicators of job stress got higher we found that they spoke less to their wives and they expressed less negative emotion with both wives and children when they returned home. For example, for the men who described themselves as happily married, there was a strong *negative* correlation between their experience of stress at work and their expressions of negative emotion, both with their wives (r = -.71) and with their children (r = -.67). Our analysis was based only on occasions when the men in the CELF families were with other family members. The focus here is the *quality* of the interactions that fathers had with their wives and children during their first hour home as a function of stressors at work. We learned that for the more happily married men and men who reported little emotional distress involvement in those interactions seemed to decrease as stress at work increased.

On the other hand, among the husbands who were not as happy in their marriages and among the men who described more emotional distress, a more stressful job was linked with signs of negative emotion spillover after work. Within this group, as ratings of stress at work increased, so did the indicators of vigorous social behavior. During the first hour at home, they did *more* talking with wives and their social responses to wives were *more* intense and elaborated. Perhaps most important, they also expressed *more* negative emotion, with wives as well as with children. In contrast to the correlations presented above for the happily married men, among the men who described lower levels of marital satisfaction, there was a moderate *positive* correlation between their experience of stress at work and their expressions of negative emotion, both with their wives (r = +.30) and with their children (r = +.34). In short, the men who said that they were less happily married and who experienced more emotional distress showed evidence of negative emotion spillover; they appeared to be both more active and involved in social interaction—and more negative—as stress at work increased.

None of these patterns were observed in the wives' responses. Whether or not they were happy in their marriages and whether or not they reported symptoms of emotional distress, there was simply no connection between what a wife and mother's life at work was like and how she responded to family members after work. But the husbands' data did tell a story. At least on the two weekdays that we studied them, the men in the CELF families behaved differently depending on two factors: how much stress they described at work and how "distressed" they said they were. In our analysis, "distress" could mean either how much anxiety and depression they reported generally experiencing or how satisfied they were in their marriages.

STRESS HORMONES AND THE MARITAL ENVIRONMENT

Although the husbands' social behavior seemed to "tell a story" about how their workdays were carried home with them, it was a different piece of the CELF puzzle that yielded a series of significant patterns for wives. Cortisol is a stress hormone that is released into saliva and that shows a regular daily pattern (peaking in the early morning and decreasing across the day). CELF participants were given portable vials so they could sample their saliva at home and at work, and they turned in three days of samples, taken at regular intervals in the morning, late morning, afternoon, and evening.

CELF researcher Darby Saxbe mapped each spouse's average cortisol trajectory, using all twelve samples across three days to get a sense of each person's daily decline in cortisol, something known as a diurnal slope. Earlier studies had established a relationship between this diurnal slope and other measures of health and well-being; for example, several studies of women with cancer found that women with flatter cortisol slopes, in which cortisol starts out lower in the morning and decreases less over the day, reported more fatigue and even had earlier mortality than women with steeper slopes.[13] Other studies linked flatter cortisol slopes with depression, burnout, and chronic stress, and one study found that working mothers who reported more relationship problems had flatter slopes of cortisol as well.[14] Given this body of evidence, we were curious whether the marital satisfaction of the couples in the CELF study would correlate with their diurnal patterns of cortisol. As it turned out, it did—but only for the wives. Women who reported greater marital dissatisfaction had flatter slopes of cortisol, the same pattern linked with more health problems and life stressors in other studies. For husbands, cortisol and marital satisfaction did not appear to be linked.[15]

Wives' marital satisfaction not only predicted their cortisol slope but also seemed to affect their pattern of recovery after a busy day at work. To explore the question of how the workday affected evening cortisol levels, we used the same measures of workload and negative social interactions at work mentioned above. Whereas Wang's analysis matched job stress ratings to only two weekdays of videotaping, the cortisol analysis could capitalize on all three days of job stress ratings provided by the CELF couples because cortisol samples were collected on each of these days. On the highest workload days, both husbands and wives actually showed lower than usual cortisol levels in the evening—suggesting an exaggerated overcorrection by the structures in the brain and body that regulate cortisol. For women, however, marital satisfaction affected the trajectory of this recovery, such that the "overcorrection" appeared only among happily married women. Women in more unhappy relationships not only showed flatter cortisol during the day, but weaker recovery after busy days at work.[16] While it may seem odd that the cortisol results emerged only for women, it actually dovetails with previous findings in the public health and epidemiology literature. It has long been known that marriage carries an overall health benefit for men: married men get a boost in longevity and well-being across the board, when contrasted with single men. In contrast, women appear to be more sensitive to the quality of the marital environment. For example, studies that have contrasted happily married, unhappily married, and single women have found that happily married women appear healthiest, while unhappily married women tend to fare worse than single women.[17] The fact that maritally dissatisfied women in the CELF study had flatter cortisol slopes and impaired recovery from work suggests one physiological mechanism through which poor marital quality may specifically affect women's health.

Why was marital satisfaction so important for wives' cortisol patterns but not for husbands'? Was there something about the quality of the marriage that might affect women's everyday stress more than that of men? Perhaps women in unhappy marriages were doing a greater share of the work around the house. In other words, measures indicating dissatisfaction with marriage might be a proxy for an unfair domestic arrangement. To test this question, Saxbe used the scan sampling

of activities data to see what spouses were actually doing at home. As
described in the appendix, a researcher recorded the locations and primary activities of every family member at regular ten-minute intervals.
For example, a tracking entry tells us that at 7:20 A.M. on Day 1, Macy
was located in the kitchen and that she was engaged in the activity of
packing lunches for her kids. At the same time her husband, Andre,
was in the bathroom, taking a shower. Saxbe worked with a research
assistant to sort more than five thousand activity entries into categories
like "housework," "leisure," "childcare," and "personal care." She compared husbands' and wives' activities over four days of scan sampling
and found striking differences. Within the average couple, compared
to wives, husbands spent about twice as much of their time at home
engaged in leisure, such as watching television, reading the newspaper,
or listening to music. And they spent only about two-thirds of the time
doing housework as did their wives.

Looking at the activities data in relation to evening cortisol levels,
even more interesting results emerged. Unsurprisingly, people who spent
more of their time at home doing housework showed less "recovery" at
the end of the day—that is, their cortisol levels didn't drop as much from
the afternoon to the evening—and parents who devoted more of their
time to leisure activities showed greater recovery. What seemed to matter most, however, was not parents' *absolute* allotment of housework or
leisure time but the time they were spending *relative* to their spouse.
In other words, in couples where women were spending a lot more time
doing housework than their husbands and a lot less time in leisure, those
wives were more likely to show diminished recovery at the end of the
day.[18] This result confirmed our initial hunch that women's cortisol patterns might reflect their feelings about the division of the labor within
their households. It came as a surprise that, while there was evidence of
job stress being carried back into the family by both husbands and wives,
the findings for fathers related to their behavior at home and the findings
for mothers related to their stress hormone levels. If we had focused on
only one "system"—their overt social behavior, for example, but not cortisol—we might not have captured different patterns of results for men
and women.

PUTTING IT ALL TOGETHER

How were social withdrawal, negative emotion spillover, and flattened
cortisol slopes manifested in the CELF families? From having viewed the

videotapes many times we knew that the CELF fathers didn't go around yelling or screaming at their children and wives, and they didn't completely ignore them either. What exactly was being reflected in higher or lower response intensity scores for those thirty-second slices of video, or higher or lower levels of cortisol, at different times of day? To understand these patterns better, it helps to look closely at a couple of scenes from family life. Focusing exclusively on the CELF families in which fathers reported high levels of stress at work, we identified one who reported a low level of distress on one indicator (marital dissatisfaction) and one who reported a high level of distress on both indicators (marital dissatisfaction and neuroticism). The early part of their evenings at home after work should help us to understand what social withdrawal and negative emotion spillover look like in the lives of middle class families.

ANDRE: A QUIET PRESENCE

Andre illustrates social withdrawal as a response to job stress. His ratings of both workload and the quality of his social relationships at work indicate above-average levels of job stress, and his marital satisfaction score was higher than any other father's in our study. Here's a man who is very happy in his marriage and stressed by his job. Let's see what happens when he returns home from work. On the first weekday of video recording the family followed their common routine of going out to dinner. Because the videographers weren't prepared to film in a restaurant— this family was one of the first to participate in the CELF study and this scenario had not been anticipated—their dinner was not captured on tape. Once the family returns home from the restaurant, Andre immediately tends to his aquariums, a favored hobby of his. During this time, Andre occasionally responds to comments made by his wife, Macy, and children, Peter (age ten) and Nancy (age eight), who are nearby, but doesn't initiate conversation. He seems very calm and relaxed as he works with the aquariums.

When those tasks are completed, Andre asks Peter if he needs help with homework, but Peter wants to work on origami with his dad. For the next forty minutes, while sitting on the floor of Peter's bedroom, father and son patiently work together to try to create a complex shooting star design by folding paper. They are following instructions from a book, and both are very involved and focused on the project. At times Andre reads and patiently guides Peter's folding; at other points Andre takes the origami and silently works to figure it out himself. Peter occasionally reads to his father from the origami book; Andre hears and answers "mmhmm" but doesn't look up. There is little talking but plenty of collaboration, watching, and experimenting with different approaches. There is a quiet connection between father and son, as they both appear to be absorbed in the task and cooperate with each other to reach the goal. As they work together, their mood remains positive, with occasional smiles and giggles, and neither gets frustrated or upset.

When Nancy enters the room and sings a silly song that she learned at Girl Scouts, she could be perceived as annoying and disruptive. Neither Andre nor Peter, however, seems bothered by the song that Nancy keeps repeating; they remain focused on the task. Not long after, father and son decide to stop and continue the project tomorrow. There are twenty-eight steps to produce the shooting star, and they've gotten about halfway through. Andre, however, continues to work on it for a few more minutes. They then carefully store the not yet completed paper star for the next day.

As the children transition to their bedtime routines, Andre and Macy quietly go through paperwork at the table. Most of it comes from school, and they occasionally consult about decisions (e.g., choices of after-school activities for the children), but most of the time they work side-by-side in silence. During that time, Macy tells Andre about a problem with a planned school field trip in Peter's class; there isn't enough space on the bus for all the children. Andre volunteers to help out by going on the field trip, and Macy fills out the volunteer form for him. For the most part, Macy and Andre are focused on reading, filling out forms, and other paperwork and don't say much to one another. Even when Nancy comes into the room and joins her parents at the table, again singing a silly song, Andre ignores her and stays on task.[19]

It's easy to see why, when the CELF coders checked in every ten minutes, Andre earned low scores for response intensity, talking, and negative emotion. We don't know if he "felt too tired to talk," as the participants in previous studies have reported, but he did seem to prefer to focus his attention on tasks—such as tending to the aquariums, origami, and paperwork—over conversation. It's interesting to observe this very happily married man jump into family activities—making origami with Peter, looking at paperwork, arranging to attend a school field trip. He doesn't go off to watch television or read a newspaper alone. He's physically near his family, often collaborating with them, and there is no sign of negative mood or annoyance. At the same time, he doesn't choose to capitalize on the many opportunities for conversation with wife and children that are presented. Those are the kinds of opportunities that the father in our next family is quick to grab.

STEVE: AN IRRITATED TENSENESS

Steve presents an interesting contrast to Andre. His ratings of workload and negative social interactions at work were also above average, in fact even a bit higher than Andre's, indicating a high level of perceived job stress. But his marital satisfaction score was below the average score of other CELF husbands and far below Andre's rating. Moreover, his score on the neuroticism scale was almost twice the average score. According to the findings described earlier, his behavior when he returns home from work might tell us something about what constitutes negative emotion spillover in the everyday lives of middle-class fathers.[20]

Like Andre, this father also jumps into family activities as soon as he gets home. Steve checks in with everyone and their activities, asking questions about school, the children's day, and meal preparation. He reminds his wife to take her vitamins, takes the children on an errand with him, and gets involved in tasks that are of direct relevance to his family. He's proactive in engaging the children and finding opportunities to teach them about the world. At the same time, there are numerous instances in which he complains, criticizes, and expresses irritation, almost all directed toward his wife, Dinah. In fact, within just the first fifteen minutes of his arrival home, we see a number of behaviors in rapid succession that could be a reflection of a negative emotion spillover process. For example, soon after his arrival home, he and Dinah have a brief conversation about the fact that he was not able to find a bill that he was supposed to mail that morning. When Dinah reminds him that items to be dropped in the mail are always left on the table by the front door, he responds in an almost prosecutorial style.

STEVE: I told you it wasn't that big of a deal, right? Didn't I?

DINAH: Um, no, you didn't.

STEVE: I didn't?

DINAH: No . . .

STEVE: I remember tapping the words "slightly consternated."

DINAH: Oh.

STEVE: You don't remember that?

DINAH: Yeah.

STEVE: You do remember that?

DINAH: Mm hmm.

STEVE: Then I'm correct.

DINAH: Does that mean ((*pause*)) that it's no big deal?

Eight-year-old Gwen enters the kitchen at that moment and asks when she will be going to the home of her mother's cousin, Fran. While Dinah explains that Fran has been sick, Steve responds to his daughter's question by saying, "Not for a long, long time," and chuckles. After a pause, he adds, "until she gets a house. Her place is too small to hang out at, Mag." It's hard not to view these comments as a slight against his wife's cousin. A bit later, while sitting on a small balcony outside their bedroom, Dinah talks to the researcher about how important this cousin is to her, and her eager anticipation of a family gathering at which they will hang out together. Dinah explains that Fran's "energy and excitement about life" has always "rejuvenated me" and acted as a source of inspiration. Steve must know all this, so his put-down of a treasured cousin in front of the camera must have stung.

Less than a minute after Steve's comments about Fran, he asks Dinah if she and their five-ear-old son, Miles, had found a library book that was missing. When mom reports that they are looking for it, he replies, "Doesn't look like he's looking for it . . ." In what appears to be an effort to vouch for her son, Dinah tells her husband that Miles has been working hard all afternoon and that they will find it, not to worry. Shortly after that, in response to his wife's question about whether he had gotten a chance to fill out some school forms for Miles, Steve comments that he received "a chilly reception tonight." Dinah sounds hurt and misunderstood as she replies, "No, I'm sorry." Her husband then adds, ". . . racing home to get one of those."

A few minutes later, Dinah seems to make one more attempt to turn things around. She describes how she helped Miles to choose a magazine to order through a program at his school. She says, "It was really cool because I had him write down his favorite choices, and I had him rate them. And then he added the numbers up." The process resulted in Miles choosing to order a subscription to *Highlights Magazine*. Despite Dinah's pleased tone, Steve is quick to criticize the choice by saying that they've had that magazine in the past and either the old copies are still around the house or he may have thrown them out because they were an eyesore without any good information in them. Dinah's response, "I think he can read them in the library," seems like a surrender.

With so much hostility apparently being directed toward Dinah, it seems almost like a relief when, at that point, Steve decides to take the children with him to run an errand. Steve is handy at fixing things, and he needs a part to repair the family washing machine. He and the children take a walk to a local hardware store that stays open late, and during that time he's relaxed and talkative with the children, but as soon as they get back to the house he seems to tense up. Dinah reports that the dinner she prepared is just about ready; some baked potatoes are cooling on the kitchen table. Steve walks into the kitchen and, seeming almost to be talking to himself but loud enough for Dinah to hear, asks, "Has the oven been turned off?" Then he answers his own question, with a loud "No." After a pause, he adds, "Forget to turn off the oven a lot . . . a pet peeve of mine."

Steve's behavior appears to be consistent with the negative emotion spillover findings from previous studies in which both members of a couple agreed that after more difficult days at work the stressed partner was impatient or touchy or disagreed with something the spouse said. The CELF coders assigned Steve high scores for response intensity, talking, and negative emotions. We can see that those thirty-second glimpses into his first hour at home accurately characterized what actually went on. That evening, he was an involved, curious, and active family member. It is also the case that at times Steve seemed impatient, was sometimes upset by and disappointed in his wife's responses to his questions, and admitted to being peeved. If we use Steve's family to tell us what negative spillover looks like, we don't find an overtly angry and aggressive man, scolding his children or openly insulting his wife. Instead, we find an active and involved father, whose interactions with his wife, in particular, often have a tense and even combative quality. It is easy to imagine Dinah feeling let down or hurt by his complaints and annoyed reactions during that first hour.

CORTISOL IN ANDRE'S AND STEVE'S FAMILIES

At the same time, what was happening to cortisol levels in our two exemplar families? Here, we focus on wives, not husbands, since results emerged only among them. Macy's marital satisfaction score—like her husband's—is well above the average for CELF wives. Also like her husband, Dinah has lower than average marital satisfaction; in fact, it is even lower than her husband's score. Fittingly, Macy consistently has higher morning cortisol than Dinah. She also tends to have lower evening cortisol than Dinah. In fact, on the evening that we described earlier, Dinah had one of the highest evening cortisol levels in the study. Since high morning cortisol and low evening cortisol are both markers of a steeper diurnal cortisol slope, the pattern that researchers have found to be "healthier" and more adaptive, it looks like both Macy and Dinah fit our expectations for how marital satisfaction might be linked with cortisol.

This finding seems to make sense when we remember how the husbands in our two families coped with their own workday experiences. Both fathers were under stress at work; this may have taken a toll on their abilities to connect with their families. Andre limited his conversation with family members, which contributed to a quiet, fairly low energy night at home. Steve, on the other hand, showed more tense and irritable behavior. Furthermore, the emotional valence of both husbands' behavior may also be tied to their own cortisol levels, introducing another piece to the puzzle that considers how stress physiology and social behavior may be linked. In a separate analysis, we found a statistically significant negative correlation between the men's average amount of negative emotion expression in the home and their average diurnal cortisol slopes on the two observed weeknights of the study (r = -38). For husbands, steeper cortisol slopes were associated with less negative emotion expression with family members after work.[21] This suggests that for someone like Andre—who did not display overt signs of annoyance or negative mood—taking a more withdrawn and emotionally neutral approach to interacting with family members may over time confer some of the health benefits associated with steeper or more adaptive cortisol slopes. For Steve, on the other hand, our data suggest that displays of criticism and hostility would ultimately be linked with a flatter and less healthy cortisol slope. Thinking about which family environment might be more "stressful" for the other partner, it is likely that Steve's overt touchiness and complaints presented more of a challenge for Dinah than Andre's quiet behavior did for Macy. While it is always difficult to extrapolate from only a few cases, it does seem fitting that Dinah showed a cortisol profile that is consistent with higher stress levels overall.

CONCLUSION

The way families cope with everyday stressors, like the transition from work to home, is not monolithic. Our research illustrates that individual differences in relationship quality (i.e., marital satisfaction) and personality (i.e., neuroticism) help to shape the patterns of behavior that individual working parents show in response to work stress. Negative emotion spillover and social withdrawal represent different ways of responding to a difficult day at work. Which strategy, if any, a person chooses may depend on a host of factors, including those explored in our research. Factors like marital satisfaction and the division of household labor appear to influence physiological stress as well, as our research on the hormone cortisol seems to suggest. While we found different patterns of results for husbands and for wives, the underlying theme is clear: in understanding the interplay between work and home, particularly the influence of job stressors on the family, it is important to consider an individual's gender, personality, and family circumstances. This makes the complexity and richness of the CELF study especially warranted as we explore the life of the family both inside and outside the home.

NOTES

1. E.g., Costigan, Cox, and Cauce 2003.

2. For reviews of the research literature summarized above, see Bumpus, Crouter, and McHale 1999; Perry-Jenkins, Repetti, and Crouter 2000; Repetti 2005.

3. Repetti 1989, 1994; Repetti and Wood 1997; Story and Repetti 2006.

4. More detail about the coding and inter-rater reliability process can be found in Wang, Repetti, and Campos 2011a. Inter-rater reliability is just one of several methodological issues that arise when coding naturalistic family interaction; a more in-depth discussion of these issues from the point of view of psychologists can be found in Repetti, Wang, and Sears 2011.

5. Wang, Repetti, and Campos 2011a.

6. Repetti 1989, 1994.

7. Ibid.; Repetti and Wood 1997.

8. Story and Repetti 2006.

9. Repetti and Wood 1997.

10. Costa and McCrae 1992.

11. Locke and Wallace 1959.

12. Readers are referred to the Wang, Repetti, and Campos (2011a) article for a detailed report of the neuroticism findings.

13. Sephton et al. 2000.

14. Saxbe 2009.

15. Saxbe, Repetti, and Nishina 2008.

16. Interested readers should consult Saxbe, Repetti, and Nishina 2008 for a more detailed description of these patterns in the data.

17. Kiecolt-Glaser and Newton 2001.

18. For more about these findings, see the original published report: Saxbe, Repetti, and Graesch 2011.

19. The next day Andre went on the school field trip with Peter's class. Since his evening interactions did not follow a day at work, we won't focus on them here.

20. Because Steve did not get home from work until very late on the first weekday of video recording and the CELF camera crew had already left, we focus here on the second weekday of film.

21. Wang, Repetti, and Campos 2011b.

10 Health as a Family Matter

LINDA C. GARRO

What is involved in considering health as a family matter? To start, it bears noting that a different orientation to health is far more pervasive in research and everyday life contexts. In both, health is typically construed as a largely individual-level concern—a framing of health as "personal well-being."[1] In the United States, for example, the commonplace greeting in daily life, "How are you?," provides an opening for individuals to reflect upon their personal state of health (or well-being). There are manifold sources offering guidelines concerning actions individuals can take to improve their health and well-being and/or to minimize risks to health and well-being. In research settings, individuals may be asked to rate their overall health or asked other questions designed to measure an individual's health status and/or to learn about aspects of an individual's life with the potential to have an impact on present or future health. Further, even when aspects of the social environment, including family relationships, enter into the research design, the focus typically remains at the individual level. Such would be the case, for example, when a research project explores whether variations in the health status of individuals is associated with variations in the quantity or perceived quality of relationships and/or responsibilities. Rarely does the attention shift from assessing impacts on individual health to the consideration of matters of health as lived in concert with others in quotidian social settings, such as family life contexts.

The existing research emphasis on individual-level health in medical and psychological anthropology (my own fields of academic specialization) as well as in medical sociology in North America and Europe may, at least in part, be linked to the reliance on interviews with individuals as a primary research method for both eliciting conceptual understandings about health and learning about the experiential dimensions of health. Nonetheless, methodological considerations alone are insufficient as a full explanation for the emphasis on individual-level health. Some researchers have expanded the interview's typical horizon to ask about health-relevant activities as embedded in everyday family life,[2] or relied on interviews as one tool for assessing well-being, such as in the work of Thomas Weisner, who defined well-being in relation to the sustainability of a family's meaningful daily routine and the positive "states of mind and feeling produced by participation in routines and activities."[3] Interviews, by themselves, do not preclude studying health as a family matter.

Buttressed, perhaps, by the way "objective" measures of health and well-being are geared to assessing individuals, the emphasis on individual-level health may also be linked with the proclivity to privilege subjective experience as the primary locus of health and well-being.[4] In this light, a key factor for personal well-being "is not how healthy you are, objectively, but rather how you feel about your health."[5] An illustrative ethnographic example drawing on field research in Toraja, Indonesia, is provided by Douglas Hollan. Hollan characterizes "being well" as "inherently a contingent, subjective state," a "dynamic state of being that is related to fluctuating states of body and world and the interaction between the two."[6] Still, even in this depiction of well-being as self-related experience, Hollan's rendering of the ebb and flow of a sense of well-being for one Indonesian villager across the course of a day unfolds in the context of a particular sociocultural environment, in specific sites (including the home), and in relationships with specific others (including family members). While the theoretical argument in Hollan's article centers on variation in subjective experience at the individual level, the ethnographic portrayal establishes the need for attention to the broader social surround and the intersubjective ground of health and well-being.

In this chapter, without dismissing the import of health and well-being as self-related experience or as individual-level concern, I broaden the analytic lens to explore health and well-being as ensconced in everyday family life and as bound up in relational connections with other family members. I start from the position that if the goal is to understand how matters of health, well-being, and illness enter into the microcultural context of family life, we must attend to what matters to family members in their daily lives.[7] With regard to the CELF project, an appreciation of what matters to family members is garnered through conjoint analyses of the ways family members talk about health and health-relevant matters with researchers, especially in the parental interview on health and well-being and the video recordings of family life. As each family is unique, analysis has centered on developing what I refer to as an individual "family health portrait."[8]

In comparison with research where individual-level health serves as the primary orienting framework, a family-level approach that revolves around what matters to family members situates health and well-being in a larger social arena and thus expands potential avenues of research inquiry. For instance, what do we learn about family life and raising a family when examined through the lens of health? In what ways are health and well-being matters of concern in the often hectic lives of working families? To what extent are the video-recorded observations of everyday family life illumined by health-relevant parental commentary elicited through our research—such as interview statements and comments directed at researchers during the video recordings? Do matters of individual health and well-being take on a different cast when the family sphere is considered? Does health as a family matter refer to something more than the sum of the personal health of the individuals who make up a family? Do parents perceive economic, material, or other factors as connected, positively or negatively, with family health and well-being? How do matters of health and well-being relate to other priorities, obligations, compelling concerns, and expectations, including hopes and fears, for the present and future?

These are, to be sure, broad and complex questions that cannot be fully addressed in a single chapter. Still, they encapsulate some of the issues regarding health and well-being that arise when the research gaze expands to consider health as a family matter.

This chapter draws on the family health portraits of two families in which the father smokes cigarettes and drinks alcohol (beer) on a regular basis, to explore the relationship between family well-being and these habits, especially smoking. These two families were not selected because smoking is common among the CELF families. It is not. And while there are other families in which one (or both) of the parents smokes cigarettes, a similar heightened concern about this habit was not present in these other families as it was in the two families showcased here. Rather, attention to the issue of smoking within these two families serves to illuminate the recurring "tug of the individual and the communal within the family"[9] with regard to matters of health and well-being. In different families, the contours of a socially embedded and relational view of health take different shapes and intertwine with health as an individual concern in divergent ways. The different ways in which fathers' smoking becomes a matter of moral reflection and contention in the two families offers an entrée for exploring the complex interrelationships between health as a matter of "personal well-being" and health as a matter of "family well-being."

Before turning to these two families, some additional introductory comments concerning the cultural landscape of health and well-being help to set the stage. As noted above, much of the existing research relies on interviews to explore how individuals think about health. Although not fully explored here, there are numerous points of correspondence between what CELF parents had to say and the literature reviewed in the following section.

THE CULTURAL REALM OF INDIVIDUAL HEALTH AND WELL-BEING

With health conceptualized as a notion bounded by individual bodies and minds, one claim is that the cultural ideal of a "disease-free, fit, and youthful body" serves as a desideratum and comparative benchmark in "an individualistic, industrialized, modern world."[10] Moreover, studies carried out in the United States and the United Kingdom attest to the widespread acceptance of the view that "the responsibility for health and illness is in one's own hands,"[11] a stance that situates "problems of health and their solutions principally, although not exclusively, as matters within the boundaries of personal control."[12]

Overall, and as also observed in the CELF interviews, framing health and well-being as ends that in important ways require "choice and active commitment"[13] imbues much talk about health and well-being in the United States and the United Kingdom with a characteristically moral quality.[14] Idealized cultural expectations about what one should do with regard to health take form through what will be referred to here as the model of "individual health promotion." This model brings together the positive valuation of behaviors deemed to enhance health with the moral standard that individuals should actively strive to adopt "healthy" behaviors and refrain from those considered injurious to health. The culturally grounded pursuit of health is underpinned by a "morality of the body in terms of what is good and bad. Actions regarded as good for the body are lauded while actions deemed bad for the body are to be avoided. In this moral world, for example, exercise is deemed 'good' while junk foods are 'bad.'"[15] Prototypically, the "individually-based oughts of so-called healthy behaviours"[16] are rather "conventionally defined primarily in terms of smoking, diet, exercise, and alcohol or other drug consumption."[17]

Drawing on interviews carried out in Chicago during the 1980s, Crawford asserted that "the quest for health" is "a distinctive feature of middle-class identity and belonging."[18] Thus, to "the question, 'How should I live?', the denizen of medical culture answers, 'Healthfully'. Behaviors are modified and lifestyles constructed in response to information about dangers to health."[19] Whether or not the individual health promotion model, and its associated optimal behaviors, carries as much directive force as Crawford suggested, the apparent widespread consensus among the middle class in North America and the United Kingdom that one "should" live in relatively close accord with the behavioral mandates of the individual health promotion model increases the vulnerability of individuals to moral critique, censure, and self-blame for the observed or presumed failure to live as one "should." The "morality of the body" demands an accounting if blame is not to be assigned to the individual. Conversely, the achievement of health and efforts to comply with the directives of individual health promotion are marks of moral virtue.

From the perspective of individual health promotion, parents are charged not only with optimizing their own health but also with optimizing the health of their children and, beyond that, for socializing children to appreciate their own independent responsibility with regard to health and well-being. A family in which individual health is accorded its moral due is a family in which the parents demonstrate an appropriate level of adherence to the mandates of individual health promotion through talk and other action. A failure to do so, or being assessed as failing to do so, places parents at risk of being seen in an unfavorable moral light by others. They may also come to judge themselves as being at fault. Interestingly, an analysis of video recordings of family mealtime interactions found that "American families devoted most of the dinner discourse to what children must eat for physiological and moral reasons."[20]

Still, not all influences on individual health are seen to lie within the purview of individual responsibility. For example, in the CELF interviews, "stress" as part of everyday work and home life as a potential source of ill health and diminished well-being was at times conceptualized in ways analogous to air pollution—a feature of one's general environment, but largely outside one's personal control, that has deleterious impacts on health and well-being. Such an explanatory framework establishes connections between lived experience and states of health and well-being in ways that offer possibilities for eliding the discourse of personal control.

While steps may be taken by an individual to minimize or avoid expo-
sure to such sources of ill, notions of personal blame or responsibility
may not inform whatever deliberations lie behind such actions.

So far, the discussion has centered on what leads someone to be
healthy or not, on the causes of good or ill health, without setting bounds
around the concepts of health and well-being. At a definitional level,
while some scholars do not explicitly distinguish health from well-being,
others find it useful to characterize health as a component of well-being
that signals attention to physical well-being. For example, as part of their
efforts to develop "a cross-cultural comparative schema" for research purposes, Mathews and Izquierdo posit several "experiential dimensions" of
well-being.[21] One is characterized as "a physical dimension of well-being,
involving how individuals conceive, perceive, and experience their bodies
in the world."[22] A further subdivision of this physical dimension differ-
entiates between "conceptions of and experience of pleasure (short-term
physical well-being) and health (long-term physical well-being)."[23] While
other scholars do not necessarily define the realm of health exclusively in
relation to the physical (or the long-term), neither is it the case that the
discussion of the physical is absent from studies of health. In much scholarly work, to speak of health is to implicitly include physical wellness.

On the other hand, the notion of well-being may be preferred by
scholars when the emphasis is on subjective states, for example, when
privileging "happiness" as "the most essential part" of well-being.[24] In
anthropological writings, the use of "well-being" may also gesture toward
a "broadening of the concept of health" to include "people's views and
rationales concerning good feelings and good lives."[25] Mathews maintains, "Well-being is not only a matter of physical health; it has an existential component as well. In order to fully experience well-being, people
everywhere need to feel that their lives are worth living."[26]

Despite such efforts, it remains inherently problematic to set definitive
boundaries around the conceptualization of health or to clearly delin-
eate what is further entailed by the notion of well-being. Instructive in
this regard is Blaxter's book, *Health*.[27] At the end of an extensive review
of primarily European and North American research, in addition to a
consideration of health through a historical lens, Blaxter concludes that
"health" is and "has always been a slightly slippery concept." Moreover,
"the theme" of her book is "not only that a single all-purpose definition
of health is impossible, but that attempts to impose one have never been
very functional."[28]

Certainly, judging by the range of answers given by interviewees across studies in North America and the United Kingdom, there exist quite diverse ways in which the rather abstract notion of health can be defined and otherwise endowed with meaning. In a recent study carried out with an ethnically diverse sample in Chicago, after individuals provided a rating of their own health, researchers followed up and asked what the word *health* meant vis-à-vis the rating task. The responses revealed at least nine "different ways in which the idea of health can be defined and given character," illustrative of the way that "the English word *health* . . . is not unitary in meaning and indexes a wide variety of intuitions, images, and implications about personal well-being."[29] Blaxter's analysis of a nationwide U.K. survey discerned five main categories for how people defined health, namely: health as not ill; health as physical fitness; health as the quality of social relationships; health as function; health as psychosocial well-being.[30]

Perhaps unsurprisingly, interview-based health-oriented studies align with a view that there is no tidy differentiation between health and well-being. The formulation of health as "psychosocial well-being" advanced in the U.K. study, for example, comprises "expressions of health as a purely mental state, instead of, or as well as, a physical condition."[31] And somewhat comparable to the conceptualization of health as the quality of social relationships[32] is Mathews and Izquierdo's "interpersonal dimension of well-being," which pertains to "how individuals conceive, perceive, and experience their relations with others."[33] More generally, a Chicago-based study involving primarily middle-class persons asserted, "Talking about health is a way people give expression to our culture's notions of well-being or quality of life."[34] Prominent intersections for constructs of health and well-being include the importance of "feeling good" and experiencing "pleasure."[35] Along similar lines, another U.S. study of "white, middle-class men and women" concluded that the "idea of health was closely associated with the idea of 'well being'; that is, abstract notions of health and healthiness were identified with positive aspects of 'being' in the world and were grounded in lived experience."[36]

Clearly, even when the focus is on health and well-being at the level of the individual, the terrain is complex. In addition to the importance of "individual health promotion" as evidenced in the cultural stress placed on individual responsibility and personal control, this brief review gives some sense of the wide range of definitions, concerns, and issues that have emerged in previous research. As we have seen, although there is a tendency for health to be associated with the physical body and for well-being to align with subjective assessment, the terms defy straightforward definition. Rather, health and well-being are flexible, broad, and somewhat nebulous constructs, complicating any effort to demarcate the arena of health and/or well-being or to clearly differentiate between the two notions. The situation becomes only more complex when studying health and well-being as embedded in everyday life.

With this definitional discussion as a backdrop, the next sections offer minihealth portraits of two families, with particular attention to the connection between the father's smoking and familial relations of care. Going beyond the view that smoking is "bad" for the smoker's physical health and for those exposed to secondhand smoke (neither of these issues were matters of controversy in the two families), the discussion reveals how smoking, when framed as a family matter, can assume a moral cast different from when health is construed solely as a matter of personal concern. For the first family, the Morris family, this "morality of care for family" corresponds with and adds weight to the "morality of the body" at an individual level, leaving the smoker asserting his personal right to make the choice to smoke. In the second family, the Casey family, the dilemma is that these two moral demands are in direct conflict.

SMOKING AND RELATIONS OF CARE

The Morris Family

On the last day of filming, a Sunday, Dale Morris was observed smoking (for the second of three times during the video recording) outside the family home. Dale spends a lot of time outside the home, often in the garage. Furnished with a reclining chair, a refrigerator stocked with beer, and a television set, the garage was the space where Dale had been recorded drinking beer on several occasions. On this Sunday, Dale's wife, Kelly, was away on an errand and Dale was keeping an eye on the family's two adopted children, nine-year-old Mark and two-year-old Tessa. Dale and Kelly's seventeen-year-old daughter, Celia, an attentive, reliable, and frequent caretaker for her younger siblings, was also at home. With Tessa taking a nap and Celia within call, Dale supervised Mark's preparations for skateboarding and watched him take off down the sidewalk. Noticing Dale's concerted efforts to keep the lit cigarette out of view, the videographer asked Dale whether he would prefer that his smoking not be captured on film. Dale replied that he didn't care about the video recording but that "this will probably be the only time on tape that you got it." With apparent concern that Dale was not at ease smoking in the presence of the camera, the videographer told him, "I smoke" and "It's okay, it's okay." Dale repeated that it didn't matter and explained: "I just mainly don't let the kids see me." After the videographer pointed out that she had never seen him drink beer inside the house either, Dale said, "I try not to let them see any of that." He then said that it wasn't so much the drinking that was an issue as "we have barbecues and stuff like that." Smoking, in contrast, "I hide." Dale went on to acknowledge that Mark has seen him smoke but then minimized these instances by claiming, "He doesn't see me [smoking] enough to really remember type thing, and the baby I don't let see me at all." Describing a couple of strategies he used to keep his smoking out of sight, Dale asserted that most of his smoking was at work, and, he explained, "I don't really smoke that much unless—I'm about a pack a day." Overall, "I really don't smoke too much at home anyways."

Dale claimed to "love being outside," and he was indeed observed spending the majority of time outside doing chores in the yard or garage or watching sports or the evening news on the television he has installed in the garage while sipping a can of beer. Kelly's domain is inside the home, and she took on a greater share of household responsibilities and had greater involvement in childcare. Compared to other CELF families, this gendered spatial division of labor was somewhat more pronounced, as was the fact that Kelly was largely responsible for making financial decisions, even quite significant ones such as purchasing a combination rental/vacation home on Catalina Island. That the family enjoys a relatively comfortable economic position was credited, by both parents, as being largely due to Kelly's efforts.

Portraying themselves as "older" parents, Kelly and Dale were in their early forties at the time of the study. In the health interview, the children take center stage as what makes life "worth living"[37] for the Morris parents. Kelly talked about having the children as a key goal that "I wanted and we've achieved." Being an "older parent" gave Kelly an "incentive to be healthy" and "be as active as I can and keep young" in order to fulfill her plan of "being here for a while" for them. Dale followed up, saying, "That's my thing too, that's what really drives me to get up and go to work cause we're doing it for the kids." As a couple who "have always enjoyed kids," both aver that the addition of the two younger children to their family has, in Dale's words, "made us healthier people."

These parental reflections seem striking given the challenges they have faced in dealing with the health problems of their two youngest children. Both were born with substance addictions and had troubled medical histories prior to being adopted by Kelly and Dale. Kelly described the children as "drug babies" and attributed Mark's diagnosis of attention-deficit/hyperactivity disorder (ADHD) to the alcohol and several illicit drugs that his biological mother ingested while pregnant. Tessa, whose biological mother was addicted to heroin, was considered essentially recovered from the trauma of her birth circumstances.

Dale and Kelly reported that they had always hoped to have more than one child and when, after Celia, they found themselves unable to have additional children of their own, they decided to work toward adopting a child who needed a family but who was otherwise unlikely to be adopted. Both parents were committed to the view that parental dedication and providing a stable home environment were necessary in order for children to flourish in the present and succeed in the future. With regard to their children, Kelly, in particular, conveyed how she was steadfast in her efforts to "bring out the best in them" and help them find their "niche." She was confident that despite the birth circumstances of her two adopted children, she could enable their future success by creating quality environments for them (this seemed to be a challenge that gave Kelly a particular sense of purpose). Her efforts were not just confined to the family home, but extended into other environments, such as school.[38] Interestingly, Kelly also linked the decision to adopt with concern about Celia not having siblings and the implications this might have for her future: "The reason I would never ever ever have only one child is because when your parents get up in life or whatever, the burden of your parents and the burden of doing things falls on your children." Outlining the expected course of events as one where parents need the help of their children, Kelly stated, "It's nice to have that brother or sister to call and say, 'I need you, I need you now'"; "I never wanted Celia to ever have to go through any of that by herself."

At an early point in the health interview, after addressing the question "What is it like when you are healthy?," Kelly added, "I have no tolerance for sick people." She explained, "I hate dealing with sick people. I hate dealing with illnesses. I hate—," followed by Dale's interjection, "We've dealt with a lot of death." As the conversation continued, and throughout the interview, details about the heavy burden of illness and loss among extended family and others close to them bore out Kelly's laments, "I've dealt with sick people all my life" and "We've had more than our share [of sickness and loss]." At the family level, when "someone is struck with an illness it puts a lot of stress and a lot of fear into a family."

Despite Kelly's affirmation "I hate having to always be the responsible party in the family," her view of herself as a moral person includes "being there for" others. While Dale strongly feels the commitment to "be there" for others as well, he affirmed that Kelly has assumed much of the burden by repeatedly taking on the role of caregiver and by providing emotional and material support when intimates are in need. Among the challenges faced by the family are the deaths of the children's grandfathers. Dale's father, a coal miner who is described as having smoked and drunk heavily, succumbed to lung cancer. Kelly's father, who had been "sick" for Kelly's "whole life," was described as a chain smoker who consumed four to five packs a day and "died from smoking." A relatively recent loss was Kelly's oldest brother, a troubled Vietnam War veteran with a "really bad circulatory problem," who became "addicted to prescription drugs." Even though Kelly saw her brother as lacking a source of motivation and satisfaction until close to the end of his life, she concluded that he "caused his own problems" because he "abused his body way too much," eventually leading to his death. Kelly's response to the health interview question of what keeps people healthy combines "a good outlook on life" and "taking care of themselves, not abusing their bodies" by drinking, smoking, and taking drugs. More generally, both Dale and Kelly perceive the world around them as full of hazard and the future as uncertain.

Even though "being there" for others during times of disappointment, grief, and hardship can take a "huge toll on you," it is a responsibility that one owes to family. Yet the imprint of this value orientation is not just restricted to times of trouble; it is found in routine everyday life contexts as well. In a previous article concerning this family, Garro and Yarris detailed how familial interactions evidencing a sensibility of mutual care and concern, along with parental efforts to motivate younger children to act in ways that "help" others, are consistent with an implicit moral stance that a responsible person is one who helps others and responds to the valid needs of others by placing these needs ahead of one's own convenience, pleasure, or comfort.[39] In addition, sacrifice may be rewarded—a person's willing acts to help another potentially benefits the helper as well; it is more likely that others will be willing to be there and help you if you take the initiative to contribute to what others seek to achieve and be there for them across good times and bad. Given Dale's and Kelly's efforts to raise their family in a manner consistent with these values, Kelly projects a future in which her grown children willingly accept the "burden" of helping aging parents. Through everyday interactional work fostering "moral responsibility in the form of generative cross-situational awareness to others' needs and desires" and supporting the development of "social awareness, social responsiveness, and self-reliance,"[40] Kelly and Dale strove to shape what sort of persons their children would become.

Along these lines, their teenage daughter Celia's interview is illuminating. Asked about the meaning of family, she replied, "Family to me, it's just a—I don't even think of the bloodline thing, you know, being related to your family. I think it is just a group of people who truly care about each other more than anything in the world and would do anything for each other . . . So it's just people who care about you so unconditionally and take the good with the bad with the ugly." Affective relationships and acts of care, rather than biological ties, are the constituents of family. Celia, who was observed to take an active role in caring for her younger siblings and to willingly pitch in to help address small unanticipated problems, minimized her own contributions: "It's not like—it's not a big deal really for me to help out my family because they do, I think, ten million more things for me than I do for them." After listing a number of concrete acts as instances of caring for which Celia was recipient, she summarized the situation by avowing: "My family is very willing to sacrifice to help."

Because parental interactions within the Morris household were typically pleasant and not confrontational, the section of the health interview during which Dale's smoking and drinking was discussed stands out as rather tense. Kelly's grievances arise in the discussion about things that have an impact on the health of the family. At first environmental concerns—"toxins" and "pollution"—were raised, largely unavoidable especially as the family home was located close to a major international airport; and then the deleterious effects of "quick fast foods" and "preservatives" were mentioned. After Dale indicated that he had nothing further to contribute on this topic, Kelly raised the issue of "when me and Dale fight." Pointing out that "everybody" fights, Dale disclosed that "money" was "pretty much the bottom line" for their arguments. Kelly concurred but expanded the list to "money, drinking, and smoking." Kelly presented herself as a careful manager of the family's resources and complained that Dale, in contrast, "doesn't realize how much money he spends every month," particularly on cigarettes and beer. Kelly views these purchases as siphoning off fiscal resources that should be used to support the well-being of the family rather than to contribute to its vulnerability. Still, the threat to family financial stability, while important, was just the tip of the iceberg, as seen in the following excerpt:

KELLY: I just have a real problem with him drinking beer everyday and him smoking everyday and that it takes a toll on his health, he's starting to look very old, and um– his children are seeing it, and when we've got two babies that are drug addict—one's an alcho– a fetal—had fetal alcohol um it's not fair to them to see that every day.

DALE: They don't see that every day. I don't smoke in front of the kids.

KELLY: But they know that you're doing it.

DALE: No they don't. Celia does. Mark doesn't. Mark really—I don't think has a clue.

KELLY: Oh he has a clue—

DALE: mm okay and Tessa I don't—

KELLY: So he gets very upset when I bring it up he gets very pissed at me, but, you know what? I'm not going to sit there in the hospital with him every day, you know. And that's a huge thing, it's a very huge thing to me. And he doesn't think about it, but I do.

DALE: Yeah, the reason I don't is because I can go tomorrow. I, you know, I don't—I don't know I just take it a day at a time, and ((*pause*)) if tomorrow never come it never comes at least I've done what I wanted to do up until that point in my life.

Kelly's critique of Dale's smoking and drinking gains depth in relation to the familial history of loss, the adopted children's past as "drug babies," and the familial orientation to valuing acts of mutual care and concern. For Kelly, that Dale is apparently unable to contemplate the present and future toll of his smoking and drinking on both self and family is a "very huge thing." In her view, his daily indulgences are making him "look very old," thus negating other efforts to counter the effects of age and extend health as long as possible in the future to "be there" for their children. For the two children born drug addicted, having a parental role model who smokes and drinks is not "fair to them." In addition to denying the "morality of the body," Dale is denying his moral responsibility to his family by choosing to smoke and drink without taking heed of the way that threats to his own well-being are also threats to the well-being of his children and wife. Predicting a future time when Dale will be seriously ill as a consequence of his own choices, and reverberating with painful experiences of past losses associated with drug use, Kelly's scenario is one in which she refuses to take on an additional burden by being physically present at his hospital bedside as she has been for other family members in the past. By alluding to a future in which she abandons a central tenet of her moral persona, namely, to "be there" for family, the gravity of Dale's past and present actions and their future consequences are underscored. Through his own actions, Dale's entitlement to Kelly's caring presence in the hospital is forfeit. In response, Dale offers an alternative scenario in which the cause of his eventual demise is not so easily foretold given the omnipresence of other sources of danger. He highlights the fact that this is something he does for himself. His avowal that if tomorrow "never comes at least I've done what I wanted to do until that point" is an explicit refusal to accept Kelly's framing of his smoking and drinking as a family matter.

Following the interaction quoted above, Kelly expressed her strong conviction that Dale should "respect what I'm asking." She reported, "There's times when I've just pretty much told him, 'I don't want to deal with this anymore. Let's get a divorce.' Because it's just, you know, but he has made the conscientious choice not to cut back." Dale, firmly sticking to his position of personal autonomy, bluntly retorted, "I will be my own man." Although he recognized the "downside" of the effect of his smoking and drinking on his personal health, it was "part of my living" and a stance that Kelly should respect and tolerate, as these habits did not negate his ability to be a good father and husband.

In the health interview, as additional support for her construal of Dale's failure to consider others, Kelly turned next to Celia. Establishing a connection between the "toll" on Celia and Kelly's experiences with her own father, she related: "Celia hates it. She has come to me crying over it, and she hates it, and she has asked him ever since she was a baby for him to quit smoking. She has told him point blank, 'All I want for my birthday is for you to quit smoking.' So, you know, if that doesn't make him quit, when your own baby daughter doesn't make you quit, then you know it's pretty hard. And my dad died from smoking so see it's a very a double edge sword for me." Kelly's moral high ground gained further elevation as she recounted how she gave up drinking alcohol, essentially for good, when she first became pregnant, because responsibilities to other family members come first (along with childcare, she included being the designated driver for Dale). In line with the way relations of caring infuse family life, the safeguarding of family health and well-being takes precedence over personal desires. The morality of care for the family is, in part, enabled by the morality of the body.

Shying away from talk of addiction or habit, and framing smoking as a want rather than a need, Dale seeks a place to hold his ground by asserting the moral right to decide for himself, including his ability to devote part of his income to alcohol and cigarettes. Yet despite the defense Dale mounted in the health interview, his continuing efforts to "hide" his smoking while at home and to minimize his drinking in the children's presence reveal that there are limits to what it means to be his own man in the familial context. Dale's own actions confirm that not smoking inside the family home is part of the optimal home environment that both parents voice commitment to in the health interview. Yet by smoking on the home's perimeters, as well as coming home from work with clothes reeking of smoke, as one interaction tellingly revealed, Dale does not measure up to Kelly's standards of responsible parenting. And while Kelly's multifaceted critique ostensibly targets what both portray as Dale's refusal to give up smoking and drinking, it is also a statement of the ways in which family health and well-being are made vulnerable through this refusal. Kelly's placing of limits on her moral obligation to "be there" for others, to the "bad and the ugly" that she will accept from a family member, stands as a warning to Dale that his inconsistency in recognizing the moral interdependence of the family with regard to matters of health and well-being may cost him not only his personal health but also exclusion from the benefits of familial interdependence at a time when he needs that support.

The Casey Family

In the Casey family, the father's smoking and drinking is neither hidden nor censured. Both are part and parcel of family life in a way that would be unimaginable in the Morris family, and these habits are not singled out as significant threats to family well-being. But then, in contrast to the Morris family and many other families in the CELF study, the Casey family's economic situation at the time of the CELF study was far more precarious. Just a year earlier, the Casey family—consisting of Ronald, or Ronnie, the father, Melissa, the mother, Amanda, their eight-year old daughter, and Michael, their four-year old son—would not have been eligible to participate in the CELF study because they did not own a home. Although both parents were clearly pleased to be home owners, Ronnie explained that purchasing their unpretentious home was "a miracle, a blessing in itself," given that they were "barely getting by at the time" and had "very little savings."

Financial concerns have troubled Ronnie and Melissa throughout the fifteen years they have been together. Both Ronnie and Melissa have worked hard and made sacrifices in order to improve their family's financial situation and overall security, and both were optimistic that better times lay ahead. Melissa, who worked as a school counselor, had recently completed an advanced degree. Still, at the time of the research, the degree had not yet led to a markedly better job and higher salary. Ronnie worked in construction and was in the penultimate year of a five-year apprenticeship as an electrician. Ronnie's income fluctuated depending on the availability of work, and he did not accrue any "sick time."

Although the recent house purchase represented the fulfillment of a family "dream," it was also the source of financial strain, especially given the renovations that were needed to make the dwelling habitable. Ronnie maintained that "financial stability is really our main concern. It's, it's a constant juggling of bills, uh. Puttin' this off, puttin' that off." Financial worries and the constant press of everyday obligations at times led to "moments of explosion and hair pulling." Ronnie explained: "You know, we as a family have learned that there's so many things that can stress us out on a daily basis." Near the end of the video recording, Ronnie stated he was "sorry" that we hadn't caught any of these moments on film as it would help us to better understand "stressed-out families" like his.

In conversation with CELF researchers, Ronnie characterized his cigarette smoking as both a "horrible, disgusting habit" that he intended to quit and a "medical need," legitimated by his diagnoses of ADHD and bipolar disorder—a way to avert eruptions of anger when he is "stressed out." Without entering into a discussion of the validity of these diagnoses, here the focus is how Ronnie's smoking and drinking enter into everyday family life. While Ronnie's voice predominates, for he had much to say in conversations with the videographer while he smoked a cigarette outside the family home, it is Melissa, in particular, who viewed Ronnie's smoking as bound up with family well-being in ways that foreshadow potential dangers should his expressed intention to quit smoking become realized. By supporting Ronnie's emotional stability his smoking and drinking are credited with maintaining both the daily emotional well-being of the family and the family's financial well-being, the latter by enabling Ronnie to hold down a job.

It was not until the second day of filming that Ronnie made his first appearance on video. The previous evening Ronnie had been at school, arriving home after the CELF researchers had left. On days when he is not taking courses for his certification as a professional electrician, Ronnie is often the first family member to arrive home. Meeting the research team as he arrives back from the corner grocery store, Ronnie explained that he typically uses the interim between his arrival and that of the remaining family members to prepare the evening meal. On this day, between leaving work and going to the grocery store, Ronnie purchased some "emergency food" from an Asian market as he was worried that what he had planned for that evening might not be enough. As he chopped vegetables, Ronnie explained that the store-bought food was "home cooked" and not "junk food." He continued:

> 'Cause believe it or not I'm the one that tries to keep everyone away from the cheeseburgers and the french fries. 'Cause if it was up to my wife, three times a day, she could probably. But I—It's become a personal mission here. I have to get some kind of nutrition into this family otherwise it would be chaos. She was raised on taquito night, you know.

A bit later, Ronnie pointed out that it is difficult to come up with nutritious food that his family, particularly his children, will eat. Nonetheless, he stated that he enjoys cooking because "it's the one time out of the day where it's my time . . . I like it. You get to be creative and know you're doing something good for the family."

Included among the items purchased at the grocery store was some bottled beer. Prior to beginning the meal preparation, Ronnie pulled a beer out of one of the grocery bags.

> RONNIE: If you don't mind if I have a beer. I'm a little nervous with eyes on me. ((*Ronnie opens the bottle and takes a drink*)) I have a beer every one or two every couple of days out of the week maybe.
>
> VIDEOGRAPHER: Uh huh.
>
> RONNIE: Generally it gets the edge off of me so I don't unleash it on the wife and kids you know. I go through quite a bit at work.

Note that Ronnie's beer consumption, initially attributed to nervousness, is put forward as a general strategy for protecting family members from his work-related strain and the effect it has on him. On another occasion, Ronnie referred to being "hepped up" by caffeine and needing to drink beer to calm down.

During her video-recorded home tour, Melissa included the outdoor picnic table where "Ronnie does his little smoking." And indeed, near the end of the family dinner, Ronnie announced he would be "back in a minute" and sat down at the table for a smoke. These departures are a recurring activity that punctuates the rhythm of everyday life and may be accompanied by a comment that he needs to smoke or take a "nicotine break." On this occasion, Ronnie and the videographer chatted about the upcoming Christmas holidays, and then Ronnie brought up his smoking. In the transcript below, note the parallels to how Ronnie talked about his beer consumption as protective of others.

RONNIE: I plan on quitting ((*pause*)) smoking after the holidays.

VIDEOGRAPHER: Yeah?

RONNIE: I quit for eight months last year, then I bought the home. It was either start up smoking again or people were going to get hurt. ((*pause*)) I was really: stressed out. It was very stress—stressful moment in my life, I'm ((*pause*)) I didn't know stress until we bought this house. It was just uhh—I was in shock for months after the fact. ((*long pause*)) Doesn't look like much to some, but ((*pause*)) there's still a lot of work. I (only) have so many more plans for this house.

The health interview provided another platform for Ronnie to introduce the topic of smoking. Near the start, in response to a general question about the meaning of health, Ronnie reported: "Hasn't meant much, I guess, until the past couple of years. I never took care of myself." Then, defining health as being "able to function well every day," he stated, "I abuse myself but, yeah, that's basically it. Just to be able to function well everyday mentally, physically." He raised the plan to stop smoking after the holidays again and retold the story of quitting and relapsing with the stress of the house purchase. Then Ronnie disclosed a relatively recent change in his eating habits, revealing his avowed "mission" to feed his family nutritious foods as also relatively recent. Ronnie recounted that he had been quite overweight ("pushing 300 pounds") and that there is a "definite difference" in the way he eats now. He said of the past: "I didn't care. I felt, you know, it's my life. We're here for a blank of time anyways, you know. I'm going to live happy." Characterizing himself as "not much of a down-the-road type of guy" and more of a "now" person, he nonetheless realized, "I want to be able to have the time and health to spend not only with my kids growing up but possibly their kids." On another occasion during the video recording he mentioned a number of past abuses and violent traumas that could have led to his death, leading him to conclude, "[I] truly have God on my side." But this realization only led to another question: "Why is he [God] keeping you around?" Pointing to his home, Ronnie answered, "Well this is why. This is why. Cuz he knows what's inside you, and what you can put out, towards other, other life. And uh ((*pause*)) I know why I'm here now. Raise these two beautiful kids, and ((*pause*)) I know my purpose now."

With regard to physical well-being, in the health interview Ronnie pointed out that while he "enjoyed smoking for many years," he now appreciated that there are "so many benefits of not smoking, you know, and I lose out so much when I smoke." Ronnie became animated when he spoke of the sensory pleasures of life without smoking. And when Melissa recounted an incident when their daughter came up to Ronnie crying about his cigarette smoking and exclaiming, "I don't want you to die," Ronnie said that this hit him "hard," even though he was not ready to quit at that time.

In the next excerpt, Ronnie responded to the interviewer's request that he talk more about his smoking. Melissa's responses and reactions are revealing. Although ADHD had not yet entered the conversation, Melissa drew a connection between nicotine and the type of medication often used to treat ADHD.

> RONNIE: Sure. What do you want to know? It's a disgusting habit. There's no benefit in it other than me having a stress—a quick stress reliever. But I quit before. I could quit again. I want to quit. You have to want to quit. ((*emphatically*))
>
> MELISSA: But it's hell for everybody else. ((*quietly*))
>
> RONNIE: Only for a little bit. ((*Melissa shakes head and mouths "no."*)) I got good there later on in time. ((*Melissa shakes head and mouths "no" again.*))
>
> MELISSA: It's a stimulant. Nicotine is a stimulant.
>
> RONNIE: It is a stimulant.
>
> MELISSA: And it kind of balances him ((*pause*)) in my own perspective, my own interpretation. When he's out of balance he's highly agitated and very um ((*long pause*)) not fun to be around, I guess you can say. And the cigarette smoking is huge on our budget, huge on our budget, but on the same token it's huge on the mental health. For him to have that balance, that it kind of balances that rest of us ((*laughing*)). I don't know—
>
> RONNIE: That's really sad. That is really sad.

Ronnie then said he would work harder to manage his agitation the next time he quit.

A bit later, Ronnie stated, "I'm ADHD," and contrasted smoking as medication with prescribed pharmaceutical treatment:

> Where she gets this balance from is I'm ADHD. My whole family is pretty much and I get really hyper, real hyper. If I'm stressed and I'm angry, I might as well be an incredible hulk. I'm just raging. And that cigarette is literally, like, becomes medication. Tried the medication thing. You know, and it's, you're like this, "Hi, how you doing." ((*spoken in a flat voice with minimal affect*)) How am I supposed provide for my family like that? I'm in construction, you know. They—get off my job kid, you know. You got to be kidding me. You become an endanger to yourself.

Through putting his physical integrity at risk while on the job and jeopardizing his chances for being hired and kept on a job, it was never a viable option to take prescribed medication instead of self-medicating by smoking.

Ronnie explained that his ADHD and bipolar disorder account for his history of "drug abuse" and his proclivity to violent outbursts outside the familial context. When Ronnie initially sought help, he told the first psychiatrist he saw, "I smoke to be normal. I smoke weed to be normal or I smoke cigarettes whatever. I drink. I—whatever abuse I was doing at the time, I told her I did it because I was normal." Ronnie sees this psychiatric consultation as failing to acknowledge his ADHD because he was told only that he was "an alcoholic drug addict." This discouraged him from seeking further help for some time. Below, Ronnie and Melissa talk about the time he sought help again.

RONNIE: It got really bad at home ((*pause*)) a couple years back. I mean bad. I don't know what was becoming of me, some certain episodes but there was a time frame there where—

MELISSA: Are you sure that's not when you quit smoking?

RONNIE: It may have been.

MELISSA: I think that's when you quit smoking.

RONNIE: But I was becoming really abusive towards her verbally, emotionally. It was eating me. I would break down and cry. I would cry, you know, because—And I couldn't explain to her enough (that) this is not me, it's not. I don't want to be like this to you baby you know. And we were so frustrated. I mean snapping at the kids, I was getting really scared (xxx). It was on the brink of, God,

what if I totally lose it one day and become physical
or something, you know. I went back again, another
psychiatrist. ((*pause*)) Diagnosed me, showed me the
medication, tried it a couple few times.

Ronnie discontinued taking the medication because it made him "depressed" and "dysfunctional." Although he felt he had developed strategies to deal with his "agitated moments," he found it depressing that he could not aspire to become a foreman because in "one moment of agitation" he might "break the customer's nose" or otherwise react in ways that would jeopardize his "leadership position" if not his job. Still, taking time off from work to see whether it was possible to stabilize the medication at an acceptable level was dismissed by Ronnie because it would entail a loss of income essential to the family's fragile financial stability. Nicotine is a "medical need" that serves its "medical purpose" by allowing him to function in everyday contexts. When Melissa suggested that counseling might help Ronnie handle anger more effectively, Ronnie resisted by countering that "it's not really that bad," further claiming that he has come a "long way" and providing a recent example in which he demonstrated "self-control" by "walking away" from an altercation with a stranger that threatened to become physical.

Ronnie's doubts surfaced more explicitly in another conversation when Melissa was not present. He remarked, "Melissa hates it when I don't smoke," noting that his lack of a "fuse" and his angry explosions put his marriage at risk. He admitted that he was "pretty scared about quitting smoking again." He continued: "There was a time of ugliness. I don't know. I can try and see what happens." Shortly afterward, he asserted, "It is a major desire for me to quit smoking. I've got my heart and mind set on it after the holidays." The choice of time reflected his desire to keep the holidays as happy as possible for the family. While Ronnie saw the ability to stop smoking as being under his control, regulating his "agitated moments" was seen to require considerable effort, with an uncertain outcome and inevitable rough spots. The "medical need" to smoke so that he doesn't hurt someone makes his past relapse less of a personal failing. Still, Ronnie hoped for a better future: "I'm always looking for the better me."

In the past Ronnie's quest for personal well-being through losing weight led not only to improvements in his own diet, but his family's as well. Health as a family matter went hand in hand with health as an individual matter: there was a happy convergence of the morality of the body with the morality of care for the family. Further, as a consequence of this success, Ronnie came to see himself as having the willpower necessary to sustain significant behavioral changes. The open question is whether, or how, the apparently conflictual needs of supporting both everyday family well-being and personal well-being might be reconciled should Ronnie act on his desire to quit smoking. His last attempt to renounce smoking is remembered by Melissa as a time when "everybody else" experienced "hell," whereas Ronnie focused on the positive changes he experienced until things fell apart. For Melissa, quitting itself portends trouble; for Ronnie, the special stressful circumstances of the house purchase obligated him to resume smoking because "otherwise people were going to get hurt." At the time of the CELF research, Ronnie's cigarette smoking, and to some extent alcohol consumption, were woven into the fabric of life in the Casey family. The credit both parents bestow on the "bad habit" of smoking for maintaining the precarious equilibrium of everyday life—by decreasing interpersonal strife and helping Ronnie to "function well every day" both at work and at home—underscores that much more is at stake than personal well-being in his determination to quit smoking.

CONCLUDING COMMENTS

With a focus on the father's smoking and drinking for two families in the CELF study, and through attention to what matters to family members in their daily lives, the material presented in this chapter revolves around the analytic challenge of understanding matters of health and well-being as embedded in an individual family's way of life. Through the lens of health as a family matter, I have sought to convey at least some of "the sense in which experience is situated *within* relationships and *between* persons."[41] Linked to compelling concerns within distinctive local moral worlds, the two families evidence variability in the way that a socially embedded and relational view of health as a family matter connects with health as an individual matter. In closing, I want to comment briefly on the way the prevailing cultural idealization of individual health promotion takes on differential meanings in the everyday lives of these two families.

While both fathers maintain that it is their children who imbue their daily round of activities with meaning, what is at stake for them in the context of everyday family life with regard to smoking, drinking, and their children differs tremendously. For Dale, it matters that his younger, medically vulnerable children not see him smoking, or at least only infrequently, so that he does not acquire the identity of being a smoker and thus offer a dangerous role model. In framing smoking, in particular, as a want rather than a need, he does not offer an accounting for his unwillingness to quit that addresses either the morality of the body or the morality of caring for family. And while Dale does not deny his responsibility for his actions and their present and possible future consequences, he advances the claim that health and well-being are also to be found in doing what one wants to do in the present, especially given the way omnipresent dangers in the world make everyone's life course uncertain. That Dale and Kelly do not regularly come into open conflict over Dale's smoking and drinking but have reached some sort of truce or perhaps stalemate was evident during a short break in the health interview when Dale expressed his surprise that Kelly had brought up issues that he thought they had settled long ago. Kelly simply replied, "This is my chance."

Living closer to the financial edge and with a pervasive foreboding of the potential for discord and aggression, Ronnie's smoking and drinking are seen to help keep disorder at bay. The drain on the family budget is, in Melissa's view, money well spent as it buys "mental health" and "balances the rest of us." Smoking for Ronnie is not a want but a need, and as such its role in supporting the smooth functioning of family life is evident to both parents. Ronnie's ambivalence centers on the way his self-inflicted "abuse" has been necessary for him in order to "function well" and be "normal." As one of two breadwinners in a family in which both paychecks have difficulty stretching to meet the bills, much is at stake in the preservation of Ronnie's ability to function. Further, the abusing of self is preferable to abusing others, especially when the others are those who make your life worth living. If Ronnie's smoking and drinking are not quite moral virtues, neither are they moral failings. Yet Ronnie expresses awareness that the current state is a catch-22 because the ongoing self-abuse has the potential to lead both to his early demise and to placing the well-being of those he loves in jeopardy. He pins his hopes for the future on having enough personal strength and self-control to succeed in his quest to quit smoking in a way that would meet the demands of both the morality of the body and the morality of caring for family. Still, if he is unable to find a way to meet the demands of both, it seems likely that his familial obligation to provide for his family in the present will continue to trump his obligation to take steps to promote his personal health.

For both of these families, the economic resources needed to support the smooth running of their households and to enhance overall economic security are seen to be achieved through the joint efforts of both parents while remaining vulnerable to many factors outside their control. As smoking and quitting smoking are construed, in the end, as volitional acts, it is intriguing that the moral cast of smoking as a family matter partakes of the way smoking is seen to be intertwined with the family's financial well-being. Among other concerns, Kelly portrays Dale's smoking as a financial drain and as a potential damper on her aspirations for her children's future: ensuring the availability of economic resources that can be drawn upon to promote their children's success is an essential parental obligation (among others) in Kelly's eyes. In the Casey family, despite their somewhat tenuous financial standing given the debts they incurred purchasing and refurbishing their home, both parents expressed considerable pride in their new home and their efforts to improve it over the past year. Just as Ronnie's most recent effort to stop smoking exposed the accompanying interpersonal and economic risks associated with quitting, it revealed how his smoking played a contributory role in the family's achievement of a key marker of middle-class status, the purchase of their own home. In distinctive ways, the two cases examined disclose how viewing health as a family matter draws attention to the material underpinnings of family well-being.

Although the individual health promotion model and the notion of health as personal well-being stand as the backdrop to the sketches of health as a family matter presented here, they fall far short as conceptual cultural tools for understanding the complexity of health as embedded in everyday family life and as bound up in familial relations. While the Morris and Casey parents offer perspectives on both individual- and family-level health that reflect their unique circumstances, compelling concerns, and past experiences, what they share with other families in the CELF study are visions of health and well-being that take shape in everyday family life in concert with others.

NOTES

1. Shweder 2008, 69.
2. See, e.g., Backett 1992.
3. Weisner 1998, 76; see also Weisner 2009.
4. Cf. Mathews and Izquierdo 2009, 12, 255–57.
5. Baumeister 1991, 213. Cf. Blaxter 2004, 54–55; Izquierdo 2005.
6. Hollan 2009, 211, 224.
7. Cf. Wikan 1990; Kleinman and Kleinman 1991.
8. For additional examples of this approach, see Garro 2010, 2011; Garro and Yarris 2009.

9. Ochs and Kremer-Sadlik, this volume.

10. Adelson 2000, 4.

11. Blaxter 1997, 748.

12. Crawford 2006, 408; see also Crawford 1984.

13. Crawford 1984, 70.

14. Backett 1992; Crawford 1984.

15. Conrad 1994, 393.

16. Backett 1992, 266.

17. Blaxter 2004, 89.

18. Crawford 2004, 506.

19. Ibid.

20. Ochs, Pontecorvo, and Fasulo 1996, 9.

21. Mathews and Izquierdo 2009, 262.

22. Ibid., 261.

23. Ibid., 262.

24. Ibid., 2.

25. Thin 2009, 37, 36.

26. Mathews 2009, 167.

27. Blaxter 2004.

28. Ibid., 148.

29. Shweder 2008, 71, 69.

30. Blaxter 2004, 51–53; 1990, chap. 3.

31. Blaxter 2004, 53.

32. Ibid., 52.

33. Mathews and Izquierdo 2009, 261.

34. Crawford 1984, 62.

35. Crawford 1984; Backett 1992.

36. Saltonstall 1993, 8.

37. Mathews 2009.

38. A full discussion of these efforts is provided in Garro and Yarris 2009.

39. Garro and Yarris 2009.

40. Ochs and Izquierdo 2009, 391, 394.

41. Jackson 1996, 26.

11 Time for Family

TAMAR KREMER-SADLIK

The cover story of the first 2010 issue of the *Economist* was dedicated to the fact that during the coming months women's participation in the workforce would exceed men's. While women's increased economic capital and independence is and should be celebrated, the prevalence of dual-earner families is frequently viewed as one of the major social changes contributing to the modern family experience of time shortage and hurriedness in everyday life.[1] Parents often complain that they have too much to do and not enough time to do it. Juggling longer working hours,[2] increased scheduling of children's activities,[3] and greater pressure to be involved in all aspects of children's lives (see chapter 7, this volume) not only render parents exhausted at the end of the day but also leave them uncertain about their ability to do a good job on all fronts.[4]

As working parents are faced with the daily challenges of fulfilling the demands of their two primary roles as workers and parents, time is at the root of their daily negotiations. Daly has argued that an inherent duality in the attitude toward time resides at the intersection of work and home.[5] Work, he suggests, is regulated by "clock time" in which time is to be used "to maximize efficiency and achieve optimal functioning in the organization."[6] In contrast, home is regulated by "care time," which is oriented to the other and his or her needs. Clock time calls for productivity, organization, planning, and control through which one's performance can be regulated and evaluated. Care time, conversely, is marked by unpredictability, attentiveness, and flexibility: the changing nature of needs determines one's actions. Daly proposes that this difference between clock time and care time is at the heart of the difficulty of balancing work and family life. Further, our cultural preference for efficiency and productivity makes it harder to carve out time for care, resulting in a concern that care time has been subjugated to the demands of clock time.

The expression "to carve out time" alludes to the idea that one needs to take time that is already assigned elsewhere and reallocate it. It brings to light the matter of agency and control over time allocation, and it implies a moral plane within which the effort of carving out time for family is viewed as the "right" thing to do. This chapter explores the degree to which parents experience a sense of control and responsibility over their allocation of time for family and its relation to parents' evaluations of their own "good parenting." It argues that time for family, ways of achieving it, and its consequence for parents' morality are culturally defined and are dependent on local views regarding parenting and individual versus shared responsibility for family well-being.

WORK TIME AND FAMILY TIME CONFLICT

As Finch has noted,[7] the family is an arena where parents' moral identities are regularly at stake for they are positioned as moral agents responsible not only for themselves but also for the well-being of their children. The need to resolve the conflict between work and family demands inadvertently is a locus where parents display their moral character. A number of studies have shown that parents regularly express a moral imperative to put their children's and family's needs first.[8] At times CELF parents unequivocally stated this preference. Excerpt 1 below shows how Arturo, father of an eight-year-old girl and a five-year-old boy, while discussing his work experience, indicates that his priorities had been very clear.

Excerpt 1

> Work is important for me, *but to me family is more important and my kids are more important.* So, that's why I work where I work and I don't work in a private company where I have to work until nine o'clock. I've done that in Spain; I worked two jobs and I worked late. So, *I prefer to be here* at si– and pick up my kids at five o'clock and see them—or six and see them every night.

Arturo positions the family against work and emphatically states that his children come first. He uses his past experience when work held a more important part in his life ("I worked two jobs and I worked late") as evidence that he is familiar with the demands of work and that he has chosen to control the degree to which work infringes on his family life by working in the public sector and being able to be home at five o'clock. By presenting himself as commanding the situation and making choices (e.g., "I prefer to be here"), Arturo depicts himself as a moral actor and a good parent who puts his family before his career, and thus as one who has resolved the work-family conflict.

Yet finding solutions to this conflict is not always easy for many mothers in our study who feel that work dominates much of their time. In the next excerpt Susannah, mother of an eight-year-old boy and a one-year-old girl, faces a conflict between her need to be at work and the need to attend to her children. Susannah has been trying to get in touch with her sister all evening to find out if she can take the kids to school the next morning. This is a departure from Susannah's usual routine in which she drops off her son at the home of her sister, who then drives him and her own children to school. This time Susannah's sister may need to take her own son to the doctor's office in the morning, which means she may not be able to drive Susannah's son to school. When at 9:00 P.M. Susannah is still unable to reach her sister, she calls her brother-in-law and complains that she must figure out the morning arrangements because she needs to inform her boss immediately of the time she will arrive at work.

Excerpt 2

> This is the thing, I can do one or the other. I can go into work late because—so I can take Jason to school, or I can leave work early to pick up the kids but I can't do both . . . *This is my dilemma.*

In essence, Susannah's problem is the result of a mismatch between her work and her children's school schedules. In order to resolve this problem, she is obliged to involve her extended family and ask for help. The overlap between work and home life is further evident as she is expected to make a work call to her boss that same evening to inform him of her morning schedule.

The tension between time for work and for family caused some of CELF mothers to feel that work is taking a toll on their ability to participate in family life. Ann, mother of an eight-year-old girl and a five-year-old boy, commutes to work and therefore returns home late. In the excerpt below she discusses the fact that she cannot arrive home on time to join her husband and children for dinner.

Excerpt 3

> Weekday meals are a totally different beast, I can't—I can't even—And the reason that they're a totally different beast is because of our commuting schedule and our work schedule, and then the fact that they've usually eaten dinner before I've gotten home . . . When I was a girl, um, my family always sat down to dinner at 6 o'clock and everybody

was always there. *And I would like to do that. I would love to do that. Can't do that. Can't. Not—not right now, not with my work schedule.* And I, I don't want to make that kind of rule, 'cause in my house it was a rule. My mom made it a rule and she made it a rule because she knew if she didn't make it a rule, my dad wouldn't come home. So, I—I *can't make that rule 'cause I can't guarantee that I'm going to be home, um, and I don't want to make it a rule and have my kids every night go, "you missed dinner, you broke the rule."*

Ann makes a causal connection between her work schedule and her inability to share dinner with her family. Ann's wish that things could be different ("I would love to do that. Can't do that") intimates that she is not happy with this situation. In comparing herself to her mother, who was able to enforce the rule that everyone would be home for dinner, Ann presents herself as an imperfect mother who cannot bring her family together at the end of the day. At the same time, avoiding rules about dinnertime is a way for Ann to diminish the importance given to dinner and to dodge the possibility of being judged and criticized by her children for not arriving home at an earlier time.

Similarly, other mothers felt a sense of inadequacy when work prevented them from being able to be with their children or participate in their lives. Debra, mother of a twelve-year-old boy and an eight-year-old girl, recounts below how sometimes her work hours cause her not to see the kids for almost forty-eight hours.

Excerpt 4

So sometimes it's terrible because I'll drop the kids off in the morning and then I won't come home till late and they're already sleeping. And the next morning I might have an early morning meeting and they're still sleeping. So it's like, you know, close to forty-eight hours. So, they're—I mean, they're used to it, but I don't feel good about it.

Debra describes the way work may infringe on her time with her kids as "terrible." Though she suggests that the children are used to the situation, she admits that she is unhappy about it.

Observations in the home reveal that Debra's daughter, Kate, shares her mother's feeling. One afternoon while at home with her father and brother, Kate calls her mom at work to ask when she is going be home and to tell her that she misses her and wishes she were home already. Another night at bedtime, as Debra kisses Kate goodnight and switches off the lights, a whispering conversation between the two divulges that though Debra's early-morning meeting the next day may not be out of the ordinary, it is not simple for both mother and daughter to accept its consequence.

Excerpt 5

MOTHER: Good night sweetie. See you in the morning, OK?

You know what, I have an early morning meeting so Dad's going to take you.

DAUGHTER: OK.

MOTHER: Oh and I have a late-night meeting.

DAUGHTER: So I'm going to see you tomorrow—tomorrow?

MOTHER: Maybe I'll see you in the morning, if you're up.

DAUGHTER: What time is the—

MOTHER: I have to leave around 7.

DAUGHTER: Well, I'll be up by 6, I think.

MOTHER: OK. Sweet dreams.

Both Debra and Kate treat the early-morning and late-night meetings as a familiar situation, yet their tone of voice and unrealistic hopes of seeing each other early the next morning reflect some discontent. Indeed, as seen in excerpt 4, Debra admits that she is dissatisfied with the situation, that "she doesn't feel good about it." Like other mothers, Debra's negative self-evaluation suggests that she perceives her inability to dedicate more time to the family as a personal inadequacy and an individual failure to be a good parent.

When CELF mothers expressed guilt about work interfering with their family life, they often suggested that the negative impact was minimized because they were able to compensate by coming up with compromising solutions. For example, Ann, who could not arrive home on time for weekday dinners, explained that therefore she attempted "to make weekend meals more of, you know, family meals." And Debra, whose work meetings took her away from her children for long stretches of time, made sure to note "my hours are pretty flexible other than the meetings, so I try to make up those hours." The attempts to provide solutions to this undesirable situation further reflect these mothers' sense of responsibility for the failure to find a good balance between their time for work and family.

A Note on Gender

Daly reminds us that time is gendered in that the ways in which men and women divide their time and responsibilities between work and family not only reflect their personal choices but also reveal culturally dominant ideologies of gender, parenting, and family life.[9] Indeed, research has shown that there are significant differences between the way men and women experience the issue of work-family conflict and the matter of family time.[10] Coltrane has suggested that traditional gender roles tend to emerge during the child-rearing phase, increasing the time pressures on women in comparison to men.[11] Roxburgh has found that women are increasingly more time pressed as the number of their roles increases (i.e., caregiver, worker, homemaker, volunteer, etc.) in comparison to men with multiple roles.[12] Bernas and Major have shown that women with high-quality work relationships experience a greater sense of work-home interference in comparison to men with similar work situations.[13]

Though the matter of gender differences regarding work and family time is not the primary focus of this chapter, it is important to note that, as the excerpts above show, concerns and struggles about finding a balance between the demands of work and family were raised almost exclusively by the mothers in our study. These mothers tended to evaluate their own moral worthiness in relation to the management of their time. In the rare times when fathers brought up the matter of balancing work and family life, like Arturo in excerpt 1, they presented themselves as in control of the situation ("that's why I work where I work and I don't work in a private company") and the problem as resolved ("I prefer to . . . pick up my kids at five o'clock and see them—or six and see them every night").

A Cross-Cultural Perspective

We have seen that the CELF parents, in particular mothers, feel that it is their duty to reconcile work and family time demands. However, the strong sense of personal responsibility for the mismatch between work and family is not necessarily shared by dual-earner parents in other countries. A cross-cultural study that compared the Los Angeles parents' discourse on family-work conflict to that of the Italian iCELF working parents highlights interesting differences in their perspectives.[14]

Unlike the CELF parents, when researchers asked the iCELF parents questions related to work and family life, the Italian parents tended to reject their possible negative implication. Excerpt 6 below illustrates how in response to whether he brought paid work home, an Italian father replies that they have work obligations that must be attended to while at home.

Excerpt 6

Besides, there's e-mail, so, I mean, the technological world is really small, right? So *there are things that we have to deal with also on*

Saturdays and Sundays, on weekends. But, I mean, *they are part of the normal routine.*

By mentioning the weekend in particular, this father recognizes the expectation that this time will not be spent on work-related activities. But rather than express discomfort or guilt, he puts forth the argument that the presence of work in family life is natural and expected. Similarly, another Italian father describes his wife's frequent business trips and thus her absence from the home on weekends as "part of our life."

But this attitude was not that of the Italian fathers only; in the next segment an Italian mother responds to a researcher's question about the number of hours she spends on work-related activities while at home by launching into a story about an essay her eight-year-old son wrote at school.

Excerpt 7

> Carlo wrote an essay. It was "My Mom and I." They had to tell what they usually do. Like "In the morning I get up, I go to school. In the afternoon I do sports and in the evening I watch TV. While my mom, in the morning she commutes, in the afternoon she works, in the evening she sits at the computer. ((*laughs*)) How embarrassing, in front of the teachers. ((*laughs*))

The mother answered the interviewer's question by describing her son's essay in which he exposes her propensity to work at home in the evenings. The lack of variety in her son's description of her daily activities reveals his perception that all she does is work. Rather than deny this description, justify her choices, or express discomfort for being "exposed," this mother laughs off this embarrassment as a humorous "faux pas."

The most striking difference between the CELF and iCELF parents was the absence of expressions of guilt. "Failures" to put family first were not viewed as breaking with personal moral integrity; rather the Italian parents framed them as commonplace and unmarked. This comparative study suggests that the disparity in the perception of the work-family conflict among the American and Italian parents resides in a broader cultural difference related to these parents' beliefs about the degree of responsibility they have for the well-being of their children and families. While both sets of parents believed that family comes before work, the American parents, especially the mothers, emphasized and felt responsible for the disjuncture between this ideal and their reality. They conveyed a sense of inadequacy and guilt when work imposed on family time and tried to remedy the situation with compromise. In contrast, the Italian parents presented their reality as satisfying and the intrusion of work into family life as normal and neutral. They did not express guilt or attribute blame but acknowledged the breach of the ideal with humor and irony.

FAMILY TIME AS QUALITY TIME

Time for family does not only refer to the ability to find a balance between work and family demands; it also refers to the way family members spend their time together. In recent decades in the United States the notion of family quality time gained popularity to make up in quality for what may be missed in quantity, primarily because, with the increase in women's presence in the workforce, both parents are away from home for many hours of the day.[15] This time is often viewed as unstressed and uninterrupted, a time when the whole family engages together in special activities, typically geared to children's interests, such as family game night or visits to the zoo.[16] Parents are bombarded with numerous publications and websites that encourage them to make time for quality time that the whole family can share and offers strategies for creating it.[17] Among those media sources are special websites run by respected institutions and individuals such as universities, government agencies, pediatricians, and HMOs, which brings credibility to their recommendations. The weight of these institutions and the value of research findings and professional expertise thus increase the likelihood of parents espousing this view of family time.

Indeed, many of the CELF parents when talking about ways of being together often evoked the quality time ideology. In interviews in which parents were asked to describe their daily schedule, twenty-seven of the thirty-two families (84 percent) talked about the weekend as their time to be with the family and especially with the children, often listing special activities that they engage in. In excerpt 8 below David and Julia, parents of an eight-year-old boy and a five-year-old girl, explain that their family spends special time together on weekends.

Excerpt 8

> FATHER: Sometimes on the—on the weekend Saturday and
> Sunday it depends, we decide to go to, like, *we belong to*
> *several places like the zoo or the aquarium . . .*

MOTHER: And we—we do a lot of hiking now . . . We've taken up *a lot of hiking with the kids . . .*

FATHER: So it's—it's *fun with the kids.* And they like it. We enjoy it.

Both parents stress the activities that they do together as a family. David notes that they have memberships to child-oriented places like the zoo and the aquarium, implying that they can visit those places on a regular basis. And Julia adds that they have also begun a new child-friendly activity, hiking, which they now engage in frequently. David summarizes the purpose of these activities as a good time with the kids that is pleasurable for all.

In excerpt 9 below Fred, father of a nine-year-old girl and a six-year-old boy, also notes that the parents' weekends are reserved for their children and for special activities.

Excerpt 9

We *pretty much really try to have* our weekends available for the kids. Um. So, you know, it . . . could be going to a movie, going to the park . . .

Fred's use of the adverbial phrase "pretty much" suggests that this is done most of the time. He depicts this time as something they "really try to have" rather than simply "have," thus framing it as a goal that not only requires effort but also entails a level of uncertainty regarding whether the parents will be able to achieve it. The labor of finding time to be together is further marked in the need to make the weekend "available" for the children, suggesting that the parents' time ("our weekend") is usually dedicated elsewhere and that they need to reorient it to the kids.

Finally, in excerpt 10 below, Alice, mother of two boys, ages eight and two, explicitly and unequivocally labels Sunday a family day.

Excerpt 10

I never work on a Sunday. *I have to have a day of just family.* You know what I mean? I mean I have *a family day.*

Stating that she never works on Sunday, Alice positions work in opposition to family, making it clear that a family day is a day dedicated solely to the family without any distractions, especially work ones. Framing family day as something that is necessary—"I have to have a day of just family"—Alice presents this kind of day as mandatory.

Similarly to the interviews in which parents noted special times and activities as "family" ones, parents' charts, in which they described activities occurring on each day of a typical week, also contained notations that depicted activities as primarily dedicated to the family. A number of parents used the word *family* to define and categorize certain activities. For example, Jacqueline, mother of eight-year-old and ten-year-old girls, noted on the chart that on Friday and Saturday evenings the family watches a "family movie" and on Saturday and Sunday mornings they eat a "family breakfast." The use of the word *family* here denotes a certain type of activity that can be enjoyed by the whole family and especially the children. The movie that the family would watch is likely to be appropriate for children, and the weekend breakfast, unlike weekday breakfasts, which is unmarked, is likely to include certain foods preferred by children such as pancakes and waffles.

In many of the families' charts parents chose to note specific time slots on weekends that were dedicated to the family. Katrina, for example, mother of an eleven-year-old girl, an eight-year-old boy, and a six-year-old girl, wrote in her chart that "family time" is the activity that takes place on Saturday between 7:00 and 9:00 P.M. and on Sunday between 7:00 and 8:00 P.M. Using this term without providing additional details suggests that Katrina assumed that family time is a known and shared concept. In addition, scheduling "family time" using clearly defined beginning and end points treats family togetherness as structured and predictable.

The excerpts and charts reveal that many parents in our study perceived a prescribed way of being together. In line with the ideology of family quality time, they viewed time for family as special, differentiated from other times when the family might be together. They felt that family time was a necessity and that achieving it could require some effort and was not guaranteed. Finally, by emphasizing that those special days and events were for the family, these parents also intimated that inherent to these important times is the notion that the family experienced these moments without the presence of people who were not members of the immediate family. Thus family togetherness is not only for the purpose of engaging in special activities together but also for separating the family from the rest of the world.

The idea that being together as a family includes being closed off from the rest of the world is made explicit in the next excerpt, in which Jeri and Jeff, parents of an eight-year-old girl and two boys ages four and one-and-a-half describe their Sunday schedule.

Excerpt 11

> FATHER: Usually. Yeah we don't usually plan much. *We plan for us.*
>
> MOTHER: We just try to, yeah, and *we say "no" to people that ask us for plans* sometimes.

In describing their family's typical Sunday this couple indicates that they make plans only for the family and that they turn down invitations to spend time with other people to secure the family's togetherness. The desire to set the family apart from the rest of the world in a marked time and in special activities captures a certain view of the family as a confined unit that exists and cares for itself away from the hassle and bustle of society, in which the well-being of and connectedness between family members is achieved in isolation from other relationships.

Jeri goes on to explain that she and her husband work hard to bring the whole family together and to clear their Sunday schedules so as to have a family day.

Excerpt 12

> Then on Sundays *we try our hardest*—it's definitely a family day to us. *We don't leave each other or the kids* on Sundays, *unless we have to. I worked this past Sunday,* but—but we usually do not leave each other on Sundays.

By emphasizing their efforts to be together, Jeri depicts her husband and herself as moral parents who do the right thing and are prevented from achieving a family day only when greater demands are put on them ("unless we have to"), as she admits happened the previous Sunday when she had to work.

The perception of family time as a private time coupled with particular "right" ways of being together emphasizes parents' overall sense of responsibility for the need to put personal effort into carving out these special times and eliminating all other activities, people, and demands. And once all that work is done, time together is expected to be a successful experience for everyone.[18] This prescribed design for family time risks setting up parents for failure as they find themselves under pressure to bring all the components together for this time to count and to be successful. We recognize this pressure in parents' discourse when they list the type of activities that would qualify for family time and explain that they *try* to find the time to organize such activities. This pressure is also evident when parents express regret and sometimes guilt when obstacles, such as work, restrict them from achieving family together-ness. The anxiety about achieving the proper family time echoes the responsibility that CELF mothers expressed when they felt burdened by and accountable for their difficulty of effectively separating their work and family life.

Cross-Cultural Perspective

In a study that compared CELF and iCELF parents' approaches to time spent with family, we found some important differences in the way they described and interpreted times family members were together.[19] For a start, the Italian parents never marked in their charts activities that were specifically for the family. In fact, the term *family* was never used to describe or define any of the activities they noted. Furthermore, there is no corresponding idiom in the Italian language for the English term *family time*. Instead, an examination of the Italian charts suggests that social activities that included the family rather than being oriented to the family were marked.

An Italian mother, for example, marked in her chart that on Saturday afternoon the activity was "passeggiata mare," or going to the beach. There is no explicit mention of who might participate in this activity; yet from interviews we know that the family regularly goes to their home in the country on weekends. So it is possible to conclude that the family will take part in this activity. Rather than note that this is an activity that will bring the family together, togetherness is an assumed state.

The description of Saturday evening in the same chart further high-lights how the experience of being together is associated with a social event and setting rather than with the participants. In describing the activities taking place on that evening, the mother wrote, "21:00—cena, camino, figli + amici + amici figli—serata." The term *serata*, derived from the word *sera* (evening), describes the experience of being together. The suffix *-ata*, as in *serata* and *passeggiata*, denotes a lasting social experi-ence and emphasizes the leisure design of that time. The setting of the *camino*, Italian for "fireplace," evokes qualities of warmth and intimacy, and the reference to participants also beyond the nuclear family—*amici* (friends), *amici figli* (children's friends)—in contrast to the American par-ents' discourse—expands time together to include others than the family.

In the Italian parents' interviews we also found that they did not seem to separate the family from the social world.[20] In excerpt 13 below, a Roman father of two children, ages nine and thirteen, when asked if he ever devoted time to his paid work while at home on the weekend, responded by describing a common occurrence when the family spends time with clients who are also good friends.

Excerpt 13

> We have friends who are our clients. They have children, and they
> are my children's friends. And we meet and we go out for dinner.
> Now, we will leave, we go together. We are a big group, (.) and—and
> mh *one couldn't say whether this is part of the [work] world.* Yes. No.
> Who knows?

In choosing to describe this dinner outing in response to a question about the separation of work and family, this father challenges the notion that these two worlds need to be separated. And by questioning whether "one could say whether this is part of the [work] world" he problematizes this ideal—and also, we argue, the idea of a time designated exclusively for the nuclear family. This father, like other Italian parents, presents time with family as diffused across other participants who share activities together.

The comparison between the Italian and American parents' charts revealed the tendency of the Americans to view togetherness as an activity-driven, exclusive time for the nuclear family only and the proclivity of the Italians to characterize times together as more fluid across activities and participants. Further, the Los Angeles parents tended to put emphasis on the personal effort required to carve out special time and activities for the family, whereas the Roman parents did not associate effort with being together with the family. We concluded that the Italian parents in our study felt less burdened by the pressure to "be together" at a certain time engaging in special activities and consequently felt less responsible to carry out an idealized family time.[21]

Quality Moments

In spite of their adherence to a formal quality family time ideal, it turned out that CELF families often experienced spontaneous, nondesigned togetherness. In a study of the video-recorded daily activities of family members, we found that parents and children took advantage of routines to connect with one another.[22] Everyday activities offered families "quality moments," unplanned, unstructured instances of social interaction that serve the important relationship-building functions attributed to quality time. In a spontaneous game of hide-and-seek when a child hid a socked foot in a pile of laundered socks the mother was folding or in a playful father-daughter conversation while standing at the cashier line during a weekly food shopping excursion, these quality moments, though brief, afforded family members opportunities to connect by displaying mutual interest and positive affect.

In that study we proposed that these moments often went unnoticed by parents primarily because of the dominance in the United States of the quality time model of organized special activities in designated time slots for the nuclear family. We felt that this oversight was unfortunate for two reasons. First, when one fails to recognize these quality moments, one risks ignoring and not fostering the ongoing relational "work" that family members engage in through social interaction during any time together. Second, affirming quality moments may diminish the repercussions associated with the pressure to achieve the idealized family time and the guilty feelings when it is not accomplished.[23] Gaining an awareness of mundane quality moments, we proposed, may render parents' subjective experiences of everyday family interactions more positive and fulfilling.[24]

But is the experience of time famine and of the struggle for family time rooted in individuals' subjective experiences? Parents' ethnotheories about how one should raise a family are heavily influenced by the constraints and values of the culture they live in.[25] And in talking about their practices and choices, parents expose the cultural resources available for them to present and understand their world.[26] Thus it is suggested that our CELF parents' discourses about time for family divulge not only their own views but also the collective voice of their community. Through discussions of their management of and concerns about time for family, they unveiled two encompassing cultural approaches to time: (a) time's definition is rooted in the activities that inhabit it (e.g., family time must include certain activities); and (b) time involves intentional, purposeful control over the occurrence of these certain activities in certain time slots (e.g., parents need to find and allocate specific time slots to the family time activity). This attitude toward time emphasizes one's individual responsibility for how time is used and the preference for exerting control over it.

Indeed, the CELF parents' excerpts in this chapter evidence this cultural propensity for taking full responsibility for the effort and struggle to control time for family. What seemed to be dominant in the parents' discourse was the feeling that they were faced with private challenges regarding time that they had to resolve with individual solutions and that they were alone in this battle. In being different, the iCELF examples allowed us the realization that this attitude was not shared by the Italian parents, suggesting that the need to master time and to control how it is used is linked to specific American cultural norms and ideals about family, time, and responsibility. When parents recognize the role of culture in the "time for family" predicament, they may begin to view their inability to produce the ideal family time as not necessarily a personal "failing" and have a more positive outlook on their family togetherness.

NOTES

1. Bianchi, Robinson, and Milkie 2006; Daly 2001a, 2001b; Darrah et al. 2007; Robinson and Goodby 1997.

2. Gornick and Meyers 2003; Jacobs and Gerson 2004.

3. Hofferth 2009.

4. Galinsky 1999; Hays 1996; Kremer-Sadlik 2008.

5. Daly 2001b.

6. Ibid., 9.

7. Finch 1989.

8. Hays 1996; Kremer-Sadlik 2008; McCarthy, Edwards, and Gillies 2000.

9. Daly 2001b.

10. Bernas and Major 2000; Christiansen and Palkovitz 2001; Coltrane 2000; Gerson 2004; Roxburgh 2002, 2006.

11. Coltrane 2000.

12. Roxburgh 2002.

13. Bernas and Major 2000.

14. Fatigante, Kremer-Sadlik, and Fasulo 2007.

15. Daly 2001a, 2001b; Gillis 2001; Plionis 1990.

16. Kraehmer 1994.

17. Kremer-Sadlik and Paugh 2007.

18. Gillis 2003.

19. Kremer-Sadlik, Fatigante, and Fasulo 2008.

20. Ibid.

21. Ibid.

22. Kremer-Sadlik and Paugh 2007.

23. Galinsky 1999; Daly 2001a, 2001b; Gillis 2001.

24. Kremer-Sadlik and Paugh 2007.

25. D'Andrade and Strauss 1992; Harkness and Super 1996, 2006.

26. Wetherell 2003.

12 The Good Enough Family

ELINOR OCHS AND TAMAR KREMER-SADLIK

THE BURDENS OF MORALITY

When working parents slide into bed after a long day, they often feel quite exhausted without exactly knowing why. This volume lays bare the fleeting but consequential moments in which working parents dedicate themselves to the family as an enterprise. Ethnographic video recordings captured the myriad efforts they exerted to achieve daily routines; photographs documented the ever-needing-to-be-tidied-up intimate spaces; in-depth interviews exposed parental desires and frustrations; and cortisol sampling revealed the hidden story of individual family members' stress levels over the course of their day.

CELF parents were constantly responding to situational exigencies that arise in the course of a day. That in itself was enervating. But, in addition, parents' handling of these exigencies was subject to moral examination, which further burdened them. Sometimes moral examination took the form of explicit judgments. More pervasively, parents sensed that their actions and decisions, as well as those of their children, were accountable to standards set by a tribunal of educators, physicians, spiritual leaders, scientific authorities, neighbors, other parents, and the popular media. CELF parents faced family life in an era of heightened insecurity about the future and disjuncture with the middle-class American Dream that once held so much promise for post–World War II parents.[1] They felt that they had to double up on their efforts to protect their families and give their children every possible advantage in a very fragmented and unstable twenty-first-century American society.[2]

Decades ago the psychoanalyst Donald Winnicott introduced the concept of "the good enough mother," who need not be perfectly intuitive but rather good enough to provide a secure environment and adjust to her child's needs and desires at different points of maturity.[3] "The good enough mother" concept presumed the mother to be the natural anchor of the family and source of success or failure of the infant's developing self. Subsequent scholars discussed the strains of being a good enough mother in relation to other roles, commitments, and desires of women.[4] Some advocated a rethinking of "care" as an ethical enterprise.[5] "The good enough family" was promoted, wherein responsibility for self-aware and resilient children and families lies in the hands of all family members.[6] Yet what constitutes "the good enough family" remains elusive to working parents in the fast-paced twenty-first century, in which moral frameworks are constantly updated. What also eludes scholars and family members alike is how "the good enough family" is achieved through family practices. Parents in the CELF study faced everyday situational imperatives to make "good enough" decisions and perform "good enough" actions for themselves and their family, and it was not always easy.

Immersed in the experiential particulars of one's own family, it is tremendously difficult for family members to reflect upon what an "ordinary" family is and how an "ordinary" family acts.[7] Sometimes, however, the presence of a CELF researcher or a video camera moved a family member to transcend the ordinary to reflect upon and even contest the conditions of his or her family life. These reflections indicated a pressure-filled striving to be "the good enough family" and the worry that the moral standard is beyond reach. In the discussion that follows, we distill commonalties and variation in the day-to-day production of an ethical family life.

THE MORAL GAZE

While the panoptical gaze of social authority has been analyzed in schools, prisons, asylums, and other institutions, the family is the quintessential site for moral assessment.[8] After all, what is more consequential than acts that cast the die for children's physical, social, and emotional development or the resilience of couple relationships. In the everyday lives of CELF families, the panoptical regard operated both from without and within the family, as one's actions and stances as mother, father, son, daughter, and spouse or partner were subject to constant evaluation.

Inside the family, parents judged children's behavior from morning to night, and spouses constantly directed moral glances at one another. For example, parents often told children what they "need to" do. Dinnertimes echoed with "You need to sit down"; "You need to eat"; "You gotta eat your lima beans"; "If you are going to burp, you need to excuse yourself." At the same time, children often resisted: "I don't want to eat"; "I don't need peas"; "I would rather starve than eat this." In one family, a father despaired, "He doesn't eat any greens," to which his child responded, "Stop lecturing us with fruits and vegetables!" From a Foucauldian point of view,[9] parents used discipline to control and educate their children to be "ethical subjects," while children struggled for the freedom to assert their own counterdesires.

Similarly, wives and husbands often scrutinized one another's actions and attitudes.[10] During dinnertime in the Khakkar household, for example, the mother, Raya, briefly left and returned to the table to find that her husband, Sam, had let their son Dar leave the table without finishing his hamburger:

> RAYA: Where is his plate?
>
> SAM: I don't know, he didn't finish it.
>
> RAYA: No, he has to finish his burger.

After this admonishment, the younger son, Moni, joined his father in laughingly revealing that the hamburger had already been thrown away. Raya's moral injunction against her spouse qua father was swift: "Why did you let him get away with it?"

A similar moral judgment between spouses transpired in the Slovenski family. Susannah spent much of the afternoon monitoring her son to make sure that he completed his homework. When her husband, John, returned home and looked over the homework, he found errors and criticized her for not teaching the child so that he could do the exercises independently. After John finished going over the boy's homework, Susannah looked at him and inquired, "Did I do it right?" In this utterance Susannah opened the possibility for her husband to criticize her by voicing her insecurity and eliciting his opinion of the quality of her assistance, which he provided.

> JOHN: Yeah, but you didn't tell him how he has to get those numbers
>
> SUSANNAH: What? Yes I did!
>
> JOHN: He said all he has to do is change the things. And I said "Do you know how the numbers came out?" And he said "No."

When John blamed her directly for failing to do the right thing, Susannah was put on the defensive. She then called her son to "testify" that she worked with him to understand how to solve the math problems. Our video recordings evidence her arduous efforts to this end in the midst of caring for a toddler, cooking, and her son's lackluster attention. In the end, however, the homework answers were incorrect.[11]

Parents, especially mothers, were also prone to self-reflection, sometimes self-disparaging, sometimes frustrated at the corners they had to cut to get through the day. Mothers themselves also voiced their unhappiness that they had to assume the daily burdens of going over homework with their children. To get a sense of its physical and mental toll, let us listen in on the "confessions" of Jeri and her friend Shelly, who chatted about teachers and homework while their daughters were playing together. Shelley began by complaining about a teacher who gives a lot of homework, and Jeri commiserated.

> SHELLY: But it's the homework that you don't want to [sit and straddle
>
> JERI: [That's right yeah.
>
> SHELLY: All—every day ((*pause*)) you know.
>
> JERI: HHH!

The use of "straddle" here alludes to the existential condition that mothers face when they leave the workplace, namely, that they begin a "second shift" of domestic undertakings.[12]

Shelly and Jeri went on to expand the emotional toll of just thinking about their children's homework.

> SHELLY: I wake up in the morning and I think about okay what's Becky going to—got to do for homework today.
>
> JERI: I know ((*pause*)) I *know!* [it's just—it's like going through school all over again.
>
> SHELLY: [It's makes me crazy. And then I come home and the first thing I say to her is "Did you get your homework done?" instead of "Hi. How was your day?"
>
> JERI: Right.
>
> SHELLY: Hhh.

Here we see how homework looms as a huge hurdle for mothers to manage from the time they wake up. Our video recordings show that the topic of homework assignments dominated conversations between mothers and their children immediately upon first contact after school and work.[13] This exchange captures a mother's guilt moment: Rather than being the "good mom" who shows care and interest ("How was your day?"), she is the bossy, nagging mother who has to make sure the homework is done.

At this point the two mothers turned their normalizing judgments away from themselves to their daughters to critique the quality of their homework.

JERI: She usually gets it done though.

SHELLY: Uh ((*pause*)) she rushes through it sometimes
((*pause*))
I have to look at it.

JERI: But yeah.

SHELLY: She ((*pause*)) she ((*pause*)) says I got it—
Her—her big thing is to say "I got it done" but then I look it over and it's

JERI: Not correct.

SHELLY: Really sloppy.

JERI: Right.

SHELLY: And really fast.

Having raised these issues, the two mothers returned the moral gaze to themselves, this time justifying with embarrassed laughter their morally compromised response to the homework quandary.

JERI: Well I get to the point where I'm so tired I give Anna the answers. ((*laughs*))

SHELLY: ((*laughs*))

JERI: I'm just like.

SHELLY: "Here let me do it for you."

JERI: I'm just like
((*Pause*))
I try my hardest but I'm like "Yeah yeah that's it."
((*laughs*))

Throughout this conversation Jeri and Shelly portrayed homework as an ethically conflicted activity that marred their relationship with their children and their own integrity. They treated themselves as objects of moral inspection.[14] Both confessed to giving answers and doing the homework for their daughters. Jeri justified these lapses as the result of being "so tired" and trying "my hardest." The mothers finished each other's sentences and laughed together at their untenable predicament. Of course, this behavior was exactly what the father in the previously mentioned example was criticizing—the fact that his wife ended up giving the child the answers rather than making sure he knew how to do it alone. The conversation between Jeri and Shelly provides insight into why mothers commit such moral transgressions—because homework activity is so lengthy, rife with tension, unpleasant, and tiring. Indeed, CELF video recordings attest to just how time-consuming homework is.[15]

This kind of morally charged conversation about homework is going on all around the country. The defensive sensibilities expressed by these two mothers form a backdrop to the panoptical gaze of those husbands who arrive home later in the evening and who upbraid their partners for providing inadequate help with children's homework. The good child, the good mother, the good father, and the good partner—all infuse the practice of homework. Or, putting it another way, practices like homework entail certain standards of conduct that are part of the "ordinary ethics"[16] of being a family. These ethical entailments, in turn, may be sources of contestation, liberation, or transformation, adding a certain open-endedness to one's family and one's day. As such, ordinary family ethics involves continuous self-production and a dynamic form of social engagement that can be emotionally and physically taxing.

THE MORAL COSTS OF PRACTICAL LIFE

It was not the intention of this volume to rethink the contours of morality and ethics, which have been subject to considerable academic debate over the centuries. Yet our study speaks to the locus of ethics in ordinary contexts. We agree with Eagleton, who argues that "the ethical is not a seductively unattainable ideal but a common material practice. We are speaking of the shape and texture of average lives, not of the aesthetic splendour of isolated acts."[17] When one thinks about daily life, the notion "mundane" comes to mind, meaning both "ordinary" and "prosaic." Morality in this context would seem to be a run-of-the-mill disposition to be good that is built into seamless and routine ways of living. It turns out, however, that this picture is far from complete. The day-to-day workings of family life are punctuated with episodes of frisson wherein what is moral is contested.

Working parents struggle with the pull of a moral regime that their own parents lived by and that no longer seems tenable.[18] A common American image from textbooks to cinema is that each new generation forges ahead, crosses frontiers, and does not look back. In addition, the rapid rise of the dual-income family has meant that parents have had to improvise a "good enough" way to raise a family. Families may continue to eat dinner, for example, but what they eat is often a prepackaged "convenience food." As such, the ordinary ethics of each nuclear family is cobbled together from childhood experiences and present-day exigencies and aspirations of family members.[19]

CELF working parents experienced disjunctures between idealized images and actual lived ways of being a family. The moral criteria for being a good parent, a good family, and a good worker were reexamined on a daily basis. It was not simply that parents transgressed some "principle" of goodness. They also expressed guilt, frustration, and ambivalence regarding the way that managed raising a family. Jeri and Shelly, for example, regretted how they took over their children's homework assignments to save time. Other women felt bad that they were unable to take time off from work to volunteer in their children's classes, not matching an ideal of being a good mother.[20] Some fathers returning from work hoped that their family would welcome them home but also recognized that their spouse and children were engrossed in homework, dinner preparation, and media activities. Fathers either found a way to penetrate the walls of consciousness of the rest of the family or, more often, resigned themselves to being ignored. One returning father who tried unsuccessfully to compete with a video game for his sons' attention muttered, "God forbid they should know anything else besides play, huh?"[21]

Parents at times conveyed conflicting messages to their children about what is ethical. They told their children what they expected, but their actions belied a different expectation. In one family, a father directed his son to get himself dressed, signaling a desire for his child's autonomy, but he then caved in to his son's demand that he untie and then tie the shoes for him and cringed when his son called him "a control freak."[22] Similarly, CELF parents asked their children what they "want to" eat, then told them what they "have to" or "need to" eat. Sometimes in these situations parents even told the children what they *want to* eat ("Rory, you want to eat everything"). As the philosopher Zizek noted, this practice exhibits an extreme mechanism of power, in that parental desires are decreed to be the desires of their children.[23]

In this manner, the existential condition of the family is that ordinary ethics is far from a taken-for-granted sensibility and more a daily challenge. The studies presented in this book have explored the unfolding of this ethical endeavor, highlighting how this daily project evidences discrepancies between culture, historically rooted principles and aspirations, and more immediate situational contingencies, as parents operate within the fine lines of doing that which is right, possible, necessary, inevitable, rational, and easiest in the quest to raise a family. At times parents relinquished that which they espoused as "the right way" for a more practical and easier alternative.

It is striking that some innovative tactics that parents adopted to simplify their lives generated unforeseen complexities, with the family as a whole unhappily bearing the consequences. For example, many parents used "time-saving" preprepared meals that can be easily microwaved, although they disclosed in their interviews that they wished they could serve home-cooked healthy meals. These frozen packaged meals, however, often turned out be a source of discontent during mealtimes, in that they could not be easily modified. Children frequently complained that they disliked something about the combination of ingredients in these meals and insisted that they be served an entirely different microwaved meal from a list of choices that were stocked in the freezer that parents rattled off to them. These complaints and ensuing negotiations negatively colored the family gathering.[24] Over time such practically motivated strategies and situational decisions affect the felicity of the family.

COMMUNAL AND INDIVIDUAL MORALITIES

An important ethical consideration for CELF families was how to accommodate the individual wants of family members in relation to the family as a communal enterprise. Individualism and communalism have often been portrayed as historically and socioculturally rooted polar ethical sensibilities. As discussed in philosophy and the social sciences, individualism favors autonomy, freedom, agency, creativity, desire, will, personality, character, charisma, intention, subjectivity, and the self. Communalism, in contrast, promotes civic consciousness, public good, duty, citizenry, regularity, continuity, collective responsibility, and socially distributed knowledge and labor.[25] In some paradigms, communalism is the moral albatross that dulls and constrains individual will and self-knowledge, from which individuals are beckoned to free themselves.[26] In other perspectives, individualism is viewed as an ever more sweeping globally decadent presence:[27]

> Some see a preoccupation with self-development as an offshoot of
> the fact that the old communal orders have broken down, producing
> a narcissistic, hedonistic concern with the ego. Others reach much
> the same conclusion, but trace this end result to forms of social
> manipulation. Exclusion of the majority from the arenas where the

most consequential policies are forged and decisions taken forces a concentration upon the self; this is a result of the powerlessness most people feel.

In the first approach the communal order gives way to self-preoccupation; in the second, self-preoccupation is a response to being left behind by prevailing powers.

From an anthropological perspective, however, communal and individual, like interdependence and autonomy, are not principles that differentiate entire societies but rather coexist in variable guises and to varying degrees of importance and elaboration within a single social group.[28] Indeed, lifelong human development and learning universally involves a combination of a strong sense of self-knowledge, self-differentiation, and self-reliance plus the ability and will to enter into webs of social coordination, empathy, and support with others to achieve common goals. In the contemporary United States and other societies, certain freedoms and potentialities associated with individualism (including the freedom to resist the status quo and to pursue alternative ideals) tend to be exalted, while the excesses of single-minded self-advancement and indulgence are deplored. As such, individualism is morally Janus-faced.

Looking at CELF households, we did not see evidence that the "communal order" of the family had broken down or that individual family members typically privileged their own desires over family concerns. Rather, what we observed in most families was a socially and culturally structured ongoing tension between these two orientations. The cohesiveness of the family was a focus of considerable moral inquietude of CELF parents, who talked about the need to carve out of the busy week a special "quality time" to be together. Parents often voiced the concern that they fell short of their own ideal. CELF researchers came to the conclusion that such feelings of inadequacy stemmed in part from the fact that parents idealized family time as a "special time" apart from others in which the whole family participated in a planned event. Curiously, many *spontaneous* moments of intimacy and enjoyment between parents and children tended to go unrecognized as family time.[29]

The tug of the individual and the communal within the family is also seen in the use of private and public home spaces, participation in family dinners, reuniting and withdrawing after work, familial fallout of individual health habits, and limited opportunities for parental leisure in the face of housework and childcare.[30] Across these contexts, individual desires often uneasily came into play with communal goals.

Home Spaces and Possessions. The domestic architecture of contemporary middle-class homes of CELF families embraced both communal and individual values. In contrast to societies where dwellings consist of an open space, CELF houses constructed before 1980 maintained the culture-historical arrangement of rooms oriented for communal/family activity, especially the kitchen, separated from rooms identified as more personal and private, especially the bedroom.[31] Household possessions enhanced the communal/individual distinction of spaces. While hallways and other living areas in CELF households were decorated with family photographs, heirlooms, or mementos, bedrooms, especially children's bedrooms, were branded as personal havens.[32] Children's names appeared on the bedroom door, trophies, and awards; walls were plastered with their artwork, logos and images of favorite sports teams and celebrities, and collections of beloved stuffed animals and other toys.

While there is a trend in U.S. remodeling toward opening up kitchen, dining, and family rooms to enhance communality, there is also an architectural drift toward enhancing private spaces within the home. Newer homes are larger, providing bigger and more rooms (e.g., home offices, more bedrooms and bathrooms) for inhabitants to distribute themselves at some distance, if they so choose. Of particular relevance is the observation that the most frequently remodeled space in CELF homes was enlargement or creation of a master suite, perhaps as a hoped-for Shangri-la retreat.[33]

Dinnertime. The confluence of the desires to come together as a family and to pursue individual aspirations revealed itself at dinnertime. Family members, especially parents, voiced a desire to eat together, yet they sometimes missed dinner because of competing individual commitments.[34] In some households, family members who were at home tried to eat together. In other households, the moral freedoms of individualism prevailed: the family ethos allowed family members to eat dinner at different times or in different rooms. The centrifugal pull of family members away from the dinner table was promoted by another cultural property of contemporary mealtimes. In some families, family members ate individuated packaged meals. While most parents expressed a desire for their children to eat with them, the children sometimes wanted to take their own self-contained food away to consume while pursuing an interest.[35]

Reuniting after Work. As soon as working parents walked through the front door after work, the desire to unite with the rest of the family often conflicted with individual pursuits of family members in the walled-off rooms within the home. Children were absorbed in television, computer games, or homework.[36] Spouses were often mired in meal preparation or childcare. In many CELF households it was hard for parents to accept that they were nearly invisible to the rest of the family. If we look a little deeper, however, we find a somewhat different story, one that features workplace stress seeping into family life. Working fathers more than mothers tended to withdraw from the family after they returned home from work, perhaps as a way of compensating for a difficult day at work. In contrast, CELF mothers did not have the same luxury of alone time as did fathers, a fact related to their involvement in housework and childcare.[37] Although the CELF study took place in twenty-first-century middle-class households at the end of the day in "tony" Los Angeles, these divergent paths regarding engagement in individual and communal activities followed socioculturally rooted gender expectations.

Healthy Living at Home. Morality is not simply a set of abstract understandings of right and wrong but also a heuristic for acting in the world.[38] Family members are constantly making big and small decisions about what to do and worry about the consequences for themselves and others who touch their lives. Decisions that benefit the ego may have costs for the family, while those that give priority to the family may have personal costs. It is not a far stretch to realize that some of these consequences have an impact on the health of individuals and families.

Nowhere is health as a family matter more evident than in the ensnaring emotional and moral ecology of an individual family member's health-adverse habits. CELF interviews captured the distress of certain parents who appeared unable to do what is right for both themselves and their family by curbing a bad habit (e.g., smoking or drinking). In these cases, moral responsibility for the health and well-being of the family was laden with intraindividual and family-level conflict.[39] Such conflicts evidence how far everyday middle-class family life actually is from being mindless and unheroic, as cast by a host of scholars.[40] At the end of his famous surrealist poem *Plutôt la Vie,* written in 1923, André Breton advises, "And since everything has already been said/Choose life instead."[41] Perhaps if Breton could look through the ethnographic lens of the present study, he might find home life rife with reflexivity and human drama, where unhealthy habits can be fiercely contested and relegated to the shadows of the homestead or reluctantly embraced and painfully (not robotically) written into the family habitus.

Housework and Childcare. There is nothing new under the sun to say about the endless efforts entailed in housework and childcare. From self-reports and interviews scholars have been well aware that women continue to bear the lion's share of these efforts.[42] And our observations of CELF families as well heartily confirm striking gender asymmetries and working mothers' dissatisfaction in the division of domestic labor. Given this, we can conclude that the socially distributed engagement in activities for the common good of the family and for individual ends is linked to abiding gender asymmetries. Importantly, these gender asymmetries may be consequential to women's health. After difficult workdays, women's stress hormones did not decline as much as those of their spouses. In these households working women were not getting ample time to recuperate alone.[43] Indeed, a number of the working mothers in the CELF study voiced frustration over the load that they carried on the home front. An implication of such dissatisfaction is that gender asymmetries in household work may affect women's sense of well-being and, consequently, the couple relationship as a vibrant social and emotional unit.

Although many women in the CELF study expressed similar sentiments of displeasure regarding their unequal burden, some did not. Instead, they emphasized the importance of having the collaboration of their partners, whatever it might be, in managing the family and home. In these families, there appeared to be an ethos of "us,"' that is, "we work together and share common goals." These families were characterized by a moral orientation that seemed to mitigate the consequences of the unequal division of household work for the emotional quality of the family relationships. These households were characterized by a sense that the whole family acts as a *team*, working together toward communal goals of caring for the home and one another, *regardless of relative contribution of each member*. This orientation assumed that family members were attuned to situational needs and were expected, able, and willing to help.

School-aged children played a major role in the social and emotional dynamics of communal and individual orientations in families. In practical terms, the children occupied two potential social roles: objects of care and active contributors to the smooth-running household. As one may guess, children took up the first role far more than the second.[44] Although children in a few households sometimes were loving caregivers of their younger siblings,[45] far more often children eight years and older required considerable help from parents to accomplish their homework and basic tasks, even getting dressed.[46] This dependency struck us as an enigma, given the value that Americans place on autonomy.[47] Moreover, parents often had a devil of a time getting children to help with practical tasks that had to be done. Part of the reason that many working mothers in the study multitasked, we concluded, was that they got little help from their children, even when requested. The entire family was implicated in the domestic division of labor, not just the couple relationship.

These socialization patterns lend insight into why family members' sense of teamwork, shared goals, and "pitching in" when situations called for help was more important than equally dividing domestic labor for some CELF working mothers. The notion of family-as-team and teamwork that operated in several households in our study is a fuzzy ideology, yet these families seemed to use "team" as a loose metaphor for family members' cooperation and give-and-take. However, while actual teams crucially rely upon team members knowing the rule-bound parameters of their own and others' positions and operating according to game guidelines as well as thinking on their feet to meet contingencies, "family-as-team" seems to rely upon team members cooperating primarily out of their care and concern for the well-being of the family and out of their attunement and responsiveness to the practical situation at hand.

At the core of an ordinary ethics of "family-as-team" is the Lockean idea that voluntary free will or goodwill, as opposed to filial or connubial sacrifice or divine commandment, motivates action.[48] It assumes that a child (or spouse), for example, will contribute to the common good of the family and cooperate in the social distribution of domestic work because he or she is both a moral agent and inclined to be helpful rather than because of role expectations associated with a implicit family contract. In this sense, placing a value on family members' spirit of teamwork is highly individualistic: it depends on a person's psychological disposition and agentive freedom to act in situations. Dependence on voluntary displays of goodwill to get a task accomplished can be far more a roll of the dice, however, than dependence upon a sense of duty.

Indeed, it has been argued that human beings are never quite free to choose the obligations they enter into, either because freedom is constrained by an evolutionary impulse that favors altruism toward family members as a means of maximizing their fitness[49] or because infants come into a social world saturated with role expectations and then operate accordingly. Moreover, a voluntaristic sense of teamwork minimally assumes that parents have ensured that their child has been socialized to (1) notice what needs to be done in a situation, (2) be empathetic and willing to help, and (3) have the practical skills to complete the desired task. This socialization zeitgeist, however, was in evidence in only a handful of households. In highly child-centered middle-class families, most parents tended to be deeply accommodating to the perceived needs and wishes of children, who in turn were often absorbed in their own enterprises.[50]

ETHNOGRAPHIC WHAT-IFS

A good deal of the CELF study has relied on ethnography. Ethnographers are keenly aware that their presence as observers changes the dynamics of the social order they seek to understand. Yet, all things considered, there withstands an anthropological conviction that ethnography is an amazing gateway to the orderly and not-so-orderly lives of individuals as they act, think, and feel alone and in concert with others. Immersing ourselves in households in the rush of early mornings, late afternoons, and evenings over the course of a week privileged us to the little intimacies that make having a family fulfilling and that make having a family so utterly demanding. Sometimes the CELF study has been compared to reality TV, and to some extent it harks back to the 1970s documentary of the Loud family, *An American Family*, without its close-ups, divorce plans, and sexual identity revelations, and the reality series *The Osbournes*, without its theme song and heightened eccentricities. Like the Louds and the Osbournes, CELF family members knew, or at least thought they knew, each other all too well; faced challenges that were both of their own making and handed to them by the times in which they were living; and operated as if each day was a major accomplishment that required the support of others.

The televised series cut through the hours of footage to present crisply edited family life. In contrast, the CELF study steadfastly went through more than 1,500 hours of video recordings and many other data points we gathered to follow family dramas and satisfactions from their inception to their denouement. One distinct advantage of looking through unedited ethnographic video recordings is that we can see how family lives unfold minute by minute. Unlike an edited family reality show, with its cuts and fade-outs from one scene to the next, CELF family living just went on, drifting here and there, and we kept our eyes glued, following right along. Also, the CELF study had its eye on thirty-two families and not just one, which is far too many lives to distill and edit down into a nonfiction narrative for a television episode. For CELF, however, this breadth gave us the distinct advantage of tapping into the sociocultural and psychological threads that characterize middle-class family life in twenty-first-century Los Angeles. And we could also see how the same family moment—coming through the door after work, dinnertime, bed-time—could be so differently managed from one household to another.

Now that the filming is over and we have looked carefully at what transpired between parents and children and between spouses, we are tempted to imagine the way a family scene might have turned out if a family member had acted differently. We have spent our academic efforts documenting and analyzing what transpired. Can we, as ethnographers, also ask, "What *could* have happened if . . . ?" No one can wave a magic wand to transform a family structure that is entangled in ideologies, practices, expectations, and values. But families might gain some insight into their own practices from the spectrum of different strategies and relational dynamics that distinguish one CELF family from another. What would happen if a routine practice in some households was adopted by other families? Sometimes a what-if alternative comes from knowing how families do things in other societies. Could it be useful to know how Swedish and Italian middle-class households manage to raise families and to imagine what if a particular strategy drifted into one's own house-hold? And sometimes a "what if" alternative is simply a modest, possible, and perhaps "logical" modification that might make a big difference in diminishing tensions between individual and communal pursuits and other moral conflicts in twenty-first-century U.S. families. The CELF study in its entirety allows consideration of the power of seemingly small behaviors and decisions in shaping how family life unfolds.

The idea of creating a what-if world that tweaks existing institutional paradigms and practices has been integral to the scholarship of Russell, Vygotsky, and Luria,[51] among others. Over the past several decades, for example, cultural psychologists have introduced techniques of "remedia-tion" as a means of improving children's learning beyond what traditional schools typically offer.[52] Remediation reconfigures learning settings in ways that are supportive and conducive to cognitive change. In this per-spective, change is lodged not so much within the individual as through activities that bring the individual and others into different kinds of cog-nitive and social engagement. Here the individual and the communal are not opposing forces but rather collaborative resources for the potential well-being of both.

In this spirit, we consider a few what-if possibilities that hold some promise for changing members' perspective on and experience of being a family. Without disabusing parents of the social and economic uncertain-ties that the twenty-first century has brought, we put forth a few what-if options that may strengthen families from *within* through everyday practices that support family members and the family as a community. Our hope is that entertaining a few of these possibilities may in itself be a remediation tool for alleviating the practical and moral weight that parents, children, and spouses shoulder, even if the alternatives are not actually implemented. In line with Vaclav Havel's view that the seat of change lies in heightened awareness ("Consciousness precedes Being, and not the other way around"),[53] the cognitive activity of reframing assumptions and practices may open the landscape of what a family should be and do. Below we put forth a selection of what-ifs to ponder.

What if working parents were routinely greeted when they returned home? Anthropologists have long noted that greeting someone is equivalent to a gift, in the sense that it gives support and respect to a person's face.[54] When we greet a family member, we acknowledge him or her as a valued human being and smooth the way to more sustained social interaction. In this important and universal manner, a greeting is a gateway to intimacy. The briefest of greetings—a "Hi Dad!"—takes only a few seconds, and more elaborate "How are you" greetings usually occupy ninety seconds or less.[55] Rewiring families to engage in this modest ritual could mitigate some of the effects of a day's stressful experiences by offering affection and a moment to air information and feelings and receive support. In that greetings are exchanged, they have the potential to instantly bring family members up to date and emotionally connected to each other's lives.

What if parents relied more on delegating tasks to children and less on eliciting their voluntary help? The few families in our study that had socialized their children to routinely do tasks experienced fewer conflicts around housework help than the many families who primarily depended upon a child's goodwill to help out.[56] That is, households that delegated tasks generally ran more smoothly than households in which parents had to request children's voluntary help in each situation. A great boon to family well-being would be to assign responsibilities to children and apprentice them into how to competently perform these responsibilities at an early age.[57] While it may be monumental to contemplate such a shift in family tectonics, what if once or twice a week each family member completed preassigned tasks, such as cleaning one's room or watering the garden, in addition to daily chores such as clearing the dishwasher or setting the table? Everyone may get a sense that they are working together toward a common goal of making everyday life run more smoothly. Moreover, parents, and especially mothers, may feel less burdened by caring for it all on their own.

What if parents secure eye contact when asking children to perform tasks and remain close at hand to ensure the tasks are at least begun? CELF parents who looked a child in the eye while issuing a directive and hung around while the child followed through with what was asked were far more effective than parents who called out directives from another room and were enmeshed in many tasks at the same time.[58] Keenly aware as we are of the many pressures on working parents when they return home, we believe that establishing mutual eye gaze and sustained parent-child focus may actually save time and emotional fallout from children's failure to act as requested.

What if fathers returning home offered mothers the opportunity to withdraw from the family and took over the tasks that needed to be completed? CELF mothers arrived home on average two hours before fathers, who worked longer hours. These two hours were tremendously exacting for working mothers, as observed in other studies as well.[59] If mothers could withdraw at some point, they could get a chance to recover from a difficult working day followed by the early evening intensity of housework and childcare, and they could rejoin the family when they felt more resilient.

What if parents paused while shopping to consider the impact of their consumption on their densely cluttered home and the seemingly unending task of housekeeping? This "what if" may be difficult to implement in the face of the desire to use dual-parent incomes to purchase objects for the family, yet the inclination toward hyperconsumerism ends up giving considerable distress to families. Many CELF parents felt that they were being choked by the many objects piled up around the house and up to the ceiling of the garage. Tidying up was overwhelming and a source of friction between parents and children, as children's bedrooms were bursting with mountains of toys and other possessions. At the cash register, it may be worthwhile for middle-class parents to project the exertion and hassle that that the purchase will exact from them once it is placed in the home.

What if parents did not fill their refrigerators and freezers with individual packaged snacks and meals and drinks for children? That children often complained about what was being served for dinner as they came to the table, insisted on different meals, and tried to take their food to another room to eat by themselves may all be tied to the ubiquity of pre-prepared single-serving food items in many homes.[60] Refrigerators chock full of easily microwaveable pizzas, pastas, and other dishes offered children the opportunity to snack and lose their appetite before dinner. In addition, these multiple food options may have given children at the dinner table reason to demand that an alternative meal be provided and for a parent to comply. Rather than enhance the family mealtime experience, these all-in-one food items created additional work for parents and were handy for children to take away to consume elsewhere in the house. What if once or twice a week parents and children made dinner together from scratch? Dinner would more likely be a shared meal in which family members invested attention, thought, time, and effort.

What if once or twice a week family members ate dinner later in the evening when everyone has returned home? Given that fathers' work schedules sometimes precluded their presence at the family dinner table, we wondered why dinner was served before the time fathers returned home. Most fathers were back in the house by 7:00 P.M. Why not serve dinner after that hour at least some nights of the week? Dinner at that hour may have a greater chance of bringing everyone together around the table to touch base about their day and plan logistics of upcoming events.

What if families sometimes became more aware of the little moments of pleasure and togetherness that everyday activities afford? CELF parents, like many other working parents, often felt guilty about not having enough time to be together with their children, yet studies repeatedly show that families spend more time together than ever before.[61] It seems that part of the problem lies in what counts as being together. CELF parents often talked about their desire and need to achieve family time with their children engaged in special activities, such as watching a family movie, going to the beach, or going to a theme park.[62] These activities required planning, effort, time, and money and elevated expectations for a grand time—and possible disappointments when the event turned out to be not so successful. Yet intimate moments peppered the routines of many of our CELF families when parents and children shared a joke, a hug, a story, or a concern, offering families many opportunities to connect and experience togetherness.[63] If parents became more aware of these moments, they might feel less concerned about the amount of time they spend with their kids and less burdened by the need to organize special activities for the family.

THE DEVIL IS IN THE DETAILS

In profound ways the everyday lives of twenty-first-century families are orchestrated by social and economic conditions that have given rise to dual-earner households, 24/7 workplaces, and child-rearing practices geared to ensuring children will be successful in a much less secure future world. At the same time, there are many aspects of family life that cannot be accounted for by these large-scale forces. The idiom "the devil is in the details" refers to the critical impact of seemingly low-level details of structure and content on the success of an endeavor—be it a building, a legal document, or mathematical model—that one should not overlook. As applied to families, the devil lies in the details of their everyday practices: how family members cooperate to get to work and school in the mornings and reconnect at the end of the day, how opportunities for positive family moments together are created, how conflicts arise and take their course, how family members get access to time alone after difficult days and to leisure moments, how homework is managed, how meals are prepared and eaten, how many possessions are purchased and fill homes, how couples coordinate housework, how children are socialized to be attentive and responsible, and how health management is a daily family consideration.

The devil in these details is the reciprocity of practical assistance and emotional support. We end this volume with the possibility that the "good enough family" depends on the ability and willingness of family members to attune to the commitments and yearnings, as well as the disappointments, weaknesses, and transgressions, of one another and the family as a social and emotional enterprise. A prerequisite for such coordination is a consciousness and sensibility, part instinctual, part socialized, that propels family members to "read" and act upon family situations, that is, to get a pulse on who needs attention and practical and emotional support and what needs to be done.

Family coordination is deeply informed by broader sociocultural expectations and conventions regarding practices and social positions, by the capacity for empathy, and by a flexibility to respond to a curve ball— an unanticipated challenge. Coordination does not necessarily lead to harmonious family interactions; indeed, at times coordination involves assertiveness, confrontation, disagreement, and/or reproof, as when a parent reprimands a child for being irresponsible. In our observations, family coordination does not work well when it depends only upon the goodwill of each family member. It works best when family members can count on one another to carry out delegated responsibilities and when they work in concert. Like a well-rehearsed dance, everyone knows how to contribute to an activity without (in the moment) being directed. At the conclusion of the CELF project, all the researchers were awed by the incredible coordination that family life in the twenty-first century demands. CELF parents performed remarkable, sometimes heroic, feats of coordination in an effort to raise a family in which members thrived individually and together.

NOTES

1. Ortner 2003.
2. Kremer-Sadlik and Gutiérrez, this volume.
3. Winnicott 1953, 1964.
4. Chodorow 1989, 2001; Doane and Hodges 1992.
5. Hochschild 1997; Hochschild and Machung [1989] 2003; Holloway 2006.
6. Govier 1998.
7. Duranti 2010; Husserl [1913] 1982.
8. Foucault 1979.
9. Foucault 1979, 1984, 1988.
10. Kremer-Sadlik, Izquierdo, and Fatigante 2010.
11. Ibid.
12. Hochschild and Machung [1989] 2003.
13. Wingard 2006a, 2006b.
14. Foucault 1988.
15. Willinghanz and Wingard 2005; Wingard 2006a, 2006b; Kremer-Sadlik and Gutiérrez, this volume.
16. Lambek 2010.
17. Eagleton 2009, 302.
18. Christensen and Schneider 2010; Gillis 1996.
19. Bourdieu 1977.
20. Kremer-Sadlik, this volume.
21. Campos et al. 2009; Ochs and Campos, this volume.
22. Ochs and Izquierdo 2009.
23. Taylor 2005.
24. Ochs and Beck, this volume.
25. Eagleton 2009; Weber 1946.
26. Foucault 1979, 1984, 1988; Lacan 1968, 2006.
27. Giddens 1990, 122.
28. Spiro 1993.
29. Kremer-Sadlik and Paugh 2007; Kremer-Sadlik, this volume.
30. See, in this volume, Graesch; Ochs and Beck; Repetti, Saxbe, and Wang; Garro; Arnold; Klein, Izquierdo, and Bradbury; Klein and Goodwin; Kremer-Sadlik and Gutiérrez.
31. Graesch 2007.
32. Arnold et al. 2012; Arnold, this volume.
33. Arnold et al. 2012.
34. Ochs et al. 2010; Ochs and Beck, this volume.
35. Ochs and Campos, this volume.

36. Campos et al. 2009; Ochs and Campos, this volume.
37. Graesch, this volume.
38. James 1977.
39. For detailed analysis, see Garro, this volume.
40. Eagleton 2009.
41. Breton 2003, 68–69.
42. Hochschild 1989, 1997.
43. Repetti, Saxbe, and Wang, this volume.
44. For details, see Klein and Goodwin, this volume.
45. See Goodwin and Goodwin, this volume.
46. Klein and Goodwin, this volume.
47. Ochs and Izquierdo 2009.
48. Jeske 2002.
49. Dawkins 1976.
50. Ochs and Izquierdo 2009.
51. Russell 1932; Vygotsky 1978; Luria 1979.
52. Newman, Griffin, and Cole 1989, ix.
53. Havel 1990.
54. Duranti 1997; Goffman 1963; Goody 1972.
55. Campos et al. 2009.
56. Klein and Goodwin, this volume.
57. Weisner 2001.
58. M. H. Goodwin 2006; Klein and Goodwin, this volume.
59. Schneider and Waite 2005; Hochschild and Machung [1989] 2003; Bianchi, Robinson, and Milkie 2006.
60. Ochs and Beck, this volume.
61. Bianchi, Robinson, and Milkie 2006; Daly 2001b; Gillis 2001; Kremer-Sadlik and Paugh 2007.
62. Kremer-Sadlik, this volume.
63. Kremer-Sadlik, this volume; Kremer-Sadlik and Paugh 2007; Goodwin and Goodwin, this volume.

The CELF Study

Private life in the United States and elsewhere is idealized as out of the public eye, concealed, protected, and relatively sacred. We have laws and rules of decorum that draw boundaries between public and private worlds. Public life implicates conducting oneself as expected for an audience, while in private life people feel that they can be less conventional and freer to be more one's self.[1] Goffman notes that the contemporary middle-class home is often conceived of as a "backstage" region where family members feel that they do not have to perform for others, although certain areas of the house, like the bedroom and bathroom, are more backstage than others.[2]

Social scientists have long thought that the public-private distinction is highly cultural and that private realms are as socially orchestrated as public ones. Yet social scientists have been relatively reticent to actually cross over the public-private threshold, directly enter into, and observe intimate life-worlds. This reticence is particularly apparent in the case of making visible the private worlds of middle-class American families. Entering these middle-class homes, where privacy is conceived of as a cultural entitlement of the highest sort, is a fearsome challenge. Moreover, in 2001 when we began our study, we had to overcome parents' trepidation that their private lives could become someone else's reality show or circulated on the Internet. Given these sociohistorical conditions, CELF researchers treaded carefully and gratefully. And in the end we have amassed an extraordinarily rare and rich archive of the backstage realms of twenty-first-century middle-class households that are otherwise out of bounds. The CELF photographic archive displays rooms as they are lived in and possessions as they are used and casually placed. We can read these photographs for what they reveal about the meaning of home and middle-class informality and intimacy. The corpus of video recordings represents sometimes self-conscious but mostly habitual ways in which family members engaged one another as they moved through their day.

Researchers trying to fathom how contemporary working parents strive to raise a family dream that they can be a fly on the wall observing the countless tasks, activities, concerns, and accomplishments that consume families' waking hours. CELF cannot claim fly status, given that we entered homes with cameras and handheld tracking devices, sampled stress hormones, interviewed family members at length, and asked them to complete psychological measures, yet we came relatively close to assuming this vantage point. The CELF team was not invisible, but researchers who entered the homes of families gracious enough to open their doors were ethnographers trained to be participant observers, that is, to be attuned to the activities and sensibilities of persons around them, to sometimes withdraw into the woodwork or outside, to sometimes lend a helping hand, and to sometimes be sounding boards for someone wanting to be heard.

THE CELF FAMILIES

The thirty-two families that participated in the CELF study were recruited through school flyers and newspaper ads and by word of mouth. Families that contacted CELF were screened by telephone to ensure that they met criteria for inclusion in the study. Families that made the decision to join the study signed consent forms. These described the study procedures and the different ways in which CELF researchers would be using the data collected. The forms also specified that families could withdraw from the study at any time with no penalty. Each family received a payment as a token of our appreciation for having participated in our study.

All participating families were composed of two parents and two to three children, one of whom was seven to twelve years old. Both parents worked at least thirty hours outside the home. In addition, the families owned and paid a mortgage on a home. In total, the CELF corpus comprised 64 adults and 73 children. The children included 35 girls and 38 boys, aged from one to seventeen. The age of CELF mothers ranged from thirty-two to fifty (mean 40) and fathers, from thirty-two to fifty-eight (mean 42).

Thirty households were headed by heterosexual parents (mother and father), and two were headed by same-sex parents (two fathers). As a

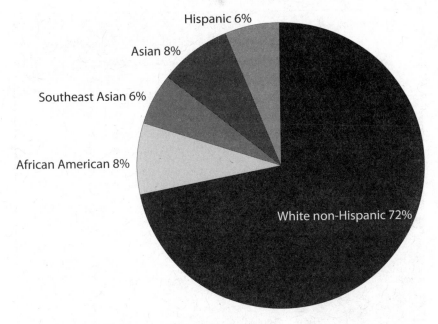

Figure A.1. CELF parents' self-identified ethnicity.

whole the ethnic composition of the CELF families represents the spectrum of ethnicities in the greater Los Angeles area.

Some CELF parents self-identified generically as "White," "Hispanic," "Black," "Asian American," or simply "American." Other parents self-identified more specifically by country of origin (e.g., "German, Canadian," "Yugoslavian Bosnian," "Indian") or religion (e.g., "Jewish," "Protestant," "Hindu") or both (e.g., "Russian, Jewish"). (See Figure A.1.)

Some families were multiethnic, each parent bringing a different background into the household. For example, in the Tracy family, the mother self-identified as Afro-Cuban and the father as "Euro Caucasian."

The CELF families resided in the greater Los Angeles area—from the San Fernando Valley to Torrance on the north-south axis and from Los Feliz to Santa Monica running east to west (Map A.1). All the families can be characterized within the loosely bounded socioeconomic category of the American middle class. It has long been argued that some combination of income, equity, education, occupation, and lifestyle distinguishes one's position in the class hierarchy.[3] In the United States the middle class occupies a broad swath that includes upper- and lower-middle-class

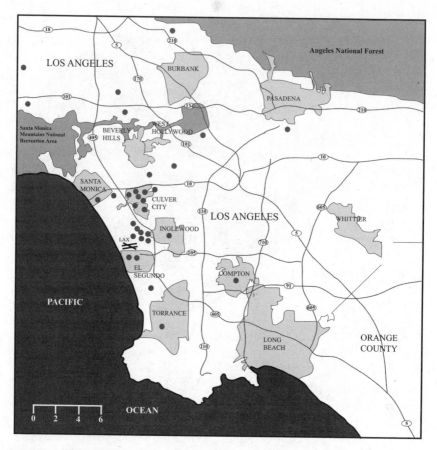

Map A.1. Distribution of CELF families in the Los Angeles area.

persons. The noted anthropologist Sherry Ortner depicts the middle class as "the most inclusive social category; indeed, it is almost a national category. In many usages it means simply all those Americans who have signed up for the American dream. . . . It is everybody except the very rich and the very poor."[4]

The majority of CELF parents were well educated, 37 percent having earned a bachelor degree and 30 percent a graduate degree. Parents' occupations were quite varied and included lawyer, dentist, engineer, accountant, teacher, business owner, sales executive, librarian, nurse, technician, office clerk, pilot, fireman, and sheriff, among other lines of work. Most parents (53 percent of fathers, 43 percent of mothers) worked 40 to 49 hours a week, some worked over 50 hours (29 percent of fathers,

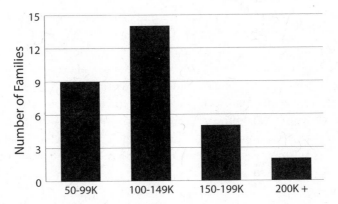

Figure A.2. CELF household income.

10 percent of mothers), and some between 30 and 40 hours (12 percent of fathers, 26 percent of mothers). The median family income was $115,000, way above the median in the Los Angeles area at the time, which stood at $43,518 (Figure A.2). As noted above, each family owned its home, paying a monthly mortgage. Most homes were modestly sized, but some were quite expansive, with big backyards.

THE CELF TEAM

The CELF team drew on expertise from academia and multimedia technology. Researchers came together from the disciplines of anthropology (including archaeology and medical and linguistic anthropology), applied linguistics, education, psychology (including clinical and social psychology), and sociology.[5] Although this volume focuses on the lives of Los Angeles families, the CELF project team collaborated closely with European colleagues who established parallel projects in Sweden (sCELF) and Italy (iCELF),[6] also funded by the Alfred P. Sloan Foundation. As seen in chapters 7 and 11, these cross-cultural collaborations offer rich, multifaceted understandings of commonalties and divergences in family ideologies and practices, in the context of historically rooted and shifting sociocultural and economic conditions in the United States and Europe.

What makes CELF rather unusual is that faculty, postdoctoral fellows, and graduate and undergraduate students worked closely with multimedia specialists to conduct a single cross-disciplinary and multimedia study of family life. Researchers spent a year designing the study in such a way that we could benefit from existing methods from our respective fields and introduce novel interdisciplinary methods and media advances to unravel the dynamics of raising a family in the twenty-first century. We then built a CELF digital laboratory to develop research-relevant software and manage the video and audio footage, photographs, architectural blueprints, clinical measurements, and other data that we collected. We also created a second CELF laboratory to view, analyze, and present data. From 2001 to 2010 the CELF research team met at least once a week to guide data collection, monitor data management, and discuss analyses. At the same time, researchers on specific projects collaborated continuously to code data and develop insights.

THE CELF ENDEAVOR

The CELF project began in 2001 and closed its doors in 2010. Data collection itself—that is, actually entering family households—took place between the years 2002 and 2005. We turn now to the overall scope of the CELF research effort. CELF designed new methodologies and adapted existing research tools to apprehend family moments that matter, perspectives that transcend these moments, and the toll of everyday challenges on family members and relationships.

"A Week in the Life"

At the heart of the CELF study is the documentation of one week in the life of thirty-two families. Three kinds of documentation captured these family life-worlds: (1) video recording, (2) scan sampling, and (3) Cortisol collection and daily mood and event reports.

Video recording

CELF researchers used two prosumer digital video cameras to record family life on two weekdays, Saturday morning, and Sunday morning and evening (Figure A.3). On weekdays family members were recorded from the time they woke up until they left for school and work in the mornings and then again when they reunited later in the day through the time when the children went to bed at night. The cameras focused on working parents interacting with their children and partners but captured children's interactions with siblings and friends as well. Using cameras with a wide-angle lens to capture the expanse of family activity and two microphones (a camera-mounted microphone and a wireless lavaliere microphone) to capture sound in the hustle and bustle of daily life, videographers filmed family members in and outside the

Figure A.3. Video recording family life.

home—accompanying them in cars, during extracurricular activities, at restaurants, on errands, peace marches, medical visits, and elsewhere. The videographers were trained to be participant observers and attuned to social situations and members' sensibilities. Wireless microphones allowed recordings to be made at a distance, reducing the intrusiveness of the cameras. Approximately fifty hours of video were recorded for each family.

Scan sampling
Borrowing a tool from behavioral psychology and ethological studies, CELF researchers tracked family members at timed intervals while they were at home. Every ten minutes across all four days of filming, each family member's location, focal activities, and objects used in activities inside the house and in the surrounding yard space were recorded using a handheld computer. Trackers were trained to remain on the periphery of home spaces and out of the way of family members. Scan sampling within this confined space allowed researchers to capture the behaviors of *all* family members at the *same* moment in time (Figure A.4). This method

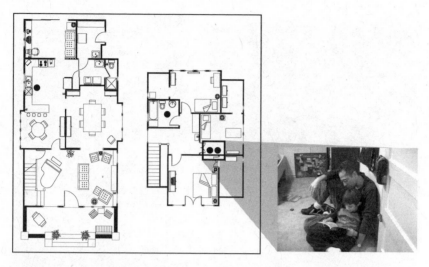

Figure A.4. Scan sampling captures family members' locations and activities: here black circles represent one parent and a child reading in bedroom, one parent in kitchen, and a child in bathroom.

systematically documents family members' use of spaces in the home, the type of activities that take place, and the objects that are used at any given time. As such this method provides a snapshot of family life that complements what is captured by the field of view of the video camera lens. Approximately 530 tracking observations were made in each family.

Cortisol sampling and mood and daily event reports

On three weekdays (the two weekdays of video recording plus one additional weekday), both parents and all children above the age of eight provided saliva samples to measure the levels of cortisol, a hormone that marks stress, at four times during the day: (1) early morning, just after awakening; (2) late morning, just before lunch;(3) afternoon, just before leaving work or school; and (4) evening, before bedtime. Saliva samples were frozen and shipped for analysis to an off-campus facility. At each sampling point in the day, these family members filled out a form rating their mood in relation to a list of twenty-five adjectives that describe positive, negative, and depressed moods. In addition, at two points in the day (just before lunch and just before leaving work or school) the parents completed a rating scale of their workload and social interactions at work, and children completed a rating scale of positive and negative academic and social events experienced at school.

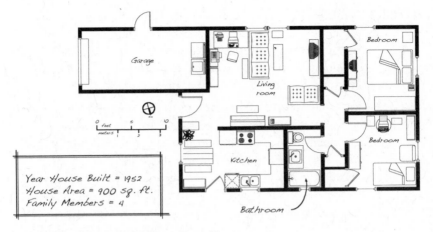

Figure A.5. Architectural floor plan of home.

Prior to "A Week in the Life"

Before this documentation of a week in the life of thirty-two families, CELF researchers gathered important information about family members and their home, which provided a rich sociocultural, psychological, and personal backdrop to the stream of household activity that we captured over the course of the week. Parents filled out questionnaires about family background, childcare arrangements, financial resources, social networks, and daily schedules. Parents were then interviewed regarding their perspectives on educational practices, social support, and family routines. These interviews were audio recorded. Family members were also asked to complete standard measures of personality (NEO Personality Inventory) and of the effects of stressful life events (Life Events Inventory).

In addition, considerable information was gathered about the family home:

(1) Parents provided a history of when the home was built, when it was purchased, and when and how it was remodeled in any way.

(2) Each space in the house was measured, and an architectural map was drawn for each home, which noted locations of major objects such as furniture (Figure A.5). This map was later used to identify spaces when researchers tracked family members' locations during the week of observations.

(3) Over five hundred photographs were taken of spaces and objects for each family in the study, including 360-degree panoramas of each room. Among other uses, these photographs allowed CELF archaeologists to identify, categorize, and count the mountains of possessions visible in each room of the house.

(4) Each parent and child above the age of five conducted an individual video tour of their home. Researchers left a video camera with each family and asked that each family member walk through the home and yard, filming and talking about home spaces and the objects therein. The recorded home tours gave researchers access to how each adult and child viewed the "same" locations and objects from different vantage points. Moreover, in the course of conducting the home tours, family members revealed a range of positive and negative emotions and moral sentiments about what they saw, providing crucial perspectives on the material habitat of middle-class families at the beginning of the twenty-first century.

After "A Week in the Life"

After documenting a week in the life of each family, CELF researchers returned to the family for an additional visit. The purpose of this visit was primarily to garner greater insight into how parents and children view themselves individually and as a family. Among other rewards, the return visit opened a window into family members' hopes, expectations, and realities in achieving emotional and physical well-being.

The focus of meeting the parents was to elicit their reflections on family and health. An in-depth interview with parents was video recorded and involved two parts:

1) Both parents discussed in depth (for approximately two hours) how health concerns affect their family life, including their assessments of each family member's overall health, chronic medical conditions, and recent health-related events. The researcher also asked parents to talk about what it means to achieve well-being and to be a healthy person, what it takes to stay healthy, and health habits in their own family.

2) While a camera was rolling, one or both parents opened their refrigerators, cupboards, pantries, and medicine cabinets and talked about the inventory of their contents, including rationales for certain purchases and which members of the family consume

which items. These descriptions of stockpiled food, medicine, vitamins, and other health-related items stored in the house illuminated shopping and meal preparation practices, food categories, and cultural understandings of nutrition, cuisine, and the path to health and well-being.

During this visit a CELF researcher interviewed each child about his or her family routines, responsibilities, and social relationships; what it is like living with working parents; and thoughts about what he or she might do later in life. In addition, the researcher asked each child eight years of age or older to complete a psychological measure of self-esteem (in academic, athletic, social, and other domains) and perception of social support from family, friends, and teachers (Harter Self-Perception Scales).

Finally, researchers left additional psychological measures for each adult family member to complete (CES-Depression Inventory, Marital Adjustment Test, and Life Events Inventory [focused on marriage]). These assessments of psychological well-being and the quality of the couple relationship were relevant to interpreting couple's interactions, the emotional tone of their communication, and levels of stress documented across the week of video recordings.

POSTPRODUCTION

Several post–data collection efforts ensured that the data corpus was organized and accessible to CELF researchers.

Video/Audio Postproduction

Research assistants created an activity log of each video recording of family interaction, using a set of key terms to mark important family moments (e.g. homework, housework, job-related work, recreation, errands). All video recordings of family interaction, home tours, and interviews were then transcribed using vPrism software, which allows researchers to synchronize video images and transcription (Figure A.6). The customized vPrism software program was developed to allow researchers to code frame by frame directly on the video the frequency and duration of key features of the recorded data (e.g., presence of family member, location, activity, time). All codes are Boolean searchable, thus sub-corpora can be generated rapidly based on various criteria (e.g., use of screen media, multitasking, couples together, siblings together).

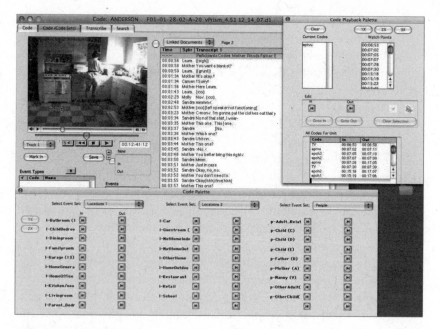

Figure A.6. vPrism synchronization of video and transcript.

Digital Image Postproduction

All photographs were marked for image content (e.g., family member, home space, food, toys, school objects) and entered into a searchable image database (Figure A.7).

Questionnaire Postproduction

All questionnaires were scanned and responses entered into a searchable database. Psychological measures were scored and entered into the database.

THE CELF ARCHIVE

In its entirety the UCLA Sloan CELF project has yielded an extraordinary archive of information regarding the state of American middle-class working parents and their children at the start of the twenty-first century. The CELF Archive is stored at the University of California, Los Angeles, and serves as a historically significant resource. The CELF Archive includes raw as well as digitized, coded, and transcribed data to facilitate analysis as follows:

Figure A.7. Digital image database.

- 32 sets of family members' socioeconomic and other background information
- 32 historical accounts of family homes
- 32 home floor plans
- 32 sets of family members' scores on psychological measures
- 1,540 hours of video recordings of family interactions, home tours, and health interviews
- 260 hours of audio recordings of interviews on education, social networks, and daily routines
- 1,170,629 transcribed lines of talk (in family interactions, interviews, and home tours)
- 1,250 activity logs with key terms of all recordings of family interactions
- 274,958 vPrism codes on video recordings
- 16,935 scan sampling observations
- 20,860 photographs of home spaces and artifacts
- 1,136 cortisol assays (649 adult, 496 child)
- 1,136 family members' self-reports on mood and experience (collected with cortisol samples)

The CELF Archive forms the basis for the analyses of family life reported in this volume. Each chapter elucidates the complexities of daily life and the challenges and achievements experienced by working families as they do their best to be a "good family."

NOTES

1. Goffman 1959; Sennett 1974.
2. Goffman 1959.
3. Beeghley 2006; Bourdieu 1984; Ehrenreich 1989; Warner, Meecker, and Eells 1949.
4. Ortner 1998b, 8.
5. CELF is administered by Elinor Ochs, Center Director; Tamar Kremer-Sadlik, Director of Research; Paul Connor, Digital Laboratory Director; and our administrators, Adrian C. Meza, Johanna Romero, Mary Hsieh, and Aleksandra van Loggerenberg. CELF Core Faculty: Jeanne Arnold, Thomas Bradbury, Linda Garro, Charles Goodwin, Marjorie H. Goodwin, Kris Gutierrez, and Rena Repetti. CELF Postdoctoral Fellows: Margaret Beck, Belinda Campos, Jeffrey Good, Anthony P. Graesch, Carolina Izquierdo, Wendy Klein, Chi-Young Koh, April Leininger, Alesia Montgomery, and Amy Paugh. CELF Graduate Student Fellows: Mara Buchbinder, Leah Dickinson, Rachel George, Jeffrey Good, Anthony P. Graesch, Wendy Klein, Tali Klima, Heather Loyd, Angie Mittman, Angela Orlando, Diane Pash, Darby Saxbe, Merav Shohet, Karen Sirota, Jaqueline Sperling, Eve Tulbert, Shu-wen Wang, Heather Willihnganz Huffman, and Leah Wingard. Additional Research Staff: Tatyana Plaksina, Julie Bernard, Brian Ellis, Satomi Kuroshima, and Maggie McKinnely. In addition, a total of 145 undergraduates have worked for CELF transcribing and coding data.
6. The Italian Center on Everyday Lives of Families (iCELF) was directed by Clotilde Pontecorvo, and the Swedish Center on Everyday Lives of Families (sCELF) was directed by Karin Aronsson from 2002 to 2005. These centers duplicated on a smaller scale (eight families were recruited in each site) the main aspects of the CELF study methodology to examine the everyday challenges that face working middle-class families in Sweden and Italy. This international comparative project has revealed how working families handle the complex demands of home and family life across the three sites and illuminated the cultural beliefs, preferences, and institutional policies that underlie these practices.

References

Adelson, Naomi. 2000. *Being Alive Well: Health and the Politics of Cree Well-Being*. Toronto: University of Toronto Press.

Aldort, Naomi. 2006. *Raising Our Children, Raising Ourselves*. Bothel: Publishers Network.

Alexander, Larry. 2003. "Family, Youth and Consumer News." Mississippi State University website, July 7. http://msucares.com/news/print/fce-news/fce03/030707activity.html.

Alwin, Duane F. 2001. "Parental Values, Beliefs, and Behavior: A Review and Promulga for Research into the New Century." In *Children at the Millennium: Where Have We Come from, Where Are We Going?*, ed. Sandra L. Hofferth and Timothy J. Owens, 97–140. Advances in Life Course Research, vol. 6. New York: JAI.

Amato, Paul R., Alan Booth, David R. Johnson, and Stacy F. Rogers. 2007. *Alone Together: How Marriage in America Is Changing*. Cambridge, MA: Harvard University Press.

Andersen, Ross E., Carlos J. Crespo, Susan J. Bartlett, Lawrence J. Cheskin, and Michael Pratt. 1998. "Relationship of Physical Activity and Television Watching with Body Weight and Level of Fatness among Children." *JAMA* 279: 938–42.

Anderson-Fye, Elaine. 2004. "A Coca-Cola Shape: Cultural Change, Body Image, and Eating Disorders in San Andrés, Belize." *Culture, Medicine, and Psychiatry* 28: 561–95.

Antill, John K., Jacqueline J. Goodnow, Graeme Russell, and Sandra Cotton. 1996. "The Influence of Parents and Family Context on Children's Involvement in Household Tasks." *Sex Roles* 34: 215–36.

Arendell, Teresa. 2000. "'Soccer Moms' and the New Care Work." Working Paper #16. Center for Working Families, University of California, Berkeley.

Ariès, Philippe. 1962. *Centuries of Childhood*. Trans. Robert Baldick. London: Jonathan Cape.

Arnold, Jeanne, Anthony Graesch, Vincenzo Raggazini, and Elinor Ochs.

2012. *Life at Home in the 21st Century: 32 Families Open Their Doors*. Los Angeles: Cotsen Institute Press.

Arnold, Jeanne E., and Ursula A. Lang. 2007. "Changing American Home Life: Trends in Domestic Leisure and Storage among Middle-Class Families." *Journal of Family and Economic Issues* 28: 23–48.

Aronsson, Karin, and Asta Cekaite. 2011. "Activity Contracts and Directives in Everyday Family Politics." *Discourse and Society* 22 (2): 1–18.

Aronsson, Karin, and Lucas Gottzén. 2011. "Generational Positions at Family Dinner: Food Morality and Social Order." *Language in Society* 40 (4): 405–26.

Backett, Kathryn. 1992. "Taboos and Excesses: Lay Health Moralities in Middle-Class Families." *Sociology of Health and Illness* 14: 255–74.

Balli, Sandra J., David H. Demo, and John F. Wedman. 1998. "Family Involvement with Children's Homework: An Intervention in the Middle Grades." *Family Relations* 47: 149–57.

Baumeister, Roy. 1991. *Meanings of Life*. New York: Guilford.

Bazelon, Emily. 2008. "The Mac-and-Cheese Effect: Why Family Dinner Makes Working Parents (Especially Moms) Feel Better." *Slate*. www.slate.com/id/2195143.

Beck, Margaret. 2007. "Dinner Preparation in the Modern United States." *British Food Journal* 109 (7): 531–47.

Beck, Margaret E., and Jeanne E. Arnold. 2009. "Gendered Time Use at Home: An Ethnographic Examination of Leisure Time in Middle-Class Families." *Leisure Studies* 28: 121–42.

Beeghley, Leonard. 2006. *Social Stratification in America: A Critical Analysis of Theory and Research*. 6th ed. Boston: Allyn and Bacon.

Before Sunset. 2004. Dir. Richard Linklater. 80 min. Warner Independent Pictures.

Belk, Russell W. 2001. *Collecting in a Consumer Society*. New York: Routledge.

Belkin, Lisa. 2007. "The Pangs of Family Mealtime Guilt." *New York Times*, June 14.

Bempechat, Janine. 2004. "The Motivational Benefits of Homework: A Social–Cognitive Perspective." *Theory into Practice* 43: 189–96.

Bernas, Karyn H., and Debra A. Major. 2000. "Contributors to Stress Resistance: Testing a Model of Women's Work-Family Conflict." *Psychology of Women Quarterly* 24 (2): 170–78.

Bianchi, Suzanne M. 2000. "Maternal Employment and Time with Children: Dramatic Change or Surprising Continuity?" *Demography* 37 (4): 401–14.

———. 2011. "Changing Families, Changing Workplaces." *Work and Family* 21 (2): 15–36.

Bianchi, Suzanne M., John P. Robinson, and Melissa Milkie. 2006. *Changing Rhythms of American Family Life*. New York: Russell Sage Foundation.

Black, Steven P. 2008. "Creativity and Learning Jazz: The Practice of 'Listening.'" *Mind, Culture, and Activity* 15 (4): 279–95.

Blair, Sampson. 1992a. "Children's Participation in Household Labor: Child

Socialization versus the Need for Household Labor." *Journal of Youth and Adolescence* 21: 241–58.

———. 1992b. "The Sex-Typing of Children's Household Labor: Parental Influence on Daughters' and Sons' Housework." *Youth and Society* 24: 178–203.

Blaxter, Mildred. 1990. *Health and Lifestyles.* London: Routledge.

———. 1997. "Whose Fault Is It? People's Own Conceptions of the Reasons for Health Inequalities." *Social Science and Medicine* 44: 747–56.

———. 2004. *Health.* Cambridge: Polity Press.

Bolin, Inge. 2006. *Growing up in a Culture of Respect: Child Rearing in Highland Peru.* Austin: University of Texas Press.

Bond, James T., Ellen Galinsky, and Jennifer E. Swanberg. 1998. *The 1997 National Study of the Changing Workforce.* New York: Families and Work Institute.

Bourdieu, Pierre. 1977. *Outline of a Theory of Practice.* Trans. Richard Nice. Cambridge: Cambridge University Press.

———. 1984. *Distinction: A Social Critique of the Judgment of Taste.* London: Routledge.

Bradbury, Thomas N., ed. 1998. *The Developmental Course of Marital Dysfunction.* New York: Cambridge University Press.

Bradbury, Thomas N., and Benjamin R. Karney. 2010. *Intimate Relationships.* New York: Norton.

Bradley, Robert H., and Robert F. Corwyn. 2004. "'Family Process' Investments That Matter for Child Well-Being." In *Family Investments in Children's Potential: Resources and Parenting Behaviors That Promote Success,* ed. Ariel Kalil and Thomas DeLeire, 1–32. Mahwah, NJ: Erlbaum.

Bradley, Robert H., Robert F. Corwyn, Harriette Pipes McAdoo, and Cynthia Garcia Coll. 2001. "The Home Environments of Children in the United States: Part I: Variations by Age, Ethnicity and Poverty Status." *Child Development* 72 (6): 1844–67.

Brannen, Julia. 2005. "Time and the Negotiation of Work-Family Boundaries: Autonomy or Illusion?" *Time & Society* 14: 113–31.

Breton, André. 2003. "Choose Life." In *André Breton Selections,* ed. Mark Polizzotti, 68–69. Berkeley: University of California Press, 2003.

Broege, Nora, Ann Owens, Anthony P. Graesch, Jeanne E. Arnold, and Barbara Schneider. 2007. "Librating Measures of Family Activities between Large- and Small-Scale Data Sets." *Sociological Methodology* 37 (1): 119–49.

Budig, Michelle J., and Nancy Folbre. 2004. "Child Care vs. Child-Minding: Measuring Activities, Responsibilities, and Time." In *Family Time: The Social Organization of Care,* ed. Nancy Folbre and Michael Bittman, 51–68. New York: Routledge.

Bumpus, Matthew F., Ann C. Crouter, and Susan M. McHale. 1999. "Work Demands of Dual-Earner Couples: Implications for Parents' Knowledge about Children's Daily Lives in Middle Childhood." *Journal of Marriage and Family* 61: 465–75.

Burman, Bonnie, R. Mangolin, and R.S. John. 1993. "America's Angriest

Home Video: Behavioral Contingencies Observed in Home Re-enactments of Marital Conflict." *Journal of Consulting and Clinical Psychology* 61: 28–39.

Burt, Sandra, and Linda Perlis. 2006. *Raising a Successful Child: Discover and Nurture Your Child's Talents.* Berkeley, CA: Ulysses Press.

Campos, Belinda, with Anthony Graesch, Rena L. Repetti, Thomas Bradbury, and Elinor Ochs. 2009. "Opportunity for Interaction? A Naturalistic Observation Study of Dual-Earner Families after Work and School." *Journal of Family Psychology* 23: 798–807.

Campos, Belinda, Shu-wen Wang, Tatyana Plaksina, Rena L. Repetti, Dominik Schoebi, Elinor Ochs, and Margaret E. Beck. n.d. "Positive and Negative Emotion in the Daily Life of Dual-Earner Couples with Children." Unpublished manuscript.

Capps, Lisa, and Elinor Ochs. 2001. *Living Narrative.* Cambridge, MA: Harvard University Press.

Chau, Amy. 2011. *Battle Hymn of the Tiger Mother.* New York: Penguin Press.

Cheal, David J. 2003. "Children's Home Responsibilities: Factors Predicting Children's Household Work." *Social Behavior and Personality* 31 (8): 789–94.

Cherlin, Andrew. 2004. "The Deinstitutionalization of American Marriage." *Journal of Marriage and Family* 66: 848–61.

———. 2005. "American Marriage in the Early Twenty-First Century." *Future of Children* 15 (2): 33–55.

Child Trends Data Bank Survey. 2003. www.childtrendsdatabank.org.

Chodorow, Nancy J. 1989. *Feminism and Psychoanalytic Theory.* New Haven: Yale University Press.

———. 2001. *The Power of Feelings: Personal Meaning in Psychoanalysis, Gender, and Culture.* New Haven: Yale University Press.

Christensen, Kathleen, and Barbara Schneider. 2010. "Introduction: Evidence of the Worker and Workplace Mismatch." In *Workplace Flexibility: Realigning 20th-Century Jobs for a 21st-Century Workforce,* ed. K. Christensen and B. Schneider, 1–14. Ithaca: Cornell University Press.

Christiansen, Shawn L., and Rob Palkovitz. 2001. "Why the 'Good Provider' Role Still Matters: Providing as a Form of Paternal Involvement." *Journal of Family Issues* 22 (1): 84–106.

Clark, Clifford E., Jr. 1986. *The American Family Home, 1800–1960.* Chapel Hill: University of North Carolina Press.

Clarke, Jean I., Connie Dawson, and David Bredehoft. 2004. *How Much Is Enough? Everything You Need to Know to Steer Clear of Overindulgence and Raise Likeable, Responsible, and Respectful Children.* New York: Marlowe & Company.

Clavan, Sylvia. 1978. "The Impact of Social Class and Social Trends on the Role of Grandparent." *Family Coordinator* 27 (4) : 351–35.

Coakley, Jay. 2006. "The Good Father: Parental Expectations and Youth Sports." *Leisure Studies* 25 (2): 153–63.

Coltrane, Scott. 2000."Research on Household Labor: Modeling and Measuring the Social Embeddedness of Routine Family Work." *Journal of Marriage and Family* 64 (4): 1208–33.

Coltrane, S., R.D. Parke, and M. Adams. 2004. "Complexity of Father Involvement in Low-Income Mexican American Families." *Family Relations* 53 (2): 179–89.

Conrad, Peter. 1994. "Wellness as Virtue: Morality and the Pursuit of Health." *Culture, Medicine, and Psychiatry* 18: 385–401.

Cooke, Lynn P. 2006. "'Doing' Gender in Context: Household Bargaining and Risk of Divorce in Germany and the United States." *American Journal of Sociology* 112 (2): 442–72.

Coontz, Stephanie. 2005. *Marriage, a History: How Love Conquered Marriage.* New York: Penguin.

Cooper, Harris. 1989. *Homework.* New York: Longman.

———. 1994. *The Battle over Homework: An Administrator's Guide to Setting Sound and Effective Policies.* Thousand Oaks, CA: Corwin Press.

Costa, Paul T., and Robert R. McCrae. 1992. *NEO PI-R.* [Professional manual.] Odessa, FL: Psychological Assessment Resources.

Costigan, Catherine L., Martha J. Cox, and Ana Mari Cauce. 2003. "Work-Parenting Linkages among Dual-Earner Couples at the Transition to Parenthood." *Journal of Family Psychology* 17: 397–408.

Craig, Lyn. 2007a. *Contemporary Motherhood: The Impact of Children on Adult Time.* Surrey: Ashgate.

———. 2007b. "Is There Really a Second Shift, and If So, Who Does It? A Time-Diary Investigation." *Feminist Review* 86: 149–70.

Crain, William. 2003. *Reclaiming Childhood: Letting Children Be Children in Our Achievement-Oriented Society.* New York: Henry Holt.

Crawford, Robert. 1984. "A Cultural Account of 'Health': Control, Release, and the Social Body." In *Issues in the Political Economy of Health Care*, ed. J. McKinlay, 60–101. London: Tavistock.

———. 2004. "Risk Ritual and the Management of Control and Anxiety in Medical Culture." *Health* 8: 505–27.

———. 2006. "Health as Meaningful Social Practice." *Health* 10: 401–20.

Crouter, Ann C., S.M. MacDermid, S.M. McHale, and M. Perry-Jenkins. 1990. "Parental Monitoring and Perceptions of Children's School Performance and Conduct in Dual- and Single-Earner Families." *Developmental Psychology* 26: 649–57.

Crouter, Ann C., and S.M. McHale. 2005. "Work Time, Family Time, and Children's Time: Implications for Child and Adolescent Relationships, Development, and Well-Being." In *Workforce/Workplace Mismatch: Work, Family, Health, and Well-Being*, ed. S. Bianchi, L. Casper, K.E. Christensen, and R.B. King, 49–66. Mahwah, NJ: Erlbaum.

Crowley, Kevin, and Melanie Jacobs. 2002. "Building Islands of Expertise in Everyday Family Activity." In *Learning Conversations in Museums*, ed. K. Crowley and K. Knutson, 333–56. Mahwah, NJ: Erlbaum.

Daly, Kerry J. 1996. *Families and Time: Keeping Pace in a Hurried Culture.* Thousand Oaks, CA: Sage.

———. 2001a. "Deconstructing Family Time: From Ideology to Lived Experience." *Journal of Marriage and Family* 63: 283–94.

———. 2001b. "Introduction." In *Minding the Time in Family Experience: Emerging Perspectives and Issues,* ed. Kerry Daly, 1–6. Oxford: Elsevier Science.

D'Andrade, Roy G., and Claudia Strauss. 1992. *Human Motives and Cultural Models.* New York: Cambridge University Press.

Darrah, Charles N. 2006. "Ethnography and Working Families." In *The Work and Family Handbook: Multi-Disciplinary Perspectives and Approaches,* ed. Marcie Pitt-Catsouphes, Ellen Ernst Kossek, and Stephen Sweet, 367–85. Mahwah, NJ: Erlbaum.

———. 2007. "The Anthropology of Busyness." *Human Organization* 66 (3): 261–69.

Darrah, Charles N., James M. Freeman, and J. A English-Lueck. 2007. *Busier than Ever: Why American Families Can't Slow Down.* Stanford: Stanford University Press.

David, Nicholas, and Carol Cramer. 2001. *Ethnoarchaeology in Action.* Cambridge: Cambridge University Press.

Davies, Gary, and Canan Madran. 1997. "Time, Food Shopping, and Food Preparation: Some Attitudinal Linkages." *British Food Journal* 99 (3): 80–88.

Dawkins, Richard. 1976. *The Selfish Gene.* Oxford: Oxford University Press.

De Carvalho, Maria E. P. 2001. *Rethinking Family-School Relations: A Critique of Parental Involvement.* Mahwah, NJ: Erlbaum.

de León, Lourdes. 2011. "'Calibrando' la atención: Directivos, adiestramiento y responsabilidad en el trabajo doméstico de los niños mayas zincantecos." In *Aprendizaje, cultura y desarrollo: Una aproximación interdisciplinaria,* ed. S. Frisancho, M. T. Moreno, P. Ruiz Bravo. and V. Zavala, 81–110. Lima: Fondo Editorial de la Pontificia Universidad Católica del Perú.

Doane, Janice L., and Devon L. Hodges. 1992. *From Klein to Kristeva: Psychoanalytic Feminism and the Search for the "Good Enough Mother."* Ann Arbor: University of Michigan Press.

Dovey, Terence M., with Paul A. Staples, E. Leigh Gibson, and Jason C. G. Halford. 2007. "Food Neophobia and 'Picky/Fussy' Eating in Children: A Review." *Appetite* 50 (2–3): 181–93.

Dukes, Richard L., and Jay Coakley. 2002. "Parental Commitment to Competitive Swimming." *Free Inquiry in Creative Sociology* 30 (2): 185–97.

Dunn, Janet S., David A. Kinney, and Sandra L. Hofferth. 2003. "Parental Ideologies and Children's After-School Activities." *American Behavioral Scientist* 46 (10): 1359–86.

Duranti, Alessandro. 1997. "Universal and Culture-Specific Properties of Greetings." *Journal of Linguistic Anthropology* 7 (1): 63–97.

———. 2010. "Husserl, Intersubjectivity and Anthropology." *Anthropological Theory* 10 (1): 1–20.

Eagleton, Terry. 2009. *Trouble with Strangers: A Study of Ethics.* Malden, MA: Wiley-Blackwell.

Eccles, Jacquelynne S., B. L. Barber, M. Stone, and J. Hunt. 2003. "Extracurricular Activities and Adolescent Development." *Journal of Social Issues* 59 (4): 865–89.

Ehrenreich, Barbara. 1989. *Fear of Falling: The Inner Life of the Middle Class.* New York: Pantheon Books.

Eldridge, Kathleen A., and Andrew Christensen. 2002. "Demand-Withdraw Communication during Conflict: A Review and Analysis." In *Understanding Marriage: Developments in the Study of Couple Interaction,* ed. P. Noller and J. A. Feeney, 289–322. New York: Simon and Schuster.

Elkind, David. 2001. *The Hurried Child: Growing up Too Fast Too Soon.* Cambridge: Perseus.

Farkas, Steve, Jean Johnson, Ann Duffett, Claire Aulicino, and Joanna McHugh. 1999. "Playing Their Parts: Parents and Teachers Talk about Parental Involvement in Public Schools. A Report from Public Agenda." www.publicagenda.org/reports/playing-their-parts.

Fasulo, Alessandra, Vivian Liberati, and Clotilde Pontecorvo. 2002. "Language Games in the Strict Sense of the Term: Children's Poetics and Conversation." In *Talking to Adults: The Contribution of Multiparty Discourse to Language Acquisition,* ed. S. Blum-Kulka and C. E. Snow, 209–37. Mahwah, NJ: Erlbaum.

Fasulo, Alessandra, Heather Loyd, and Vincenzo Padiglione. 2007. "Children's Socialization into Cleaning Practices: A Cross-Cultural Perspective." *Discourse and Society* 18: 1.

Fatigante, Marilena, Tamar Kremer-Sadlik, and Alessandra Fasulo. 2007. "The Emergence of Moral Parenthood within the Ethnographic Relationship." Paper presented at the panel Doing the Right Thing: The Discursive Portrayal of Good Parents and Moral Families, International Pragmatics Association (IPrA) annual conference, Gothenburg, Sweden, July 10.

Fiese, B. H., T. J. Tomcho, M. Douglas, K. Josephs, S. Poltrock, and T. Baker. 2002. "A Review of 50 Years of Research on Naturally Occurring Family Routines and Rituals: Cause for Celebration?" *Journal of Family Psychology* 16: 381–90.

Finch, Janet. 1989. *Family Obligations and Social Change.* Cambridge: Polity Press.

Fisher, Kevin. 2009. "Elite Place-Making and Social Interaction in the Late Cypriot Bronze Age." *Journal of Mediterranean Archaeology* 22 (2): 183–209.

Folbre, Nancy. 2001. *The Invisible Heart: Economics and Family Values.* New York: New Press.

Forsberg, Lucas. 2007. "Homework as Serious Family Business: Power and

Subjectivity in Negotiations about School Assignments in Swedish Families." *British Journal of Sociology of Education* 28 (2): 209–22.

———. 2009. *Involved Parenthood: Everyday Lives of Swedish Middle-Class Families*. Linköping: Linköping University Press.

Foucault, Michel. 1977. *Discipline and Punish: The Birth of the Prison*. New York: Vintage Books.

———. 1979. *Discipline and Punish: The Birth of the Prison*. New York: Random House.

———. 1984. "Docile Bodies." In *The Foucault Reader*, ed. P. Rabinow, 179–87. New York: Pantheon.

———. 1988. *Technologies of the Self: A Seminar with Michel Foucault*. Ed. L. H. Martin, H. Gutmann, and P. H. Hutton. Amherst: University of Massachusetts Press.

Galinsky, Ellen. 1999. *Ask the Children: What America's Children Really Think about Working Parents*. New York: William Morrow.

Garro, Linda. 2010. "Beyond the Reproduction of Official Accounts: Parental Accounts Concerning Health and the Daily Life of a California Family." *Medical Anthropology Quarterly* 24: 472–99.

———. 2011. "Enacting Ethos, Enacting Health: Realizing Health in the Everyday Life of a California Family of Mexican Descent." *Ethos* 39 (3): 300–330.

Garro, Linda, and Kristin Yarris. 2009. "'A Massive Long Way': Interconnecting Histories, a 'Special Child,' ADHD, and Everyday Family Life." *Culture, Medicine, and Psychiatry* 33: 559–607.

Gergen, Kenneth J. 1991. *The Saturated Self: Dilemmas of Identity in Contemporary Life*. New York: Basic Books.

Gerson, Kathleen. 2004. "Understanding Work and Family through a Gender Lens." *Journal of Community, Work, and Family* 7 (2): 163–79.

Getzels, Jacob W., and Mihály Csikszentmihalyi. 1976. *The Creative Vision: A Longitudinal Study of Problem-Finding in Art*. New York: Wiley.

Giddens, Anthony. 1990. *The Consequences of Modernity*. Stanford: Stanford University Press.

Gillis, John R. 1996. *A World of Their Own Making: Myth, Ritual, and the Quest for Family Values*. Cambridge, MA: Harvard University Press.

———. 2001. "Never Enough Time: Some Paradoxes of Modern Family Time(s)." In *Minding the Time in Family Experience: Contemporary Perspectives in Family Research*, ed. Kerry J. Daly, 19–37. Contemporary Perspectives in Family Research, vol. 3. Thousand Oaks, CA: Sage.

———. 2003. "Childhood and Family Time: A Changing Historical Relationship." In *Children and the Changing Family: Between transformation and Negotiation*, ed. An-Magritt Jensen and Lorna McKee, 149–64. New York: Routedge Falmer.

———. 2006. "Never Enough Time: Some Paradoxes of Modern Family Time(s)." In *Minding the Time in Family Experience: Emerging Perspectives and Issues*, ed. Kerry J. Daly, 19–36. Contemporary Perspectives in Family Research, vol. 3. Thousand Oaks, CA: Sage.

Goffman, Erving. 1959. *Presentation of Self in Everyday Life*. New York: Doubleday.

———. 1961. *Encounters: Two Studies in the Sociology of Interaction*. Indianapolis: Bobbs-Merrill.

———. 1963. *Behavior in Public Places: Notes on the Social Organization of Gathering*. New York: Free Press.

———. 1967. *Interaction Ritual: Essays on Face-to-Face Behavior*. Garden City, NY: Doubleday.

———. 1981. *Forms of Talk*. Oxford: Blackwell.

Gonerko, Christina, Marjorie H. Goodwin, and Eve Tulbert. 2008. *Socializing Accountability: Relations between Parent-Child Interaction and Sibling Caretaking Stylistic Repertoire*. Working Paper #78. Center on Everyday Lives of Families, University of California, Los Angeles.

Good, Jeffrey. 2009. "Multitasking and Attention in Interaction: Negotiating Multiple Tasks in Everyday Family Life." Ph.D. diss., University of California, Los Angeles.

Goodnow, Jacqueline J. 1988. "Children's Household Work: Its Nature and Functions." *Psychological Bulletin* 103 (1): 5–26.

Goodwin, Charles. 1994. "Professional Vision." *American Anthropologist* 96 (3): 606–33.

———. 2006. "Retrospective and Prospective Orientation in the Construction of Argumentative Moves." *Text & Talk* 26 (4–5): 443–61.

———. 2007. "Environmentally Coupled Gestures." In *Gesture and the Dynamic Dimension of Language*, ed. S. Duncan, J. Cassell, and E. Levy, 195–212. Amsterdam: John Benjamins.

Goodwin, Marjorie Harness. 2005. "Interaction, Language Practice, and the Construction of the Social Universe." *Calidoscopio* 3 (3): 184–95.

———. 2006. "Participation, Affect, and Trajectory in Family Directive/ Response Sequences." *Text & Talk* 26 (4–5): 513–42.

———. 2007. "Occasioned Knowledge Exploration in Family Interaction." *Discourse and Society* 18 (1): 93–110.

———. 2010. "From Task to Play: Shifting Frame in Sibling Interaction." Paper presented at session Children's Play and Multimodality, org. Ann-Carita Evaldsson and Amy Kyratzis, International Conference on Conversation Analysis ICCA10 "Multimodal Interaction," Mannheim, July 6.

Goodwin, Marjorie Harness, Asta Cekaite, and Charles Goodwin. Forthcoming. "Emotion as Stance." In *Emotion in Interaction*, ed. M.-L. Sorjonen and A. Perakyla. Oxford: Oxford University Press.

Goody, Esther. 1972. "'Greeting', 'Begging', and the Presentation of Respect." In *The Interpretation of Ritual*, ed. J.S. La Fontaine, 39–71. London: Tavistock.

Goran, Michael I., Kim D. Reynolds, and Christine H. Lindquist. 1999. "Role of Physical Activity in the Prevention of Obesity in Children." *International Journal of Obesity* 23: S18–S33.

Gornick, Janet C., and Marcia K. Meyers. 2003. *Families That Work: Poli-

cies for Reconciling Parenthood and Employment. New York: Russell Sage Foundation.

Gosden, Chris. 2001. "Making Sense: Archaeology and Aesthetics." *World Archaeology* 33: 163–67.

Gottman, John M. 1994. *Why Marriages Succeed or Fail.* New York: Simon and Schuster.

Govier, Trudy. 1998. *Dilemmas of Trust.* Montreal: McGill-Queen's University Press.

Graesch, Anthony P. 2004. "Notions of Family Embedded in the House." *Anthropology News* 45 (5): 20.

———. 2006. "An Ethnoarchaeological Study of Contemporary U.S. Houses and Households." Working Paper #59. Center on Everyday Lives of Families, University of California, Los Angeles.

———. 2009. "Material Indicators of Family Busyness." *Social Indicators Research* 93 (1): 85–94.

Grolnick, Wendy S., Carrie E. Price, Krista L. Beiswenger, and Christine C. Sauck. 2007. "Evaluative Pressure in Mothers: Effects of Situation, Maternal, and Child Characteristics on Autonomy Supportive versus Controlling Behavior." *Developmental Psychology* 43 (4): 991–1002.

Grolnick, Wendy S., and Kathy Seal. 2007. *Pressured Parents, Stressed-Out Kids: Dealing with Competition while Raising a Successful Child.* Amherst, MA: Prometheus Books.

Gutiérrez, Kris, Carolina Izquierdo, and Tamar Kremer-Sadlik. 2010. "'Middle-Class Working Families' Ideologies and Engagement in Children's Extra Curricular Activities." *International Journal of Learning* 17 (3): 633–56.

Halldén, Gunilla. 1991. "The Child as Project and the Child as Being: Parents' Ideas as Frames of Reference." *Children and Society* 5 (4): 334–46.

Harkness, Sara, and Charles Super. 1996. *Parents' Cultural Belief Systems: Their Origins, Expressions, and Consequences.* New York: Guiford Press.

———. 2006. "Themes and Variations: Parental Ethnotheories in Western Cultures." In *Parental Beliefs, Behaviors, and Parent-Child Relations: A Cross-Cultural Perspective,* ed. Kenneth H. Rubin and Ock Boon Chung, 61–79. New York: Psychology Press.

Havel, Vaclav. 1990. Address to the Joint Session of the United States Congress. Washington, DC, February 21. http://vaclavhavel.cz/showtrans. php?cat=projevy&val=322_aj_projevy.html&typ=HTML.

Hays, Sharon. 1996. *The Cultural Contradictions of Motherhood.* New Haven: Yale University Press.

Hochschild, Arlie. 1997. *The Time Bind: When Work Becomes Home and Home Becomes Work.* New York: Metropolitan Books.

Hochschild, Arlie, and Anne Machung. [1989] 2003. *The Second Shift.* New York: Penguin.

Hofferth, Sandra L. 2009. "Changes in American Children's Time, 1997–2003." *International Journal of Time Use Research* 6 (1): 26–47.

Hofferth, Sandra L., and Sally C. Curtin. 2005. "Leisure Time Activities in Middle Childhood." In *What Do Children Need to Flourish? Conceptualizing and Measuring Indicators of Positive Development*, ed. L. Lippman and K. Moore, 95–110. New York: Springer Science & Business.

Hofferth, Sandra L., and John F. Sandberg. 2001a. "Changes in American Children's Time, 1981–1997." In *Children at the Millennium: Where Did We Come from, Where Are We Going?*, ed. Sandra L. Hofferth and Timothy J. Owens, 193–232. Advances in Life Course Research, vol. 6. New York: Elsevier Science.

———. 2001b. "Changes in Children's Time with Parents: United States, 1981–1997." *Demography* 38: 423–36.

Hollan, Douglas. 2009. "Selfscapes of Well-Being in a Rural Indonesian Village." In *Pursuits of Happiness: Well-Being in Anthropological Perspective*, ed. Gordon Mathews and Carolina Izquierdo, 211–27. New York: Berghahn Press.

Holloway, Wendy. 2006. *The Capacity to Care: Gender and Ethical Subjectivity*. London: Routledge.

Hook, Jennifer L. 2006. "Care in Context: Men's Unpaid Work in 20 Countries, 1965–2003." *American Sociological Review* 71 (4): 639–60.

Hoover-Dumpsey, Kathleen V., Otto C. Bassler, and Rebecca Burow. 1995. "Parents' Reported Involvement in Students' Homework: Strategies and Practices." *Elementary School Journal* 95: 435–50.

Hoover-Dumpsey, Kathleen V., Angela C. Battiato, Joan M. T. Walker, Richard P. Reed, Jennifer M. DeJong, and Kathleen P. Jones. 2001. "Parental Involvement in Homework." *Educational Psychologist* 36 (3): 195–209.

Husserl, Edmund. 1982. *Ideas Pertaining to a Pure Phenomenology and to a Phenomenological Philosophy*. The Hague: Martinus Nijhoff.

Ingold, Tim. 2000. *The Perception of the Environment: Essays in Livelihood, Dwelling and Skill*. London: Routledge.

Izquierdo, Carolina. 2005. "When 'Health' Is Not Enough: Societal, Individual and Biomedical Assessments among the Matsigenka of the Peruvian Amazon." *Social Science and Medicine* 61: 767–83.

Jackson, Michael. 1996. *Things as They Are: New Directions in Phenomenological Anthropology*. Bloomington: Indiana University Press.

Jacobs, Jerry A., and Kathleen Gerson. 2001. "Overworked Individuals or Overworked Families? Explaining Trends in Work, Leisure, and Family Time." *Work and Occupations* 28 (1): 40–63.

———. 2004. *The Time Divide: Work, Family, and Gender Inequality*. Cambridge, MA: Harvard University Press.

James, William. 1977. *The Writings of William James*. Chicago: University of Chicago Press.

Jeske, Diane. 2002. "Special Obligations." In *Stanford Encyclopedia of Philosophy*. Stanford, CA: Metaphysics Research Lab, CSLI, Stanford University.

Johnson, M. D., C. L. Cohan, J. Davilla, E. Lawrence, R. Rogge, and B. Karney. 2005. "Problem-Solving Skills and Affective Expression as Predictors of

Change in Marital Satisfaction." *Journal of Consulting and Clinical Psychology* 73: 15–27.

Keenan, Elinor Ochs. 1977. "Making It Last: Repetition in Children's Discourse." In *Child Discourse*, ed. S. Ervin-Tripp and C. Mitchell-Kernan, 125–38. New York: Academic Press.

Kendall, Shari. 2006. "'Honey, I'm home!': Framing in Family Dinnertime Homecomings." *Text & Talk* 26 (4–5): 411–41.

Kendon, Adam. 1990. "Spatial Organization in Social Encounters: The F-Formation System." In *Conducting Interaction: Patterns of Behavior in Focused Encounters*, ed. A. Kendon, 209–38. Cambridge: Cambridge University Press.

Kiecolt-Glaser, Janice K., and Tamara L. Newton. 2001. "Marriage and Health: His and Hers." *Psychological Bulletin* 127 (4): 472–503.

Kennedy, Tracy L. M., Aaron Smith, Amy Tracy Wells, and Barry Wellman. 2008. *Networked Families*. Pew Internet & American Life Project, October 19. www.pewinternet.org/pdfs/PIP_Networked_Family.pdf.

King, Edith W. 1999. *Looking into the Lives of Children: A Worldwide View*. Melbourne: James Nicholas.

Klein, Felix, and Arnold Sommerfeld. 2008. *The Theory of the Top*, vol. 1: *Introduction to Kinematics and Kinetics of the Top*. Trans. Raymond J. Nagem and Guido Sandri. New York: Birkhäuser; Boston: Springer Science+Business Media.

Klein, Wendy, Anthony P. Graesch, and Carolina Izquierdo. 2009. "Children and Chores: A Mixed-Methods Study of Children's Household Work in Los Angeles Families." *Anthropology of Work Review* 30 (3): 98–109.

Klein, Wendy, Carolina Izquierdo, and Thomas N. Bradbury. 2007. "Working Relationships: Communicative Patterns and Strategies among Couples in Everyday Life." *Qualitative Research in Psychology* 4: 29–47.

Klein, Wendy, Carolina Izquierdo, Thomas N. Bradbury, and Francesco Arcidiacono. 2005. *Collaboration and Conflict: Insights into the Division of Household Labor among Working Couples in the United States and Italy*. Working Paper #36. Center on Everyday Life of Families, University of California, Berkeley.

Klein, Wendy, and Tamar Kremer-Sadlik. 2009. "State of the Union: Gender Roles and Support among Couples in Los Angeles." Paper presented at the Annual Meeting of the American Anthropological Association, Philadelphia, December 5.

Kleinman, Arthur. 1988. *Rethinking Psychiatry: From Cultural Category to Personal Experience*. New York: Free Press.

Kleinman, Arthur, and Joan Kleinman. 1991. "Suffering and Its Professional Transformation: Toward an Ethnography of Interpersonal Experience." *Culture, Medicine, and Psychiatry* 15: 275–301.

Klinck, Betty. 2010. "Survey: 89% Will Eat Family Dinner on Thanksgiving." *USA Today*, November 30.

Kraehmer, Steffen. 1994. *Quality Time: Moving beyond the Quality Time Myth*. Minneapolis: Deaconess Press.

Kralovec, Etta, and John Buell. 2000. *The End of Homework: How Homework Disrupts Families, Overburdens Children, and Limits Learning*. Boston: Beacon Press.

Kremer-Sadlik, Tamar. 2008. "Work-Family Conflict: A Parent's Problem." Paper presented at the Workplace Flexibility Sloan Conference, Washington, DC, May 29.

Kremer-Sadlik, Tamar, Marilena Fatigante, and Allesandra Fasulo. 2008. "Discourses on Family Time: The Cultural Interpretation of Family Togetherness in Los Angeles and Rome." *Ethos* 36 (3): 283–309.

Kremer-Sadlik, Tamar, Carolina Izquierdo, and Marilena Fatigante. 2010. "Making Meaning of Everyday Practices: The Case of Children's Extra-Curricular Activities in the United States and in Italy." *Anthropology and Education Quarterly* 41 (1): 35–54.

Kremer-Sadlik, Tamar, and Jeemin L. Kim. 2007. "Lessons from Sports: Children's Socialization to Values through Family Interaction during Sports Activities." *Discourse and Society* 18 (1): 35–52.

Kremer-Sadlik, Tamar, and Amy L. Paugh. 2007. "Everyday Moments: Finding 'Quality Time' in American Working Families." *Time and Society* 16: 287–308.

Kusserow, Adrie. 2004. *American Individualisms: Childrearing and Social Class in Three Neighborhoods*. New York: Palgrave Macmillan.

Lacan, Jacques. 1968. *The Language of the Self: The Function of Language in Psychoanalysis*. Baltimore: Johns Hopkins University Press.

———. 2006. *Écrits: The First Complete Edition in English*. Trans. B. Fink. New York: Norton.

Lacroix, Alexandre, and Martin Legros. 2010. "Mon réveillon chez Platon." *Philosophie Magazine* 45: 54–58.

Lambek, Michael. 2010. "Introduction." In *Ordinary Ethics: Anthropology, Language, and Action*, ed. M. Lambek, 1–38. New York: Fordham University Press.

Lareau, Annette. 2003. *Unequal Childhoods: Class, Race, and Family Life*. Berkeley: University of California Press.

Larson, Reed W. 2001. "How U.S. Children and Adolescents Spend Time: What It Does (and Doesn't) Tell Us about Their Development." *Current Directions in Psychological Science* 10 (5): 160–64.

Larson, Reed, and Maryse H. Richards. 1994. *Divergent Realities: The Emotional Lives of Mothers, Fathers, and Adolescents*. New York: Basic Books.

Larson, Reed W., and Suman Verma. 1999. "How Children and Adolescents Spent Time across the World: Work, Play, and Developmental Outcomes." *Psychological Bulletin* 25 (6): 701–36.

Lee, Yun-Suk. 2005. "Measuring the Gender Gap in Household Labor: Accurately Estimating Wives' and Husbands' Contributions." In *Being Together*

Working Apart: Dual-Career Families and Work-Life Balance, ed. Barbara Schneider and Linda J. Waite, 229–51. Cambridge: Cambridge University Press.

Levey, Hilary. 2009. "Pageant Princesses and Math Whizzes: Understanding Children's Activities as a Form of Children's Work." *Childhood* 16 (2): 195–212.

Levine, Madeline. 2008. *The Price of Privilege: How Parental Pressure and Material Advantage Are Creating a Generation of Disconnected and Unhappy Kids.* New York: Harper.

Lévi-Strauss, Claude. 1969. *The Raw and the Cooked. Mythologiques.* Vol. 1. Chicago: University of Chicago Press.

Locke, Harvey J., and Karl Wallace. 1959. "Short Marital Adjustment Prediction Tests: Their Reliability and Validity." *Marriage and Family Living* 21: 251–55.

Luria, A. R. 1979. *The Making of Mind: A Personal Account of Soviet Psychology.* Ed. M. Cole and S. Cole. Cambridge, MA: Harvard University Press.

Maier, Kimberly S., Timothy G. Ford, and Barbara Schneider. 2007. "Are Middle Class Families Advantaging Their Children?" In *The Way Class Works: Readings on School, Family, and the Economy,* ed. L. Weis, 134–48. London: Routledge.

Mathews, Gordon. 2009. "Finding and Keeping a Purpose in Life: Well-Being and *Ikigai* in Japan and Elsewhere." In *Pursuits of Happiness: Well-Being in Anthropological Perspective,* ed. Gordon Mathews and Carolina Izquierdo, 167–85. New York: Berghahn Press.

Mathews, Gordon, and Carolina Izquierdo. 2009. "Introduction: Anthropology, Happiness, and Well-Being" and "Conclusion: Towards an Anthropology of Well-Being." In *Pursuits of Happiness: Well-Being in Anthropological Perspective,* ed. Gordon Mathews and Carolina Izquierdo, 1–19, 248–66. New York: Berghahn Press.

McCarthy, Jane Ribbens, Rosalind Edwards, and Val Gillies. 2000. "Moral Tales of the Child and the Adult: Narratives of Contemporary Family Lives under Changing Circumstances." *Sociology* 34 (4): 785–803.

Maynard, Ashley E. 2002. "Cultural Teaching: The Development of Teaching Skills in Maya Sibling Interactions." *Child Development* 73 (3): 969–82.

Mead, Margaret. [1950] 2001. "The School in American Culture." *Society* 39 (1): 54–62.

Meissner, M., E. Humphreys, S. Meis, and W. Scheu. 1975. "No Exit for Wives: Sexual Division of Labour and the Cumulation of Household Demands." *Canadian Review of Society and Anthropology* 12: 424–39.

Messner, Michael. 2009. *It's All for the Kids: Gender, Families, and Youth Sports.* Berkeley: University of California Press.

Miller, Pavla. 2005. "Useful and Priceless Children in Contemporary Welfare States." *Social Politics: International Studies in Gender, State, and Society* 12 (1): 3–41.

Mintz, Steven. 2004. *Huck's Raft: A History of American Childhood.* Cambridge, MA: Harvard University Press.

Mintz, Steven, and Susan Kellogg. 1988. *Domestic Revolutions: A Social History of American Family Life*. New York: Free Press.

Murphy, Keith M. 2005. "Collaborative Imagining: The Interactive Use of Gestures, Talk, and Graphic Representation in Architectural Practice." *Semiotica* 156 (1–4): 113–45.

Nash, Ogden. 1933. *Happy Days*. New York: Simon and Schuster.

National Center on Addiction and Substance Abuse at Columbia University. 2010. *The Importance of Family Dinners* VI. New York: National Center on Addiction and Substance Abuse.

Needleman, Robert. 2001. "Extra-Curricular Activities." *Dr. Spock*. www.drspock.com/article/0,1510,5922,00.html.

Neumark-Sztainer, Dianna, Peter J. Hannan, Mary Story, Jillian Croll, and Cheryl Perry. 2003. "Family Meal Patterns: Associations with Sociodemographic Characteristics and Improved Dietary Intake among Adolescents." *Journal of the American Dietary Association* 103: 317–22.

Newman, Denis, Peg Griffin, and Michael Cole. 1989. *The Construction Zone: Working for Cognitive Change in School*. Cambridge: Cambridge University Press.

Nocon, Honorine, and Michael Cole. 2006. "School's Invasion of 'After-School': Colonization, Rationalization, or Expansion of Access?" In *Learning in Places: The Informal Education Reader*, ed. Z. Bekerman, N. Burbules, and D. Keller, 99–122. New York: Peter Lang.

Ochs, Elinor. 1988. *Culture and Language Development: Language Acquisition and Language Socialization in a Samoan Village*. Cambridge: Cambridge University Press.

Ochs, Elinor, with Anthony Graesch, Angela Mittmann, Thomas Bradbury, and Rena L. Repetti. 2006. "Video Ethnography and Ethnoarcheological Tracking." In *Handbook of Work and Family*, ed. M. Pitt-Catsouphes, S. Sweet, et al., 387–410. Mahwah, NJ: Erlbaum.

Ochs, Elinor, and Carolina Izquierdo. 2009. "Responsibility in Childhood: Three Developmental Trajectories." *Ethos* 37 (4): 391–413.

Ochs, Elinor, Clotilde Pontecorvo, and Alessandra Fasulo. 1996. "Socializing Taste." *Ethnos* 6 (1): 7–46.

Ochs, Elinor, and Bambi Schieffelin. 1984. "Language Acquisition and Socialization: Three Developmental Stories and Their Implications." In *Linguistic Anthropology: A Reader*, ed. A. Duranti, 263–301. Malden, MA: Blackwell.

Ochs, Elinor, and Merav Shohet. 2006. "The Cultural Structuring of Mealtime Socialization." In *Family Mealtime as a Context of Development and Socialization*, ed. R.W. Larson, A.R. Wiley, and K.R. Branscomb, 35–50. San Francisco: Wiley Periodicals.

Ochs, Elinor, Merav Shohet, Belinda Campos, and Margaret Beck. 2010. "Coming Together at Dinner: A Study of Working Families." In *Workplace Flexibility: Realigning 20th-Century Jobs for a 21st-Century Workforce*, ed. K. Christensen and B. Schneider, 57–70. Ithaca: Cornell University Press.

Ochs, Elinor, Ruth Smith, and Carolyn Taylor. 1989. "Detective Stories at Dinnertime: Problem-Solving through Co-Narration." *Cultural Dynamics* 2 (2): 238–57.

Ochs, Elinor, and Carolyn Taylor. 1992. "Science at Dinner." In *Texts and Contexts: Cross-Disciplinary and Cross-Cultural Perspectives on Language Study,* ed. C. Kramsch, 29–45. Lexington, MA: D.C. Heath.

Odgen, Cynthia L., Katherine M. Flegal, Margaret D. Carroll, and Clifford L. Johnson. 2002. "Prevalence and Trends in Overweight among US Children and Adolescents, 1999–2000." *JAMA* 288: 1728–32.

Offer, Shira, and Barbara Schneider. 2010. "Multitasking among Working Families: A Strategy for Dealing with the Time Squeez.." In *Workplace Flexibility: Realigning 20th-Century Jobs for a 21st-Century Workforce,* ed. K. Christensen and B. Schneider, 43–56. Ithaca: Cornell University Press.

Orenstein, Peggy. 2009. "The Way We Live Now: Kindergarten Cram." *New York Times,* www.nytimes.com/2009/05/03/magazine/03wwln-lede-t.html?_r = 1&emc = eta1.

Ortner, Sherry B. 1998a. "Generation X: Anthropology in a Media-Saturated World." *Cultural Anthropology* 13 (3): 414–40.

———. 1998b. "Identities: The Hidden Life of Class." *Journal of Anthropological Research* 54 (1): 1–17.

———. 2003. *New Jersey Dreaming : Capital, Culture, and the Class of '58.* Durham: Duke University Press.

Osit, Michael. 2008. *Generation Text: How to Raise Kids in an Age of Instant Everything.* New York: Amacom.

Patrick, Heather, and Theresa A Nicklas. 2005. "A Review of Family and Social Determinants of Children's Eating Patterns and Diet Quality." *Journal of the American College of Nutrition* 24 (2): 83–92.

Patterson, Gerald R. 1982. *Coercive Family Process.* Eugene, OR: Castalia.

Patterson, Gerald R., and Lew Bank. 1986. "Bootstrapping Your Way in the Nomological Thicket." *Behavioral Assessment* 8: 49–73.

Paugh, Amy, and Carolina Izquierdo. 2009. "Why Is This a Battle Every Night? Negotiating Food and Eating in American Dinnertime Interaction." *Journal of Linguistic Anthropology* 19 (2): 185–204.

Perry-Jenkins, Maureen, Rena L. Repetti, and Ann C. Crouter. 2000. "Work and Family in the 1990s." *Journal of Marriage and the Family* 62: 981–98.

Peterson, R.R., and K. Gerson. 1992. "Determinants of Responsibility for Child Care Arrangements among Dual-Earner Couples." *Journal of Marriage and the Family* 54: 527–36.

Pew Research Center Publications. 2007. "As Marriage and Parenthood Drift Apart, Public Is Concerned about Social Impact." http://pewresearch.org/pubs/526/marriage-parenthood.

Philosophie Magazine. 2010. "La famille est-elle insupportable?" *Philosophie Magazine* 45: 38–57.

Pigeron, Elisa. 2008. "'Here's the Deal': Socialization into Morality through

Negotiations of Media Time Use." Working Paper #77. Center on Everyday Lives of Families, University of California, Los Angeles.

——. 2009. "The Technology-Mediated Worlds of American Families." Ph.D. diss., University of California, Los Angeles.

Pisarski, Alan E. 2006. *Commuting in America III: The Third National Report on Commuting Patterns and Trends.* Cooperative Research Program Report. Transportation Research Board of the National Academies. http://onlinepubs.trb.org/onlinepubs/nchrp/CIAIII.pdf.

Pleck, E. H., and J. H. Pleck. 1997. "Fatherhood Ideals in the United States." In *The Role of the Father in Child Development,* ed. M. E. Lamb, 33–48. New York: Wiley.

Plionis, E. M. 1990. "Parenting, Discipline, and the Concept of Quality Time." *Child and Adolescent Social Work* 7 (6): 513–23.

Pomerantz, Anita. 1984. "Agreeing and Disagreeing with Assessments: Some Features of Preferred/Dispreferred Turn Shapes." In *Structures of Social Action: Studies in Conversation Analysis,* ed. J. M. Atkinson and J. Heritage, 57–101. Cambridge: Cambridge University Press.

Press, Sarah. 2003. "Orders, Accounts, and the Culture of Control: Directives in Parent-Child Relationships." Honors thesis, University of California, Los Angeles.

Qvortrup, Jens. 2001. "School-Work, Paid Work and the Changing Obligations of Childhood." In *Hidden Hands: International Perspectives on Children's Work and Labour,* ed. Phillip Mizen, Christopher Pole, and Angela Bolton, 91–107. Future of Childhood. London: Routledge Falmer.

——. 2005. "Varieties of Childhood." In *Studies in Modern Childhood: Society, Agency, and Culture,* ed. Jens Qvortrup, 1–20. New York: Palgrave Macmillan.

Rabain-Jamin, Jacqueline, Ashley E. Maynard, and Patricia Greenfield. 2003. "Implications of Sibling Caregiving for Sibling Relations and Teaching Interactions in Two Cultures." *Ethos* 3 (2): 204–31.

Reay, Diane. 2004. "Education and Cultural Capital: The Implications of Changing Trends in Education Policies." *Cultural Trends* 13 (2): 1–14.

Redekop, Paul. 1984. "Sport and the Masculine Ethos: Some Implications for Family Interaction." *International Journal of Comparative Sociology* 25 (3–4): 262–69.

Repetti, Rena L. 1989. "Effects of Daily Workload on Subsequent Behavior during Marital Interaction: The Roles of Social Withdrawal and Spouse Support." *Journal of Personality and Social Psychology* 57 (4): 651–59.

——. 1994. "Short-Term and Long-Term Processes Linking Job Stressors to Father-Child Interaction." *Social Development* 3 (1): 1–15.

——. 2005. "A Psychological Perspective on the Health and Well-Being Consequences of Parental Employment." In Work, Family, Health, and Well-Being," ed. S. M. Bianchi, L. M. Casper, and R. B. King, 245–58. Mahwah, NJ: Erlbaum.

———. 2009. "Bringing It All Back Home: How Outside Stressors Shape Families' Everyday Lives." *Current Directions in Psychological Science* 18 (2): 106–11.

Repetti, Rena L., Shu-wen Wang, and Meredith S. Sears. 2012. "Using Direct Observational Methods to Study the Real Lives of Families: Advantages, Complexities, and Conceptual and Practical Considerations." In New Frontiers in Work and Family Research, ed. J.G. Grzywacz and E. Demerouti. New York: Psychology Press and Routledge.

Repetti, Rena. L., and Jennifer Wood. 1997. "Effects of Daily Stress at Work on Mothers' Interactions with Preschoolers." *Journal of Family Psychology* 11: 90–108.

RMC Research Corporation. 2005. *Healthy Youth Survey 2004*. Portland, OR: Washington State Department of Health, Maternal and Child Health Assessment Section.

Roberts, Linda J. 2000. "Fire and Ice in Marital Communication: Hostile and Distancing Behaviors as Predictors of Marital Distress." *Journal of Marriage and the Family* 62: 693–707.

Robinson, John P., and Geoffrey Godbey. [1997] 1999. *Time for Life: The Surprising Ways Americans Use Their Time*. 2nd ed. University Park: Pennsylvania State University Press.

Roxburgh, Susan. 2002. "Racing through Life: The Distribution of Time Pressures by Roles and Role Resources among Full-Time Workers." *Journal of Family and Economic Issues* 23 (2): 121–45.

———. 2006. "'I wish we had more time to spend together . . .': The Distribution and Predictors of Perceived Family Time Pressures among Married Men and Women in the Paid Labor Force." *Journal of Family Issues* 27 (4): 529–53.

Russell, Bertrand. 1932. *Education and the Social Order*. London: George Allen & Unwin.

Rybczinski, Witold. 1986. *Home: A Short History of an Idea*. New York: Viking.

Sacks, Harvey, Emanuel A. Schegloff, and Gail Jefferson. 1974. "A Simplest Systematics for the Organization of Turn-Taking for Conversation." *Language* 50: 696–735.

Saltonstall, Robin. 1993. "Healthy Bodies, Social Bodies: Men's and Women's Concepts and Practices of Health in Everyday Life." *Social Science and Medicine* 36: 7–14.

Saxbe, Darby E. 2009. "A Field (Researcher's) Guide to Cortisol: Tracking the HPA Axis in Everyday Life." *Health Psychology Review* 2 (2): 163–90.

Saxbe, Darby, and Rena L. Repetti. 2010a. "For Better or Worse? Correlation of Couples' Cortisol Levels and Mood States." *Journal of Personality and Social Psychology* 98 (1): 92–103.

———. 2010b. "No Place Like Home: Home Tours Predict Daily Patterns of Mood and Cortisol." *Personality and Social Psychology Bulletin* 36: 71–81.

Saxbe, Darby E., Rena L. Repetti, and Anthony P. Graesch. 2011. "Time Spent in Housework and Leisure: Links with Parents' Physiological Recovery from Work." *Journal of Family Psychology* 25 (2): 271–81.

Saxbe, Darby E., Rena L. Repetti, and Adrienne Nishina. 2008. "Marital Satisfaction, Recovery from Work, and Diurnal Cortisol among Men and Women." *Health Psychology* 27 (1): 15–25.

Schegloff, Emanuel A. 1968. "Sequencing in Conversational Openings." *American Anthropologist* 70: 1075–95.

———. 1987. "The Routine as Achievement." *Human Studies* 9: 111–51.

Schieffelin, Bambi B. 1983. "Talking Like Birds: Sound Play in a Cultural Perspective." In *Acquiring Conversational Competence*, ed. Elinor Ochs and Bambi B. Schieffelin, 177–84. Boston: Routledge & Kegan Paul.

———. 1990. *The Give and Take of Everyday Life: Language Socialization of Kaluli Children*. Cambridge: Cambridge University Press.

Schiffer, Michael B., with Andrea Miller. 1999. *The Material Life of Human Beings: Artifacts, Behavior and Communication*. New York: Routledge.

Schneider, Barbara, and David Stevenson. 1999. *The Ambitious Generation: America's Teenagers, Motivated but Directionless*. New Haven: Yale University Press.

Schneider, Barbara, and Linda Waite, eds. 2005. *Being Together, Working Apart: Dual-Career Families and the Work-Life Balance*. Cambridge: Cambridge University Press.

Schor, Juliet B. 1991. *The Overworked American: The Unexpected Decline of Leisure*. New York: Basic Books.

———. 2004. *Born to Buy: The Commercialized Child and the New Consumer Culture*. New York: Scribner.

Schwartz, Pepper. 1994. *Peer Marriage: How Love between Equals Really Works*. New York: Free Press.

Shweder, Richard. 2008. "The Cultural Psychology of Suffering: The Many Meanings of Health in Orissa, India (and Elsewhere)." *Ethos* 36: 60–77.

Sennett, Richard. 1974. *Fall of the Public Man*. New York: Knopf.

Sephton, Sandra E., Robert M. Sapolsky, Helena C. Kraemer, and David Spiegel. 2000. "Diurnal Cortisol Rhythm as a Predictor of Breast Cancer Survival." *Journal of the National Cancer Institute* 9: 994–1000.

Shohet, Merav. 2004. "Narrating Anorexia: Genres of Recovery." M.A. thesis, University of California, Los Angeles.

Sloan, A. Elizabeth. 2006. "What, When, and Where America Eats: A State-of-the-Industry Report." *Food Technology* 60 (1): 19–27.

Solomon, Yvette, J. O. Warin, and Charlie Lewis. 2002. "Helping with Homework: Homework as a Site of Tension for Parents and Teenagers." *British Educational Research Journal* 28 (4): 603–22.

Southerton, D. 2003. "Squeezing Time: Allocating Practices, Coordinating Networks, and Scheduling Society." *Time and Society* 12: 5–25.

Spiro, Melford E. 1993. "Is the Western Conception of the Self 'Peculiar' within the Context of the World Cultures?" *Ethos* 21 (2): 107–53.

Stearns, Peter N. 2003. *Anxious Parents: A History of Modern Childrearing in America.* New York: New York University Press.

———. 2006. *Consumerism in World History.* 2nd ed. New York: Routledge.

Stevens, Daphne Pedersen, Krista Lynn Minnotte, Susan E. Mannon, and Gary Kiger. 2007. "Examining the Neglected Side of the Work-Family Interface: Antecedents of Positive and Negative Family-to-Work Spillover." *Journal of Family Issues* 28 (2): 242–62.

Story, L.B., and Rena L. Repetti. 2006. "Daily Occupational Stressors and Marital Behavior." *Journal of Family Psychology* 20: 690–700.

Super, Charles M., and Sara Harkness. 1986. "The Developmental Niche: A Conceptualization at the Interface of Childand Culture." *International Journal of Behavioral* Development 9 (4): 545–69.

Taylor, Astra. 2005. *Zizek!* 70 min. Zeitgeist Films.

Thin, Neil. 2009. "Why Anthropology Can Ill Afford to Ignore Well-Being." In *Pursuits of Happiness: Well-Being in Anthropological Perspective,* ed. Gordon Mathews and Carolina Izquierdo, 23–44. New York: Berghahn Press.

Thornton, Peter. 1984. *Authentic Decor: The.Domestic Interior.* Viking, New York.

Tolin, David F., Randy O. Frost, and Gail Steketee. 2007. *Buried in Treasures: Help for Compulsive Acquiring, Saving, and Hoarding.* New York: Oxford University Press.

Trudeau, Garry. 2004. *Doonesbury.* June 8.

Tulbert, Eve, and Marjorie Harness Goodwin. 2011. "Choreographies of Attention: Multimodality in a Routine Family Activity." In *Embodied Interaction: Language and Body in the Material World,* ed. J. Streeck, C. Goodwin, and C.D. LeBaron, 79–92. Cambridge: Cambridge University Press.

U.S. Department of Education. 2009a. "My Child's Academic Success: Homework Tips for Parents." www.ed.gov/parents/academic/involve/homework/index.html/.

———. 2009b. No Child Left Behind and Other Elementary/Secondary Policy Documents. www.ed.gov/policy/elsec/guid/states/index.html/.

———. 2009c. Partnership for Family Involvement in Education. www.ed.gov/pubs/PFIE/index.html/.

Van Hamersveld, Kristine A., and Marjorie H. Goodwin. 2007. "Temporality and Trajectory inn Parent-Child Assessment Interaction Concerning Extra-Curricular Activities." Working Paper #69. Center on Everyday Lives of Families, University of California, Los Angeles.

Veblen, Thorstein. 1899. *The Theory of the Leisure Class.* New York: Macmillan.

Voorpostel, Marieke, Tanja van der Lippe, and Jonathan Gershuny. 2009. "Trends in Free Time with a Partner: A Transformation of Intimacy?" *Social Indicators Research* 93 (1): 165–69.

Vygotsky, L. S. 1978. *Mind in Society: The Development of Higher Psychological Processes.* Cambridge, MA: Harvard University Press.

Wang, Shu-wen, Rena L. Repetti, and Belinda Campos. 2011a. "Job Stress and Family Social Behavior: The Moderating Role of Neuroticism." *Journal of Occupational Health Psychology* 16: 441–56.

———. 2011b. "Links between Observed Naturalistic Social Behavior and Hpa-Axis Activity in the Family." Unpublished manuscript.

Warner, W. Lloyd, Marchia Meeker, and Kenneth Eells. 1949. *Social Class in America: A Manual of Procedure for the Measurement of Social Status.* Chicago: Science Research Associates.

Warren, Elizabeth, and Amelia Warren Tyagi. 2003. *The Two-Income Trap: Why Middle-Class Mothers and Fathers Are Going Broke.* New York: Basic Books.

Watson-Gegeo, Karen Ann, and David W. Gegeo. 1989. "The Role of Sibling Interaction in Child Socialization." In *Sibling Interaction across Cultures: Theoretical and Methodological Issues,* ed. P. G. Zukow, 54–75. New York: Springer.

Weber, Max, C. Wright Mills, and Hans Heinrich Gerth. 1946. *From Max Weber: Essays in Sociology.* New York: Oxford University Press.

Weinstein, Miriam. 2005. *The Surprising Power of Family Meals: How Eating Together Makes Us Smarter, Stronger, Healthier and Happier.* Hanover, NH: Steerforth Press.

Weisner, Thomas. 1989. "Comparing Sibling Relationships across Cultures." In *Sibling Interaction across Cultures: Theoretical and Methodological Issues,* ed. P. G. Zukow, 11–25. New York: Springer.

———. 1998. "Human Development, Child Well-Being, and the Cultural Project of Development." In *Socioemotional Development across Cultures,* ed. S. Dinesh and Kurt W. Fischer, 69–85. San Francisco: Jossey-Bass.

———. 2001. "The American Dependency Conflict." *Ethos* 29 (3): 271–95.

———. 2002. "Ecocultural Understanding of Children's Development Pathways." *Human Development* 45: 275–81.

———. 2009. "Well-Being and Sustainability of Daily Routines: Families with Children with Disabilities in the United States." In *Pursuits of Happiness: Well-Being in Anthropological Perspective,* ed. Gordon Mathews and Carolina Izquierdo, 228–47. New York: Berghahn Press.

Weisner, T. S., and R. Gallimore. 1977. "My Brother's Keeper: Child and Sibling Caretaking." *Current Anthropology* 18 (2): 169–90.

Wetherell, Margaret. 2003. "Racism and the Analysis of Cultural Resources in Interviews." In *Analyzing Race Talk: Multidisciplinary Approaches to the Interview,* ed. Harry Van Den Berg, Margaret Wetherell, and Hanneke Houtkoop-Steenstra, 11–30. Cambridge: Cambridge University Press.

Whiting, Beatrice B., and John W. M. Whiting. 1975. *Children of Six Cultures.* Cambridge, MA: Harvard University Press.

Whybrow, Peter C. 2005. *American Mania: When More Is Not Enough.* New York: Norton.

Wikan, Unni. 1990. *Managing Turbulent Hearts: A Balinese Formula for Living.* Chicago: University of Chicago Press.

Wilk, Richard R. 1996. *Economies and Cultures: Foundations of Economic Anthropology.* Boulder, CO: Westview Press.

Willihnganz, Heather, and Wingard Leah. 2005. "Exploring Emotion Work in Interaction." Working Paper #29. Center on Everyday Lives of Families, University of California, Los Angeles.

Wingard, Leah. 2006a. "Mentioning Homework First in Parent-Child Interaction." *Text & Talk* 26 (4–5): 573–98.

———. 2006b. "Verbal Practices for Accomplishing Homework: Socializing Time and Activity in Parent-Child Interactions." Ph.D. diss., University of California, Los Angeles.

———. 2007. "Constructing Time and Prioritizing Activities in Parent-Child Interactions." *Discourse and Society* 18: 75–91.

Wingard, Leah, and Lucas Forsberg. 2008. "Parents' Involvement in Children's Homework in American and Swedish Dual-Earner Families." *Journal of Pragmatics* 41: 1576–95.

Winnicott, Donald W. 1953. "Transitional Objects and Transitional Phenomena." *International Journal of Psychoanalysis* 34: 89–97.

———. 1964. *The Child, the Family, and the Outside World.* Cambridge, MA: Perseus.

Witmer, Denise D. 2004. *The Everything Parents Guide to Raising a Successful Child: All You Need to Encourage Your Child to Excel at Home and School.* Avon: Adams Media.

Zaff, Jonathan F., Kristin A. Moore, Angela P. Papillo, and Stephanie Williams. 2003. "Implications of Extracurricular Activity Participation during Adolescence on Positive Outcomes." *Journal of Adolescent Research* 18 (6): 599–630.

Zeitlin, M., R. Megawangi, E. Kramer, N. Colletta, E. D. Babatunde, and D. Garman. 1995. *Strengthening the Family: Implications for International Development.* New York: United Nations University Press.

Zelizer, Viviana A. 1994. *Pricing the Priceless Child: The Changing Social Value of Children.* Princeton: Princeton University Press

———. 2005. "The Priceless Child Revisited." In *Studies in Modern Childhood: Society, Agency, and Culture,* ed. Jens Qvortrup, 184–200. New York: Palgrave Macmillan.

Zukow, Patricia Goldring. 1989. "Siblings as Effective Socializing Agents: Evidence from Central Mexico." In *Sibling Interaction across Cultures: Theoretical and Methodological Issues,* ed. P. G. Zukow, 79–105. New York: Springer.

Contributors

JEANNE E. ARNOLD is a professor of anthropology at the University of California, Los Angeles, and Director of the Channel Islands Laboratory at the UCLA Cotsen Institute of Archaeology. She is lead author of two recent books, *Life at Home in the Twenty-First Century* (2012) and *California's Ancient Past: From the Pacific to the Range of Light* (2010).

MARGARET BECK is an assistant professor of anthropology at the University of Iowa. Her research interests include ethnoarchaeology in the United States and the Philippines, cooking and cuisine, households past and present, and archaeological ceramic analysis.

THOMAS N. BRADBURY is a professor of psychology at the University of California, Los Angeles. He specializes in the study of couples and couple communication, with specific interests in how relationships develop and change.

BELINDA CAMPOS is an assistant professor in the Department of Chicano/ Latino Studies and an affiliate of the School of Medicine PRIME-LC Program and the Department of Psychology and Social Behavior at the University of California, Irvine. Campos's research examines the role of culture and positive emotions in shaping relationship experience and health outcomes, with a focus on U.S. Latinos.

LINDA C. GARRO is a professor in the Department of Anthropology at the University of California, Los Angeles. She received the Stirling Prize from the Society for Psychological Anthropology and is president-elect of the Society of Medical Anthropology.

CHARLES GOODWIN is a professor of applied linguistics at the University of California, Los Angeles. His interests include video analysis of talk-in-interaction, cognition in the lived social world, embodiment as interactively organized social practice, aphasia in discourse, and the ethnography of science. His publications include *Conversation and Brain Damage*, "Professional Vision," and "Action and Embodiment."

MARJORIE HARNESS GOODWIN is a professor of anthropology at the University of California, Los Angeles. Her work investigates how talk is used to build social organization, with particular emphasis on the social worlds of young girls. She is the author of *He-Said-She-Said: Talk as Social Organization among Black Children* and *The Hidden Life of Girls: Games of Stance, Status, and Exclusion*.

ANTHONY P. GRAESCH is an assistant professor of anthropology at Connecticut College, where he engages students in studies of material culture and built space. Graesch's major research interests are the archaeological study of indigenous North American households in the Pacific Northwest and the ethnoarchaeological study of objects and identity in urban America. His work has been published in a wide spectrum of social science journals and includes numerous collaborations with linguistic anthropologists, psychologists, and sociologists.

KRIS GUTIÉRREZ is a professor of literacy and learning sciences and holds the Inaugural Provost's Chair at the University of Colorado, Boulder. She is also professor emerita of Social Research Methodology in the Graduate School of Education and Information Studies at the University of California, Los Angeles. Her research examines learning in designed learning environments, with particular attention to students from nondominant communities and English learners.

CAROLINA IZQUIERDO is an anthropologist, currently a visiting scholar at the University of California, Los Angeles. Her research has centered on health and well-being among the Matsigenka in the Peruvian Amazon, the Mapuche in Chile, and middle-class families in the United States. She is the editor of the volume *Pursuits of Happiness: Well-Being in Anthropological Perspective* and has published articles in *Social Science & Medicine; Culture, Medicine and Psychiatry; Ethos; Journal of Linguistic Anthropology; Qualitative Methods in Psychology*, and *Anthropology & Education Quarterly*, among others.

WENDY KLEIN is an assistant professor of anthropology and linguistics at California State University, Long Beach. Previously, as a graduate student and postdoctoral scholar at the University of California, Los Angeles, her research focused on the negotiation of household responsibilities among family members in the CELF study and youth socialization in Indian immigrant families. Her current research examines language and disability in Japanese immigrant families in Southern California. Some of her work has appeared in *Qualitative Research in Psychology, Anthropology of Work Review*, and *Heritage Language Journal*.

TAMAR KREMER-SADLIK is an adjunct assistant professor in the Department of Anthropology and director of programs of the Social Sciences Division at the University of California, Los Angeles. Her research interests include sociocultural perspectives on family life, cross-cultural studies of parenting and childhood, language and morality, food ideologies and practices, and children's health.

ELINOR OCHS is Distinguished Professor of Anthropology and Applied Linguistics. Drawing on work in the United States, Italy, Madagascar, and Samoa, her research probes how language practices construe ways in which children and others become competent and moral members of social groups across the life span. She has been honored as a MacArthur Fellow, a Guggenheim Fellow, and a member of the American Academy of Arts and Sciences. Her publications include *The Handbook of Language Socialization* (Duranti, Ochs, Schieffelin, 2012), *Linguaggio et Cultura* (2006), and *Living Narrative* (Ochs and Capps, 2001).

RENA REPETTI is a professor of psychology at the University of California, Los Angeles. She studies how common stressors influence the daily lives and health of families.

DARBY SAXBE received her Ph.D. from the University of California, Los Angeles, where she was advised by Rena Repetti and wrote her dissertation on Center for Everyday Lives of Families data. Starting in 2013, she will be an assistant professor of clinical science in the Department of Psychology at the University of Southern California. Her research interests include stress, health, and family relationships.

SHU-WEN WANG is an assistant professor of psychology at Haverford College. Her research examines stress and coping in relationships and families, with a focus on observed social interaction and support processes.

Index